Global Networks and Local Values

A Comparative Look at Germany and the United States

Committee to Study Global Networks and Local Values

Computer Science and Telecommunications Board

Division on Engineering and Physical Sciences

National Research Council

NATIONAL ACADEMY PRESS
Washington, D.C.

NOTICE: The project that is the subject of this report was approved by the Governing Board of the National Research Council, whose members are drawn from the councils of the National Academy of Sciences, the National Academy of Engineering, and the Institute of Medicine. The members of the committee responsible for the report were chosen for their special competences and with regard for appropriate balance.

This study was supported by a grant between the National Academy of Sciences and the German-American Academic Council. Any opinions, findings, conclusions, or recommendations expressed in this publication are those of the author(s) and do not necessarily reflect the views of the organizations or agencies that provided support for this project.

International Standard Book Number 0-309-07310-3

Library of Congress Control Number: 2001099571

Additional copies of this report are available from:
National Academy Press
2101 Constitution Avenue, NW
Box 285
Washington, DC 20055
800/624-6242
202/334-3313 (in the Washington metropolitan area)
http://www.nap.edu

Printed in the United States of America

THE NATIONAL ACADEMIES

National Academy of Sciences
National Academy of Engineering
Institute of Medicine
National Research Council

The **National Academy of Sciences** is a private, nonprofit, self-perpetuating society of distinguished scholars engaged in scientific and engineering research, dedicated to the furtherance of science and technology and to their use for the general welfare. Upon the authority of the charter granted to it by the Congress in 1863, the Academy has a mandate that requires it to advise the federal government on scientific and technical matters. Dr. Bruce M. Alberts is president of the National Academy of Sciences.

The **National Academy of Engineering** was established in 1964, under the charter of the National Academy of Sciences, as a parallel organization of outstanding engineers. It is autonomous in its administration and in the selection of its members, sharing with the National Academy of Sciences the responsibility for advising the federal government. The National Academy of Engineering also sponsors engineering programs aimed at meeting national needs, encourages education and research, and recognizes the superior achievements of engineers. Dr. Wm. A. Wulf is president of the National Academy of Engineering.

The **Institute of Medicine** was established in 1970 by the National Academy of Sciences to secure the services of eminent members of appropriate professions in the examination of policy matters pertaining to the health of the public. The Institute acts under the responsibility given to the National Academy of Sciences by its congressional charter to be an adviser to the federal government and, upon its own initiative, to identify issues of medical care, research, and education. Dr. Kenneth I. Shine is president of the Institute of Medicine.

The **National Research Council** was organized by the National Academy of Sciences in 1916 to associate the broad community of science and technology with the Academy's purposes of furthering knowledge and advising the federal government. Functioning in accordance with general policies determined by the Academy, the Council has become the principal operating agency of both the National Academy of Sciences and the National Academy of Engineering in providing services to the government, the public, and the scientific and engineering communities. The Council is administered jointly by both Academies and the Institute of Medicine. Dr. Bruce M. Alberts and Dr. Wm. A. Wulf are chairman and vice chairman, respectively, of the National Research Council.

COMMITTEE TO STUDY GLOBAL NETWORKS AND LOCAL VALUES

KENNETH H. KELLER, University of Minnesota, *Chair*
KENNETH W. DAM, University of Chicago Law School (resigned)
PAUL A. DAVID, All Souls College, Oxford University
KENNETH KENISTON, Massachusetts Institute of Technology
HENRY H. PERRITT, JR., Chicago-Kent College of Law, Illinois Institute of Technology
ROBERT SPINRAD, Xerox Palo Alto Research Center (retired)
GEORGE VRADENBURG, America Online, Inc. (resigned)

German Delegation from the Max-Planck-Projektgruppe

CHRISTOPH ENGEL, Max-Planck-Projektgruppe, *Chair of the German Delegation*
KLAUS W. GREWLICH, Center for European Integration Studies, Bonn; College of Europe, Bruges; Universität Freiburg
BERND HOLZNAGEL, Universität Münster, Institut für Informations-, Tele-kommunikations- und Medienrecht
MICHAEL HUTTER, Universitaet Witten-Herdecke
RAYMUND WERLE, Max-Planck-Institut fuer Gesellschaftsforschung
MARTINA ZITTERBART, Institut fuer Betriebssysteme und Rechnerverbund (resigned)

U.S. Staff

National Research Council
HERBERT LIN, Senior Scientist
NICCI DOWD, Project Assistant (through September 1999)
MICKELLE RODRIGUEZ, Senior Project Assistant (through February 2001)
JANICE SABUDA, Senior Project Assistant

German Staff

Max-Planck-Projektgruppe Recht der Gemeinschaftsgüter
JOACHIM DÖLKEN
ANJA MOOSMANN
LORENZ MÜLLER
WOLF OSTHAUS

Preface

BACKGROUND

It is described alternatively as the "third wave," the "information revolution," or the "virtually connected world." Whatever the rhetoric used to capture the impact of information technology in general and global networks in particular, it leads inevitably to the assertion that these developments will have a profound and increasing impact on individual life, social communities, commerce, and government. But what kind of impact and how, specifically, will it occur? For some it appears to be a set of risks and threats. For others, it amounts to almost unbounded opportunity.

Both assertions may have elements of truth. Opportunities and risks are twins. Unfortunately, because most discussions of the likely effects have been rather general and conjectural, there has been little basis for judging either the optimism of the technophiles or the pessimism of the technophobes. Where opportunities are concerned, conjecture and uncertainty have few negative consequences; the ingenuity of creative people, the workings of the market, and the acceptance by society of useful new tools will determine soon enough which technological applications will find a place in our lives and in what ways. The risks are another matter. It is important to try to anticipate the social effects of a new technological development in order to understand what tools and strategies might be used to reduce the risks or minimize the negative impacts.

The societal implications of new information technologies have not been universally welcomed. Most nations, including both fundamentalist and dictatorial nations as well as liberal democracies that tend to have high respect for personal freedom, have individual values that may be threatened by new information technologies. For example, in 1996 the Bavarian Attorney General forced CompuServe to ban a couple of newsgroups on issues of homosexuality that were perfectly legal in California. Similarly, some types of Nazi propaganda that would be criminally prosecuted in Germany are constitutionally protected as free speech in the United States.

Local governments have traditionally been responsible for countermeasures against information regarded as socially harmful. However, today's global telecommunications may constrain the options available to governments for controlling information, limit the effectiveness of old policy tools, and make it more difficult for governments even to understand or identify the values held by the populace at large. Governments might lose considerable ability to influence or preserve values that are different from those elsewhere in the world, or even to manage regional differences within their own boundaries.

Many questions regarding social organization arise. To what extent is it possible to organize power along territorial lines in a world of global telecommunications? What new loci of power and influence are made possible? To what extent do global telecommunications enable power to be organized around personal interests rather than geographically based or limited communities? What is the impact of such organization on social development? How will the roles of government and of society change as a result of global networks? Will all governments—or even all democratic governments—change in the same way? Are there scenarios in which governments may use the power of networks to enhance their power?

To address some of the issues related to the impact of global networks on local values, the German-American Academic Council asked for a study in this area. In response, the U.S. National Research Council established a committee in accordance with its usual procedures. The German delegation, under the auspices of the German Max-Planck-Project Group on Common Goods, Law, Politics, and Economics, were intimately involved in all aspects of the development of this report (participating in meetings, writing, and so on), but were not formally approved as NRC committee members.

A comparison of Germany and the United States was thus appropriate for two reasons. The procedural reason is that the expertise of the committee members was more concentrated on these two nations than on others, and that it was the German-American Academic Council that asked for the study. The substantive reason is that Germany and the United States have many important similarities (e.g., a well-developed information-technology infrastructure and a commitment to democracy and the rule of law) and many important differences as well (e.g., differing values that each nation wishes to uphold). For this reason, this report is structured around an exploration of the potential impacts of global telecommunications on values of Germany and the United States—specifically some of the values associated with democracy, privacy, freedom of information, and free speech.

STUDY PLAN

In carrying out its study, the Committee to Study Global Networks and Local Values met for the first time in the spring of 1998 and six more times (including two symposia described below) to deliberate. The symposia were integral to the study, as they involved speakers from a range of disciplines and helped to expose the committee to a much broader range of input and perspectives than what was represented by committee expertise. In this role, the speakers served admirably. (Individually authored papers from these symposia can be found online at <http://www.mpp-rdg.mpg.de/dresden1.html> for Symposium 1 and at <http://www.mpp-rdg.mpg.de/woodsh.html> for Symposium 2. These papers are also available in hard copy.[1])

PURPOSE OF THIS REPORT

This report focuses on the relationship between global information networks and political, economic, and cultural institutions and norms, which, in aggregate, are referred to as "local values." The study has examined the effect of global networks on the ability of individual nations and communities to protect or perpetuate indigenous values and systems, and it has examined the policy approaches available, at least in the United States and Germany, to achieve those ends—that is, to alter, control, or otherwise affect the local impact of information networks.

This report is intended to help policymakers understand the issues, how they are linked to one another, and how action targeting one problem or issue can have effects—oftentimes unintended—on others. It combines positive and normative analyses. The positive analysis—describing and explaining the current situation, attempting to predict likely development paths and their future effects, and forecasting the consequences of

---

[1]Christoph Engel and Kenneth H. Keller, eds., 2000, *Understanding the Impact of Global Networks on Local Social, Political and Cultural Values,"* Law and Economics of International Telecommunications, Vol. 42, Baden-Baden: Nomos; Christoph Engel and Kenneth H. Keller, eds., 2000, *Governance of Global Networks in the Light of Differing Local Values,* Law and Economics of International Telecommunications, Vol. 43, Baden-Baden: Nomos.

regulatory actions—aims at making clear what the present and potential problems are. The normative analysis—assessing the seriousness of the problems, making judgments on whether they require societal action, and, if so, commenting on what the course of action might be—emphasizes the different levels and the range of formal and informal structures, institutions, and policies available to deal with the problems identified. Furthermore, the report recognizes that legislators and the traditional political structures are not the only institutions that societies depend on to deal with perceived problems. A host of less formal political institutions and actors can, at times, be more effective, as they have been in much of the development of global networks that has already occurred. Therefore, the analysis in this report is not directed exclusively to traditional policymakers, but is also intended for professional groups, commercial institutions, nongovernmental organizations, and the broad array of other entities that make up civil society.

Finally, it is worth noting that the report does not make specific policy recommendations. Rather, it offers insights that the committee hopes will be useful to policymakers in thinking about critical decisions.

ACKNOWLEDGMENTS

The committee wishes to express its gratitude to the participants in the two symposia, whose contributions were critical for helping the committee to better understand the issues. Staff of the Max-Planck-Project Group on Common Goods, Law, Politics, and Economics and the U.S. National Research Council's Computer Science and Telecommunications Board provided helpful support, both logistically and intellectually.

Most importantly, the U.S. and German delegations to the committee acknowledge each other for a willingness to overcome their cultural differences and work through the misunderstandings that often characterize multinational study teams. At first, a common vocabulary and working style seemed to elude the committee. But over time and with patience, committee members from the two delegations were able to work out a rough consensus on important concepts and definitions. (Indeed, at times the process of deliberation was self-reflective—some of the issues discussed in this report played out during the committee process.)

The committee also thanks the German-American Academic Council (GAAC) for making this project possible, noting in particular the help of Dr. Rolf Hoffmann and Dr. Johannes Belz in facilitating interactions between the committee and the GAAC.

Acknowledgment of Reviewers

This report has been reviewed in draft form by individuals chosen for their diverse perspectives and technical expertise, in accordance with procedures approved by the National Research Council's (NRC's) Report Review Committee. The purpose of this independent review is to provide candid and critical comments that will assist the institution in making the published report as sound as possible and to ensure that the report meets institutional standards for objectivity, evidence, and responsiveness to the study charge. The review comments and draft manuscript remain confidential to protect the integrity of the deliberative process. We wish to thank the following individuals for their review of this report:

Michael Froomkin, University of Miami School of Law,
James Hamilton, Duke University,
Herwig Kogelnik, Lucent Technologies,
Viktor Mayer-Schoenberger, Kennedy School of Government,
David Post, Temple University,
Margaret Jane Radin, Stanford University, and
Debora Spar, Harvard Business School.

Although the reviewers listed above have provided many constructive comments and suggestions, they were not asked to endorse the conclusions or recommendations, nor did they see the final draft of the report before its release. The review of this report was overseen by Morris Tanenbaum. Appointed by the National Research Council, he was responsible for making certain that an independent examination of this report was carried out in accordance with institutional procedures and that all review comments were carefully considered. Responsibility for the final content of this report rests entirely with the authoring committee and the institution.

Contents

Global Networks and Local Values

Executive Summary

How do global networks—especially the Internet—affect a community's political, economic, and cultural values? How do these values, in turn, affect the ways in which global networks are designed, operated, and regulated?

As a first step toward addressing some of the issues related to the impact of global networks on local values, and vice versa, the Computer Science and Telecommunications Board of the National Research Council (United States) and the Max-Planck-Project Group on Common Goods, Law, Politics, and Economics (Germany) conducted a study whose goal was to help policymakers understand the issues, how they are linked to one another, and how action targeting one problem or issue can have effects—often-times unintended—on others.

To keep the scope of the study manageable, the Committee to Study Global Networks and Local Values concentrated its work on Germany and the United States, two countries that are different enough to contrast on a variety of critical issues yet similar enough to invite useful comparisons. In addition, the study did touch on some questions from a more global perspective. Furthermore, instead of making specific policy recommendations, it sought to develop insights that will be useful to policymakers around the world in thinking about policy decisions.

THE INTERNET AS GLOBAL NETWORK

The Internet was initially created for the purpose of linking academic computer scientists' research, and the technology—most importantly, the protocols—to support the early version of the network was created to meet its needs. But while today's Internet is widely regarded as a new medium for all to exploit and use, the underlying protocols have not changed significantly since, and they still embody the values of those early days. For example, one value of that era was trust; destructive hacking was not regarded as much of a problem, and the protocols were designed with that assumption in mind. Today, much of the concern over cyber-vulnerability results from those protocols' inattention to security.

The Internet is a network of networks that is truly global. The TCP/IP protocol, on which the Internet is based, allows a network to be designed in such a way that the "intelligence" that controls interactions is located primarily at the nodes and edges of the network (i.e., under the control of information suppliers and end users rather than some "global" central authority). Thus, the Internet is not subject to strong centralized management in its day-to-day operations. Technical decisions about architecture and design are coordinated at present through an informal working group, the Internet Engineering Task Force (IETF), though this may change in the future. In particular, as the Internet becomes more important to governments and business interests, commercial and political pressures are likely to emerge that seek to change the traditional forms of Internet management.

It should be noted, however, that the success of the Internet is largely the result of the *lack* of a master plan to guide its development. In its early stages, the Internet was promoted and funded, but not designed, by the U.S. government. This is not to say that government input was irrelevant. Indeed, the government made three critical decisions—to allow the original research and education network to evolve toward a general-purpose network, to select TCP/IP for the NSFNET and other backbone networks, and subsequently to privatize the NSFNET backbone—that had a powerful influence on the Internet's evolution. Nevertheless, direct control over future development of the Internet through comprehensive action plans will be even more difficult in the future, if only because the Internet has now extended itself across so many national borders and has mobilized such a diverse ensemble of interested parties.

Because the Internet is not subject to centralized management over its operations (and arguably should not be in the future), the fact that it crosses local and national boundaries introduces new dimensions of concern for communities accustomed to exercising sovereignty within their borders. Thus, the presence of the Internet raises the essential question of how (or whether) they *should* exercise authority over this new medium.

VALUES

Public opinion tends to start from a simplistic hypothesis: global networks threaten local values. But before they take action, policymakers should first understand whether values are really the issue; what values do for the individual, society, and government; whether the values are legitimate and thus deserve protection; and how global networks might affect local value orientations.

Values help individuals understand, decide, and even exist. Values endow individuals with a normative language that allows them to distinguish and judge their own behavior. And this allows them to decide on courses of action, and to preserve self-esteem.

Values help society to convey information, facilitate coordination, and give the group an identity. Precisely because they share values, the members of a society can interpret the behavior of other members and establish expectations about it. Through the sharing and communication of values, the behavior of individuals can be coordinated and made cohesive. Building a community essentially involves aligning people with shared values.

For government, values are the link to its citizenry. They provide a basis for the development of statutes to which people are inclined to adhere. They give legitimacy to governmental action. And shared values are the bedrock of a national identity.

Individuals are not likely to have a consistent order of values, and even less are societies or states. A more appropriate picture is a basket of values that are in tension and in permanent motion. History, culture, and public discourse shape the dominant balance of these values at any given time. Nations, societies, and individuals differ less by adhering to entirely different values, and much more by how they balance them.

Values can be either formal (like tolerance) or substantive (like national pride).[1] Modern societies are characterized by strong formal and relatively weak substantive values; but no society has ever existed without some shared substantive values.

Protecting local values is not a value as such. The locally prevailing values can be inappropriate for a changed world, for example, or they can be illegitimate (like obedience to an autocratic regime).

---

[1]Formal values (American legal scholars might term these "neutral" values) are, to a first approximation, those associated with social processes—rules of behavior that facilitate discourse and, indeed, can be a key element in making a community possible—while substantive values come closer to moral convictions or beliefs. While the committee recognizes that this distinction is not always crisp, it is useful for this report. More discussion of this point can be found in Chapter 3.

THE POTENTIAL IMPACT OF GLOBAL NETWORKS ON LOCAL VALUES

Global networks can influence local values in a number of ways. The networks may enable individuals to remove themselves from the reach of a community's influence on enforcing a particular set of values. That is, if an individual dislikes a value or a set of values dominant in his or her local environment, networks enable that person to exit from the community.

Global networks give individuals access to values that differ from the ones prevailing in their society of origin, and to different ways of balancing competing values. Having been exposed to the fact that values and their balance are historically contingent, individuals can use this knowledge for questioning their society's traditional values.

Global networks may lead to a convergence of values, raising concerns over cultural hegemony. In particular, the central role of the United States in developing and populating the Internet, the predominance of English in Internet content, and the vitality of the traditionally egalitarian Internet culture all contribute to what some outside observers characterize as U.S. cultural hegemony.

Global networks enable communication that is almost devoid of context. The user often does not know the content provider. Internet use is mostly unnoticed by the physical communities to which the user belongs. This is important because values are embedded in context. Trespassers cannot be reminded of the value if the violation remains invisible.

THE INTERNET AND THE DEMOCRACTIC PROCESS

The Internet has potentially large effects on democracy and the political process generally. Established political arenas are more easily engaged through the Internet than through conventional channels, and the existence of new arenas may challenge existing institutions, especially those in government. Political actors gain leverage by virtue of the Internet's ability to facilitate organization; the Internet also allows—for better or worse—a larger degree of unmediated communication between the public and its political leaders.

The Internet can also change the political process. It enables issues to be brought to the forefront of policymaker attention in very short times, and it lets stakeholders and advocates press their cases in a multiplicity of forums. Meanwhile, the Internet and its associated technologies provide tools for policymakers to make their case to the public without intermediaries.

The Internet can change the balance between direct and representative democracy in favor of the former: it allows broader and faster public dissemination of more types of information and ideas relevant to the policymaking process. But whether the Internet will result in a more effective selection process—through which ideas can be sifted and evaluated in a reasonable and deliberate manner—is an open question.

Because of its pluralizing potential, the Internet increases the likelihood that transnational conflicts will arise—but because there is no sovereign international authority to adjudicate and, especially, to enforce, the resolution of Internet-driven conflicts is highly complex. At the same time, the Internet and information technology have the potential to fractionate the public because they allow individuals to customize the information they receive.

The Internet poses different challenges to the legal and constitutional environments in which the United States and Germany operate. To the extent that the courts are able to rely on the values expressed in their respective constitutions (rather than rights that have been explicitly articulated in the documents themselves), they will have greater flexibility to facilitate evolution of their legal and constitutional environments as the technologies and uses of the Internet change.

Finally, government reactions to the Internet may not necessarily be benign or constructive. Indeed, governments may well choose to use more traditional command-and-control regulation to deal with what they may see as problems created by the Internet. Such actions do not necessarily serve democratic and freedom-preserving interests.

FREEDOM OF SPEECH

Although both the United States and Germany recognize a constitutional right to freedom of expression, the interpretation of that right in the two countries is significantly different. Moreover, and just as important, the weight given to that right in comparison with other values is different in the two societies. As a result, the legal structures and protections that have developed to implement the right are different, and they exemplify why harmonization of the laws related to many aspects of freedom of expression on the Internet is likely to remain quite difficult.

Consider two types of speech for which the United States and Germany have different legal regimes. Hate speech—the willful public expression or promotion of hatred toward any segment of society distinguished by color, race, religion, or ethnic origin—is generally proscribed by the German legal system. Such a prohibition is not surprising given the nation's determination to avoid the reestablishment of a national socialist authority. By contrast, hate speech is generally deemed a constitutionally protected form of expression in the United States; only when such speech can lead to a hate-engendered crime is it prohibited.

A second type of speech that the two countries regard differently is speech that is deemed detrimental to minors. Both nations proscribe child pornography. But they have dealt differently with material that might be psychologically traumatic to minors. The United States has sought to pass laws that hold providers criminally liable for supplying minors with materials that are "obscene," "indecent," "patently offensive" (the Communications Decency Act, or CDA), or "harmful to minors" (the Child Online Protection Act, or COPA). CDA was held unconstitutional, and COPA was overturned at the district level and now awaits appeal. Germany has proscribed the distribution to minors of material that is "immoral, [has] a brutalizing effect, [gives] incentive to violence, crimes or racial hatred, . . . [or glorifies] the war," but these laws have not been seriously challenged in court.

The global nature of the Internet makes it extremely difficult and costly for national authorities to unilaterally implement laws and regulations that reflect national, rather than global, moral standards. But commercial law (or private law, as it is usually known in Europe), self-regulation, and encouragement of intermediation provide additional tools. Commercial law is useful when material on the network injures a clearly identifiable party (for example, if a Web site published libelous material about a person or violated someone's legally protected privacy).

Self-regulation—through site-identification and labeling schemes, age-verification software, and the provision of filtering software—allows for greater diversity of Internet material, enhanced freedom of expression, and customization of controls to fit the needs and desires of individuals. Intermediaries, such as host providers, can play a useful role in offering the public a regulating or authenticating service. That is, host providers can market their Internet access software by promising to include certain kinds of content and to exclude others. In each of these alternatives, government has a role in ensuring their quality; thus, they are examples of "hybrid" regulation, combining governmental and nongovernmental approaches to the overall regulatory process.

THE INTERNET, PRIVACY, AND FREEDOM OF INFORMATION

Potential tensions between privacy and freedom of information (FOI) illustrate contrasts between a substantive value (privacy) and a formal value (transparency in government, as exemplified by freedom of information). Privacy asserts the ability of individuals to control and restrict the dissemination of information about themselves, while FOI refers to the free availability of information related to the conduct of government business. Both public and private institutions gather, organize, store, and in some instances disseminate information about people. Thus both kinds of institutions are key actors in threats to, as well as protection of, privacy. Both are also involved in FOI issues, though private institutions play only an indirect role.

Though privacy and freedom of information are not necessarily in opposition, they do come into conflict in some instances. For example, information on individuals is collected by governments. Asserting an absolute right to privacy would argue for never releasing such information, while asserting an absolute right to FOI would argue for releasing any of it on demand. In these cases, the substantive value of privacy is in conflict not only with the formal value of transparency of state activities, but also with the public interest (in the prevention and prosecution of criminal offenses) and commercial interests (in the collection and exploitation of data).

Global networks such as the Internet have raised the stakes significantly for both privacy and freedom of information. Clearly, they facilitate dissemination of information held by both public and private institutions. But perhaps more significantly, computers and software have greatly enhanced the storage, mining, sorting, and reorganizing of data. This has increased the ability of institutions to develop comprehensive and accessible profiles—on private individuals as well as on the actions of governmental bodies—from disparate databases and put the information into useful formats.

The German and American approaches to privacy and freedom of information are opposites of each other. Germany, and European nations in general, have comprehensive systems of law and regulation that reflect strong commitments to protection of privacy. The United States has a patchwork of incomplete protections reflecting uncertain commitment to privacy. With respect to freedom of information, the situation is reversed. The United States has a comprehensive system in place that reflects its commitment to access. Germany has a patchwork system, reflecting its ambiguity about access.

In the context of the Internet, privacy and freedom of information raise many policy issues. For example, because routine consumer transactions can easily involve players in a number of countries, applying national regulations represents a major extraterritorial extension of domestic or regional law. Furthermore, attempts to find a common solution to privacy problems in a globally networked world are difficult because nations such as Germany and the United States approach privacy from very different political and legal viewpoints and traditions. Germans traditionally vest considerable trust in government to protect their privacy interests. By contrast, Americans tend to mistrust governmental institutions and have a strong tradition of relying on market forces not only to regulate the economy but also to serve many other social needs. As a consequence, Americans have been more ambivalent about turning to the government to protect their personal privacy.

Despite these differences, both Germany and the United States over the last 25 years have developed fair-information principles that reflect substantial agreement on basic questions regarding privacy. These principles include openness, individual participation, collective limitation, data quality, finality, security, and accountability. However, it should be noted that implementation of fair-information practices may differ significantly from system to system even though the same general principles or framework applies in all cases.

International law could theoretically play an important role in the legal protection of personal privacy because of the ease with which personal data can be transferred electronically across national borders. Harmonization can be effected through conventional treaties that express substantive rights and that obligate national authorities to enforce those rights through national legal institutions. But treaties work only when there is near-complete agreement on the values involved; furthermore, negotiating them is a very slow process.

An alternative to treaties are framework agreements based on "hybrid" forms of international organization. In these matrices, or frameworks, of international public law, private self-regulation is used to work out the details. Such hybrid regimes will be acceptable only if they offer new flexibility in rule making—if they tailor substantive requirements to the realities of rapidly changing technologies. They also must offer more flexibility and lower transaction costs for complaint- and dispute-resolution, and an effective state-based system to ensure compliance.

Freedom of information is a pillar of democratic societies, and one of the greatest potential contributions of global networks is enhanced public access to government information. As court decisions, legislative documents, and regulations of administrative agencies become more easily available through the Internet's World Wide Web, the rule of law is strengthened.

Such "primary legal information"—information having the force of law, such as parliamentary enactments, judicial decisions, and comparable instruments from administrative agencies such as rules and orders—must be public for effective governance. But as noted above, public records containing personal information can pose a conflict between freedom of information and privacy rights—a conflict exacerbated by advances in information technology that make it more practical to extract and cross-link personal data from public records.

Similarly, notes, drafts, and intermediate documents of public officials and bodies can give the public insights into the decision-making processes of government and administration, but how far a society should go in providing access to such records is a matter requiring further discussion. The value of transparency in the decision-making process must be weighed against the need for administrators or judges and their advisors to have candid discussions without which the quality of decisions might well be reduced. Government also needs space and time in which to assess arguments and conduct its own debates with a degree of privacy.

The international legal complications related to freedom of information are neither as pervasive nor as challenging as those related to privacy protection, and the drive for harmonization is less urgent. The differences arise because in the FOI area, the principle underlying national law is to compel disclosure of government information, while in the privacy arena the principle is to prohibit disclosure of personal information. Therefore, transborder data flows are a lesser threat to freedom-of-information values than they are to privacy values. Even under changed technological conditions, each country can pursue its own FOI policy since it exercises control at the point of origination of information.

Nevertheless, there are reasons for a nation such as Germany to try to bring its freedom-of-information principles closer to those of the United States. First, global networks expose people to governmental openness in other states, which can lead them to demand more openness and access in their own country. Second, a restrictive national policy with respect to freedom-of-information principles can be undermined to a certain extent by the dissemination capabilities of the Internet. Third, and perhaps most important, economic considerations may provide an even stronger motivation for adopting freedom-of-information principles in Germany; access to public information increases the predictability of political conditions that may affect economic actors.

COMMERCE

Values associated with commerce can be placed in three categories: those values directly related to the fairness of doing business (e.g., "fair" taxation and competition); those related to basic constitutional foundations of commerce (e.g., property and contract); and those related to other, more general institutions (e.g., the rights to privacy and to information access or delivery).

In an Internet environment, small businesses often face lower costs of entry than they might in the physical world. Thus, they can occupy new niches of promising commercial activity more easily, and large numbers of small-business entities seek to identify and construct such niches. On the other hand, "network effects" associated with the Internet environment can help lead to "winner take all" situations for larger companies that already enjoy significant market share, thus facilitating their further growth and dominance. As for taxation, the relative permeability of national borders to Internet traffic (and many of the goods and services the network can carry) is likely to increase the difficulty of imposing taxes on sales made to foreign customers through the Internet.

Enforcement of intellectual property rights in an Information Age is greatly complicated by global networks. Because these networks make it profoundly easier to copy and transmit information, old balances of property rights against "fair use" have been upset, and a new political and social equilibrium has not yet been established. The moral rights of authors, which allow an individual to try to prevent the distortion of his or her work—a concept well-recognized in the European Community but not in the United States—seem particularly challenged by the ease with which digital representations can be disseminated.

New practices in the Internet realm also appear to raise issues about contract. For example, in an electronic transaction, it is arguably harder to confirm the voluntary and informed consent of the parties involved, as contract terms are often hidden on a Web page. In other cases, computer programs make selections that imply contract acceptance. In still other cases, obligations may automatically be incurred with an acquired information product.

GOVERNANCE

The examples addressed above—commerce, free speech, privacy, freedom of information, democracy—illustrate that Germany and the United States differ on the role of the state in promoting social integration and protecting local value systems. Americans emphasize individual liberty, reliance on markets to organize economic activity in the face of technological change, and the use of a variety of nongovernmental organizations to mediate political change. Germans tend more to look to the state as a protector of values, especially when these values are threatened by market and technological forces.

Despite these differences, it is clear that for both nations, the state is an important actor in managing the impact of the Internet on these—and other—areas. States will be obliged to come to terms with how governance in cyberspace is to proceed, and in doing so will need to draw on the full range of governance mechanisms available to them.

At one level, nonregulatory mechanisms are available. Technical solutions and informal rules of behavior can help to lubricate points of friction caused by the conflict of values. For example, filtering and portals help to target the information that is accessible to individuals, and informal rules for behaviors, such as "Netiquette," facilitate interaction.

On the other hand, social conventions are nonbinding, which makes them weak tools for compelling behavior in persons unwilling to conform to such conventions. Thus, when rules are necessary, legal tools of one sort or another will generally prove more effective.

National law and regulation are likely to be of limited effectiveness, however, because global networks make national boundaries highly porous with respect to information. In principle, extraterritorial enforcement of national laws and rules is possible—assuming cooperation from other nation-states—but in practice such cooperation is the exception rather than the rule. Nevertheless, while before-the-fact denial of access to information is technically hard to achieve, the presence of individuals on sovereign soil provides a route through which local laws can be enforced. Further, intermediaries such as service providers or credit card agencies are subject to national regulation as well.

International legal harmonization is an obvious solution to conflicts over values in cyberspace. It can be achieved through agreements that allocate regulatory authority or by harmonizing the regulations themselves. The former is unlikely, however; states tend to balk at cooperating when their own laws and attitudes toward a particular issue differ from those of the state whose laws they are being asked to enforce. Only when there is consensus about an issue can international cooperation be quickly and effectively achieved.

A second possibility is the use of internationally coordinated private laws to regulate conduct on global networks. The role of the state under those circumstances is simply to interpret and judge the validity of contracts, to protect people's interests in the contracting process, and to help them in the enforcement of legal titles. In addition, tort law can establish liability, generating financial incentives for private entities to refrain from inappropriate conduct. As a general rule, national private-law systems are much better coordinated internationally than are systems of public law; thus private law may have greater potential to facilitate governance.

Finally, hybrid regulation—an arrangement that involves elements both of private cooperation and public law—has some potential. From this perspective, governance is about the allocation of power not only in a public setting but within private associations as well, and power is exercised by a multitude of actors at different levels of authority and operation. In hybrid regulation, public law provides a framework for private self-ordering that meets certain minimum requirements. Over time, this may lead to an increasingly limited role for the state, as new actors appear who assume regulatory powers that have traditionally been exercised by the state.

GLOBAL NETWORKS AND CULTURE

Global networks affect culture in three ways. First, they give rise to concerns about hegemony. Networks provide an infrastructure whose actual characteristics are largely determined by those who design and use them, and the fact is that one nation is dominant. The majority of the Internet's designers and users, and much of its hardware and software, hail from the United States. Thus some fear that the preponderance of the information available on the network is likely to reflect the interests and culture of American users more than those from less influential states.

The Committee to Study Global Networks and Local Values believes that these fears are overdrawn—at least for Western industrial nations. The reason is that these states have the resources to create language and cultural "zones" that cater to their own interests and tastes. So, for example, most German, French, and Japanese computer and Internet users can conduct all of their day-to-day activities in their native languages because content providers have already generated or translated information for local consumption. Furthermore, even if it is indeed U.S. companies that provide the bulk of the software in use, these companies realize that other nations represent markets large enough to warrant the development of software customized to their particular needs. Thus for developed nations it appears likely that the use of information networks will reflect local values rather than replace them.

For the developing world, the situation is far more complex. In the newly industrialized countries of East Asia, for example, economic globalization is considered a key to development. These nations see global networks as a tool that they have a natural advantage in adopting rather than as a threat to local culture. On the other hand, the incentives for localization of network content and applications are much fewer there than for the developed world. To the extent that the United States seeks to promote democratic change in developing nations, its efforts may be seen as promoting forms of cultural hegemony—for example, in the technical structure of global networks that make it difficult for these nations to interdict the flow of information they deem undesirable.

Second, global networks affect the distribution of power and information within and between social classes. In fact, these networks appear more likely to affect relationships between groups defined by profession and level of education than between those defined by national identity. Because Internet technology will not diffuse throughout a society in a uniform manner, and those that obtain it first are most likely to be members of privileged classes, incentives to provide societal services to all classes may wane if the privileged classes—because of their access to the Internet—are able to obtain such services on their own; this may be especially true in nations without a strong countervailing tendency toward egalitarianism. Such changes result from the differential relationships of these groups to the Internet, different interdependencies between groups that occur as a result of the Internet, and changes in the modes of operation of certain professions that affect activities unrelated to electronic networks as well as those directly related to the networks.

Finally, global networks shift boundaries between public and private spaces. Historically, those boundaries, in both principle and practice, have been largely determined by cultural norms. Which people know about us and what they know, what they physically see of us, how we feel about it and the extent to which we control it, differ widely from one culture to another. How and where one entertains, the candor and directness with which one expresses ideas, how publicly and under what circumstances one displays one's body, are all related to the boundaries between public and private spheres but follow no obvious, logical, or consistent pattern. In the physical world, it is reasonably clear how to maintain these boundaries. But network technologies have the potential to shift them in either direction, depending on circumstances and the sophistication of the user. Encryption technologies, for example, can increase the effective domain of private space; on the other hand, connecting to the Web can increase public space by exposing the contents of one's computer to inspection or alteration.

PRINCIPLES AND CONCLUSIONS

Global networks present a variety of new challenges to national governments. While in some cases governments have faced these challenges before, global networks have some potential for altering the balances of power between government and those governed that were established in pre-network eras. Nevertheless, the Internet is not the only influence on the evolution of values, and a multitude of other influences will affect such evolution as well. Thus, a government's stance toward global networks (and the Internet in particular) must be part of a larger strategy aimed at promoting the healthy evolution of a society's value set. That is, government must respond to (rather than simply resist) the many changes occurring as society becomes better educated, more diverse, and more fully connected to the wider world around it.

Because the Internet is only one factor, albeit an important one, in globalization and modernization, the focus of policymakers when policy action is necessary should be on outcomes rather than on tools or modalities. Thus they should seek to define what outcomes are desirable and undesirable rather than seek to regulate one particular instrumentality such as the Internet.

A second important point is that command-and-control regulation is unlikely to be well matched to the technological realities of the Internet. An alternative to command-and-control regulation is the use of self-regulation and intermediation within a statutory framework. This hybrid approach to regulation is likely to be more effective than command-and-control regulation in addressing many aspects of the public interest, and it serves as counterpoint to formal regulation. One reason is that global networks are characterized by a complex system of market forces—private, public, and quasi-public—and a stable balance among them is easier to achieve when stakeholders are well informed and can take an active part in shaping their roles. Command-and-control regulation often attacks a well-balanced status quo; because hybrid regulation builds on the status quo, it is more likely to be successful.

Finally, the history of the Internet's technology suggests that it would be a mistake for governments to seek to control the future development through comprehensive action plans. Indeed, despite U.S. government promotion and funding of the Internet in its early stages, at no time did some kind of master plan exist to guide the Internet's evolution. Alternatives to centralized approaches, such as coordination and self-regulation, are worth considering, though they may require new forms of hybrid public-private international regimes.

Chapter 10 discusses other principles and conclusions related to free speech, privacy, and freedom of information.

1

Introduction and Context

1.1 AIMS OF THIS REPORT

Global telecommunications—particularly the Internet—can in principle change the ability of national governments to preserve their nations' values. The ever-increasing bandwidth of communications technologies, and their diffusion internationally, makes it possible for large volumes of information to cross national borders much more easily than in the past. And because information—depending on its content and who receives it—can enhance or detract from a nation's ability to govern itself, we may reasonably expect that information technology will have a nontrivial impact on the conduct of national policy.

Clearly, no easy generalizations can be made in advance about the social and political effects of most technological developments. The influence of a new technology on a society is seldom determined solely by its technical characteristics alone. The innovations it spawns—the systemic changes it promotes or makes possible—depend on interactive, bidirectional, and iterative processes that constitute the society's social, political, economic, and cultural life. Indeed, much has been written on this subject[1] describing the intricacies of those interactions.

Global information networks are no different in this respect, although their very breadth and transformative nature make the challenge all the

---

[1]See, for example, Merritt Roe Smith and Leo Marx, eds., 1998, *Does Technology Drive History?* Cambridge, MA: The MIT Press.

greater. As the very term implies, they are not developed by nor are they contained within a single, homogeneous, or even coherent society. Much of their power and potential derives from the connectivity they provide across large distances, geographic barriers, time zones, and political boundaries.

The effectiveness of global information networks depends on some uniformity in technical standards, agreed-upon rules and operating procedures, and compatibility of hardware and software. In each of these respects, choices have to be made that are based primarily on technical considerations and the values held by the technology's first developers and users. But although uniformity or interoperability may be technically desirable, it is much less clear that it is socially desirable, at least to the extent that it limits the accommodation of local needs and values.

Moreover, as the global network diffuses more and more widely within each nation, the values, needs, and desires of a much broader spectrum of people have to be considered. The target is a moving one in several respects: the increasing level of penetration brings additional groups with different characteristics into contact with the new technology; the groups themselves evolve in their adaptation to the network; and the technology continues to develop, offering new potential uses as well as new challenges.

Taken together, these considerations suggest three kinds of questions that define the aims of this report: What can be said about the interactions between information networks and different social/political/cultural systems? How are these interactions affected by the global nature of the networks? What changes in these relationships can be expected over time?

The last question is particularly troublesome and, in a report focused on the future, particularly important. Because of the iterative and interactive nature of technology development, analyses of the present state of affairs may be either irrelevant to or misleading about the future. Who would be willing to predict with confidence that the so-called "digital divide"—the seriously skewed access at present to the benefits of information technology among different nations and different socioeconomic groups—will be a transient phenomenon or, alternatively, an embedded condition that will only intensify in the future? Are the perceived threats to civil society, local businesses, or government-taxation authority inherent in the technology or will they disappear as societies adjust to the dynamics of a new system? To what extent can one expect that, over time, there will be technological fixes for the tensions or conflicts created by the introduction of global networks?

The working hypothesis in this report is that each country is affected differently by global networks, depending on its own local values. Even when the nominal effect is substantially the same in different countries, they may perceive the impact differently; that is, their governments or their people may find it more or less disruptive. Finally, countries may react in different ways, in accordance with the structures and traditions of their governance systems.

Although it is difficult to provide answers to the questions posed above, this report attempts to explore them in some detail. The premise is that by raising the issues at this early point in the development of global networks, societies and policymakers will be encouraged to monitor developments. And they will have a framework for doing so, thus positioning themselves to take action as the dynamics of the interactions between these new global networks and local values become clearer. The discussion also highlights the importance of incorporating, both through institutional and technological design, as much flexibility into the system as possible, thereby allowing for salutary changes to cope with tensions or conflicts as they arise or are recognized. In this respect, technological "lock-in" is something to be studiously avoided.

1.2 BACKGROUND

This report focuses on and compares the United States and Germany. That choice grew out of an interest in both countries to pursue the study on which the report is based. As noted in the preface, the German-American Academic Council asked the U.S. National Research Council and the German Max-Planck-Project Group on Common Goods, Law, Politics, and Economics to undertake the task as a joint venture. Both institutions saw this as an opportunity not only to explore an issue of mutual interest but to do so in a way that could draw on scholarly strengths in both countries, provide greater clarity about the issue itself through the comparisons and contrasts that would be possible, and build a model for possible future collaborations. In this last respect, it was not lost on either institution that developing models for collaborations of this kind is one important social/political response to the very changes being brought about by the globalizing influence of information technology.

A study limited to the United States and Germany has obvious shortcomings. To be truly comprehensive in addressing the interactions between global networks and local values, one would have to examine the entire spectrum of countries. It would range from the Scandinavian nations—which are extensively penetrated by the Internet and have the greatest homogeneity and the least rigid political and social systems—to those, like North Korea, Myanmar, or certain countries in the Middle East, that tightly control or even attempt to seal themselves off from global networks.

On the other hand, comparing two industrialized, relatively wealthy, and extensively networked countries with similar but not identical political systems and similar but not identical value systems can yield insights for policymakers in both countries. The United States and Germany obviously meet these criteria. In addition, they are countries whose languages are primarily English (in one case) and primarily German (in the other), and they are sufficiently large that each has already made practical choices in deciding how to react to the influence of global networks. Their similarities serve to control the number of variables; their differences make clearer how global networks can affect and be affected by relatively well-identified local values. Furthermore, it is hoped that the comparison will offer some guidance as to how differences in judgment or reaction in the two countries might be resolved or accommodated, given the constraint that the networks must operate globally and harmoniously.

This reasoning suggests, in fact, that although a study of a broader range of countries might provide greater insight into the interactions between global networks and local values, it could actually be of more limited use to policymakers. Countries with vastly different cultures or political systems will certainly be challenged by global networks in very different ways, but there may be less to be learned that is applicable to policy choices through an explicitly comparative study of the kind undertaken here; that is, there is likely to be little in the way of policy approaches that is adaptable to one country from the other when the two are widely different and there are few options available that would harmonize policies across the much broader cultural and political gaps.

1.3 THIS STUDY

The U.S.-German committee that was assembled to plan and carry out this study (see the appendix) covered a range of disciplines, including economics, law, political science, sociology, engineering, and science and technology policy. In addition to its several planning and writing meetings, the committee organized two symposia—one in Dresden in February 1999, and another in Woods Hole, Massachusetts, in June 1999, to which individuals with an even broader range of professional, academic, industrial, and public-policy backgrounds were invited.

The Dresden symposium focused on the numerous ways in which global networks are affecting local institutions and values, or are likely to do so in the future. Commissioned papers addressed conceptual questions—such as the meaning of values and the several ways in which values are embedded in political, social, and economic institutions—as well as analytical questions concerning actual or potential impacts. The values that inhere in the global networks themselves were also considered.

The Woods Hole symposium focused on potential responses—by governments, other institutions, and less structured groups—to the new context, potential conflicts, and other changes that the penetration of global networks into local societies may likely bring about.

The papers commissioned for the two symposia have been published in their entirety.[2] These papers and related discussions also provided the committee with much of the background material on which this report is based, although its organization and content were separately determined.

1.4 GERMANY AND THE UNITED STATES: SOME CONTRASTS

The similarities between Germany and the United States are fairly apparent. The question is, How do they *differ*? Obviously, any attempt to describe two complex cultures with a few brief comments based on a limited number of characteristics is bound to lead to oversimplification. However, if one views the exercise as merely an attempt to identify political, social, and cultural differences that might give rise to different kinds of interactions with global networks, it can provide a useful starting point for this study. The following descriptions should be viewed in that light:

- *Political/social organization*. Many observers would contrast Germany and the United States by describing the former as somewhat "hierarchical" in a number of respects and the latter as rather "horizontal." Germans are more willing to delegate authority for many kinds of societal decisions, to believe in and rely on experts or on those formally charged with decision-making responsibility, and to expect that social and political problems can be approached using an orderly, rational, and formal process.

Americans, on the other hand, are increasingly impatient with representative democracy, as evidenced by the growing use of ballot referenda in many states and the number of issues that have moved from the agendas of specialized agencies to the forum of public debate. The advent of the Internet has caused many to envision a return to a style of governance much like that of early New England town meetings. Americans are now much more likely than most Europeans to turn to the Internet as a source of information rather than to designated experts.

Much has been written in recent years about the demise of citizen involvement in the United States—fewer people voting in elections, reduced participation in civic groups, and a loss of public support for a "social safety

---

[2]Christoph Engel and Kenneth H. Keller, eds., 2000, *Understanding the Impact of Global Networks on Local Social, Political and Cultural Values,* Law and Economics of International Telecommunications, Vol. 42, Baden-Baden: Nomos; Christoph Engel and Kenneth H. Keller, eds., 2000, *Governance of Global Networks in the Light of Differing Local Values,* Law and Economics of International Telecommunications, Vol. 43, Baden-Baden: Nomos.

net."[3] Some have argued that the concern may be overstated (or they have questioned some of the explanations offered for the phenomenon), but polling data show increasing numbers of Americans responding in the negative to a question asking, "Do you trust your neighbors?"

On the other hand, one explanation offered for the willingness in German society to delegate authority is the relatively high level of trust among citizens with respect to government. The trust appears to be related to the expectation that individuals in and out of government will fulfill their responsibilities. Moreover, the reaction to abuse of that trust may be all the greater in Germany, as evidenced by the strong backlash to recent revelations of fundraising improprieties in the Christian Democratic Party.

- *Social cohesion.* The United States is a highly mobile society with little attachment to place. University students often choose schools without regard to where they have grown up, routinely moving hundreds to thousands of miles to do so. Workers expect to relocate to other parts of the country several times in the course of one or several careers. Extended families do not expect to live close to one another. The country's population density is relatively low, single-family dwellings are the norm, suburban communities continue to grow, and city life is the exception rather than the rule. With place a less important factor, the Internet offers a particularly viable organizing link. E-mail is now a common mode for family communication. And with distances from home to work a major problem and public transportation very limited, new ideas such as "telecommuting" offer an attractive possibility.

Germany has a higher population density, shorter commuting distances, and relatively stable attachment to place. City life is a central feature of social structure, personal marketing, and living generally. Thus there are fewer needs for and attractions to a Web existence, and more to be sacrificed in choosing that alternative.

- *Nationalism and internationalism.* Germans, like most Europeans, have a strong sense of history and geography. They also have an international perspective: their educated classes are multilingual; their television programming is polyglot; their economic interdependence with other countries is evident in everyday life. Indeed, Germans have been leaders in the integration of Europe. Within their own country, their awareness of history and the relative homogeneity of their society create a sense of tradition, which leads to skepticism about change. At the same time, their history has sensitized them to the dangers of nationalism and led them to

[3] See, for example, Robert Putnam, 2001, *Bowling Alone: The Collapse and Revival of American Community*, New York: Touchstone Books.

the pragmatic view of the nation-state as a rational construct rather than a divine or natural order.

Americans, on the other hand, generally have little sense of history or geography. Moreover, separated by oceans from both Europe and Asia, they have an impatience with internationalism that manifests itself today as either neo-isolationism or unilateralism. Their lack of knowledge of other languages is well known. Unconstrained by an historical perspective, and ethnically heterogeneous, they are unusually open to change. It is a society with great social mobility, a widespread entrepreneurial spirit, and receptiveness to technological innovation. One observer has noted that Americans tend to look first at the opportunities presented by change, while Germans look first at the risks.

At the same time, Americans create unity by promoting a shared pride in the idea of their country as a nation of immigrants and the values it represents. That very heterogeneity saves Americans from the worst aspects of nationalism, but they do not have a sense of proportion about their role in the world. Combined with their population size and economic power, this omission often leads them to be inadvertent agents of hegemony.

- *Technical/economic factors*. In a number of ways, the efficiency of German society, its trust of government, and its commitment to narrowing economic gaps and class distinctions provide an impetus for the spread of new technologies in everyday life. Magnetic insurance cards, automated videotape rental, and information-technology-based systems for regulating and monitoring traffic have all penetrated German (and European) society more than they have that of the United States. On the other hand, the local telecommunications systems remain de facto monopolies. This creates a pricing structure that slows Internet penetration and use by raising the cost of broadband "last mile" communication links and by failing to make flat-rate access schemes available.

The more decentralized governance and market orientation structures in the United States have facilitated deep penetration of a Web culture in several ways. Competition in telecommunications has led to substantial reductions in the cost of Web connection, to flat-rate access schemes being the norm, and to the availability of many competing high-bandwidth systems via telephone lines, cable systems, and satellites. Decentralization, market orientation, and a somewhat lower level of concern for uniformity of access have led to a faster, if inhomogeneous, spread of Internet connections and use.

- *Religion*. Both the United States and Germany nominally separate church and state, but the role of religion is different in the two societies. Americans, far more than Germans, attend religious services and are involved with church, synagogue, or mosque activities on a regular basis. This is a source of perennial political conflict in the otherwise secular United States—whether it be on prayer in public schools and at public events, or the teaching of evolution, or stem-cell research. These conflicts extend to the Internet world on issues such as pornography and free speech. In German society, on the other hand, the overlap of religious and secular life appears to be relatively modest.

1.5 STRUCTURE OF THIS REPORT

In examining the influences of global networks on the two countries, this report attempts to be specific but not exhaustive. It looks at pornography and hate speech, at privacy and freedom of information, at cultural diversity and hegemony, at the local values associated with democracy, and at electronic commerce. In separate chapters, it puts these specific issues into a general framework that addresses global networks, local values, and their reciprocal influence. In so doing, it singles out issues for examination in order to illustrate how diverse the relationship between global networks and local values can be.

The body of the report is divided into three sections. The first deals with contextual issues: how the technology evolved to its present form, how that form may affect its future growth and regulation, and how we can come to an understanding of values that would be useful in this assessment. The second section uses these concepts to examine the effects of global networks on a number of specific issues, including privacy, freedom of information, free speech, and the political and commercial structures in which global networks are embedded. It also suggests alternative approaches to network governance. The third section—the penultimate chapter—raises a number of cultural issues not discussed elsewhere; it provides an opportunity to raise questions that cannot easily be approached in the U.S.-German context, and so it is more open-ended. The final chapter summarizes the high points of the report and offers conclusions.

Clearly, some very important issues are not considered here in any detail. The most obvious among them are intellectual property, electronic cash, consumer protection, and the impact of global networks on financial markets. Two factors led to the decision not to include them. First, much has already been written about these issues elsewhere.[4] Second, they appear to be sufficiently far-enough removed from the other issues considered in this report that there would be no great gain in treating them here. Given the practical limitations on the report's length and comprehensiveness, it seemed better to exclude them than to address them superficially.

---

[4]See, for example, Computer Science and Telecommunications Board, National Research Council, 2000, *The Digital Dilemma*, Washington, D.C.: National Academy Press.

2

The Evolution of Global Networks

> We shape our buildings; thereafter they shape us.
>
> —*Winston Churchill*

2.1 INTRODUCTION

This chapter examines the evolution of global networks, mainly the Internet, and seeks to relate general features of the architecture and design of these communications systems to the values inherent in or reinforced by the technology. The focus is not on specific values such as privacy, intellectual property rights, or free speech, some of which are analyzed in other chapters of this volume, but rather on two more general phenomena: how values and interests have shaped and become embedded in the specifications of technological systems, and how the technical features of such systems in turn affect the values of the communities that make use of them.

The Internet emerged as a mega-network, so to speak, of technically and socially heterogeneous electronic communications networks. There were no formal obligations imposed on participants to converge on any uniform set of technical practices or social values in developing or using the Internet. At the same time, the benefits of ever-wider connectivity achievable by the system provided strong incentives for diverse public and private entities to ensure that hardware, software, and organizational structures were compatible and complementary. Thus far, this process of de facto standardization has been limited to technical specifications for interoperability and to basic social norms and business practices that are recognized as being conducive to the further growth of "inter-networking."

The way that the Internet has evolved historically from its origins in ARPANET, and the development of the World Wide Web (WWW) from its beginnings at the European Center for Nuclear Research (CERN) in Geneva, underscore a paradox. Although the "network of networks" has provided a culturally and politically heterogeneous array of societies with global connectivity, the key technologies of the system were originally designed to suit the needs of publicly funded scientific research groups. While widely distributed geographically and situated in a variety of academic and quasi-academic institutions, these groups were nonetheless very homogeneous with regard to the values shared among their respective work cultures.

Moreover, the scientific work groups within which the Internet's core technology was formed made little provision for coping technically with such issues as content, privacy, security, and identity.[1] The relative emphases reflected a focus on resource sharing, communication, and collaboration among the original communities of designers and users, whose members were scientists and engineers selected according to criteria of technical competence and, in some cases, of national security.

It should not be surprising, therefore, that some palpable sociocultural frictions emerged as the network of networks became a universal communications facility—the "global information superhighway," in 1990s argot. The difficulties that have arisen over the control of content (based on "acceptability" concerns) on the Internet are, in some sense, a reaction to the technical and, increasingly, economic ease with which the Internet's reach can be extended into many diverse cultural settings. The set of electronic communications systems that evolved into the Internet carried with it technological design features that were in some respects quite unlike those of the existing telecommunications networks: more content can be discovered and pulled in from more sources, and more can be sent, relatively easily and inexpensively.

One consequence of these features was that they enabled the rapid spread of digital communications channels that simply bypassed established licensing procedures and other kinds of authorization that are evi-

---

[1]Of course, given the limitations on resources embodied in the first connected computing systems, an early feature was simply logging in, which could be enhanced to support different levels of security in access control. Attempts to introduce security for specific contexts or user groups date from the 1970s. See Stephen S. Kent, 1999, "Security and the Internet (circa 1980-1990)," ACM *SIGCOMM Tutorial: A Technical History of the Internet,* available online at <http://www.cs.utexas.edu/users/dragon/sigcomm/tl/kent.slides.ppt>.

dent—for example, in broadcasting. Radio and television have afforded local or national political jurisdictions the opportunity to pre-assign responsibilities for, and place a variety of restrictions on, the content and conditions of programs' delivery.

A second noteworthy dimension of the "value" conflicts that have emerged with the Internet's explosive growth stemmed from the formation, among some pioneer users of these internetworked facilities, of a new and distinctive cultural ethos of "cyberspace." This culture drew strength from the fusion of network engineers' and software programmers' enthusiasms for experimentation in this new technological domain, and it evinced an occasional anti-authoritarianism that took many faces—for example, frustration with the controlled telecommunications context in which the Internet technology arose, the extracurricular development of UNIX (a programming language fundamental to the early Internet) within AT&T, and the creativity of the "computer hacker" communities that only later became associated with destructive intent.

Popular perceptions tend to inflate the role of the Internet as the most recent among the "technologies of freedom,"[2] and they tend to intensify representations of any governmental posture other than laissez-faire as contests between a reactive authoritarian state and those who adhere to the libertarian, democratic ethos of the Internet. But although anti-authoritarianism is now part of the popular culture or ideology often associated with the Internet and its early developers and users, this aspect—given the role of large institutions in guiding and funding much of the fundamental Internet development work—should not be overstated.

Nevertheless, anti-authoritarianism was one major reason why the evolution of the Internet led to significant technical departures—with respect to network architecture, cost structures, the services it carried, and the innovative "business models" that have co-evolved with it—from previous telecommunications systems.[3] As with other technological developments, social and organizational goals affected the design and evolution of the Internet, first becoming "embedded" in specific network implementations and later manifesting themselves in protocols, technical standards, and operating procedures. This ensemble of characteristics, in turn, shaped the social conventions and behavioral norms that developed among users of the technology. Much may be learned from this history, which is presented in more detail in the next section.

---

[2]Ithiel de Sola Pool. 1983. *Technologies of Freedom.* Cambridge MA: Belknap Press.

[3]These fundamental attributes of the Internet have been chronicled in a series of Computer Science and Telecommunications Board reports: *Realizing the Information Future* (1994), *The Unpredictable Certainty* (1996), and *The Internet's Coming of Age* (2001), all National Research Council reports published by the National Academy Press, Washington, D.C.

A third major issue that needs to be addressed is the extent to which the ubiquity of the Internet's technology-based infrastructure will promote convergence in the values of the disparate user communities around the world. This is a complex matter, raising questions about whether the changing purposes for which the network of networks is being used will drive alterations in its architecture and technical features, as well as questions about the extent to which those changes can accommodate local pressures to affect network configuration or to control content through local regulatory interventions. This issue is discussed below and in Chapter 3. Without drawing premature conclusions at this point, it appears unlikely that a single, globally uniform value system will emerge. Still, one should be cautious about attempting to "predict the unpredictable,"[4] given the uncertainties that surround, and are in turn created by, the continuing rapid pace of advance in digital network technology.

2.2 EVOLUTION AND DESIGN OF GLOBAL TELECOMMUNICATIONS NETWORKS

Globally pervasive telecommunications networks, even those in the prosaic form of the public telephone and telex, are a comparatively new phenomenon. In the last decades of the 19th century telegraphy was able to acquire something approaching global reach by means of submarine cables, but the number of nodes of the "Victorian Internet" remained limited to the industrially advanced countries and their colonial possessions.[5] Even in those regions, telegraphic access tended to be restricted to the major commercial centers that lay along the seaboards or that were linked by railways. Indeed, it was not until the 1960s and 1970s that mature telecommunications systems, which had evolved as mono-functional (single-service) networks for the transmission of voice and text, achieved high penetration rates throughout industrialized countries and something approaching truly global coverage—albeit with an emphasis on major population centers.

Thus global "coverage" is not the same as a ubiquitous presence or even universal access to basic telecommunications. The great majority of the world's people still live under conditions that do not afford them basic local telephonic services, let alone global connectivity (which still relies to a considerable degree on the telephone network).

[4]David J. Farber. 2000. "Predicting the Unpredictable—Technology and Society," in *Understanding the Impact of Global Networks on Local Social, Political and Cultural Values,* Christoph Engel and Kenneth H. Keller, eds., 29-37. Baden-Baden: Nomos.

[5]Tom Standage. 1998. *The Victorian Internet: The Remarkable Story of the Telegraph and the Nineteenth Century's On-line Pioneers.* New York: Berkeley Books.

Progress, of course, has involved changes in the mix of technologies. While the telephone network continues to grow, the number of telex users has fallen as that technology has been replaced by facsimile (fax), which grew explosively during the 1980s. Around the world, all these networks have been affected by the operation and ownership largely of entities—public administrations (postal, telephony, and telegraphy authorities, or PTTs) or private regulated monopolies—that provided the services under common-carrier and universal-service regimes.

The rise of the Internet has been associated with privatization of telecommunications and relaxation of PTT control in many countries (e.g., with the introduction of competitive service from nontraditional players such as Internet service providers, or ISPs). This pattern reflects movement away from the inherently hierarchical architecture and control model of telephony and telex (both within countries and historically in the international, interconnected network environment), the rise of direct country-to-country dialing and other modern features associated with the new global network environment, and declining relative telecommunications prices (which still tend to be higher than in the United States and less likely to be flat-rate than to vary with time on the line and distance), itself a goal.

The design of the telephone system and the prevailing business models, as well as cultural and economic factors, powerfully shape the way we use the telephone, which is nowhere more obvious than in comparing user behavior across nations. For example, flat-rate local charges for business and residential customers may encourage frequent and long telephone calls (though charges do not fully explain the extent to which, in Western societies, the teenage children of middle-class householders engage in interminable after-school telephone conversations). Other evident changes beginning in the late 1990s relate to the spread of mobile (cellular) phones, and observers speculate about the cultural impact of anywhere/anytime calling behavior.

But although private communications practices, and the organization of commerce and industry, have been transformed in many respects by the diffusion of the telephone, we have no evidence that local and national cultural values have been significantly altered by the telephone's advent. Still less is there evidence to support the claim that the spread of ubiquitous telephone access, in and of itself, has been a strong force promoting convergence of social or business norms toward uniform regional and national, let alone global, value systems.[6]

---

[6]Ithiel de Sola Pool, ed., 1978, *The Social Impact of the Telephone,* Cambridge MA: The MIT Press; Christian Pinaud, 1985, *Entre Nous, les Telephones. Vers une Sociologie de la Telecommunication,* Paris: Insep Editions; Claude S. Fischer, 1992, *America Calling: A Social History of the Telephone to 1940,* Berkeley, CA: University of California Press.

Networks for data communication have a more uneven history than those for voice, although they have largely been built on the same underlying infrastructure (e.g., through the use of lines provisioned by telephone companies). Early data communications networks emerged in the 1960s and 1970s along with time-sharing computer systems. The major computer vendors developed software that supported interconnection of their machines, and consequently the early data communications networks were proprietary rather than public. Most of them were corporate networks linking different sites of a firm via leased telephone lines. Pioneer users were large corporations in the electronics and automobile industries and firms in the financial services sector; the multinationals took the lead in creating private global networks, primarily to facilitate intraorganizational data exchange.

Beginning in the 1970s, this same approach was expanded by intermediaries, third-party providers of so-called value-added networks (VANs, such as Telenet and Tymnet in the United States) to serve companies that could not afford the cost or inconvenience of developing their own networks. VANs grew in the 1980s by expanding points of presence in countries around the world, providing them with dialup and leased-line connections. Also in the 1980s, some of these companies began to offer service (e.g., GE Information Services' GE*nie) to the general public at comparatively low rates for non-business-hour use. They competed with other businesses having a "bulletin board" style as well as time-sharing roots, such as CompuServe (which introduced consumer service in 1979).

This was also the period during which VANs experimented with third-party interconnection of different businesses through the structured, controlled technologies associated with electronic data interchange (EDI). These EDI services supported the exchange of documents in standard formats through central host-computer systems; all parties to a transaction (e.g., buyer and seller) needed to be subscribers to the VAN's EDI service. VANs were treated as enhanced services in the U.S. regulatory context, making them exempt from telecommunications regulation.[7]

State-owned and regulated private monopoly-telephone-network operators around the world moved slowly to enter the growing markets for data services. A combination of regulatory restrictions and technical and managerial incompetence (reflecting, in part, emphasis on voice and lack of experience in data communications) appear to have constrained these organizations. Initially some of the PTTs in Europe, with the German Bundespost at the forefront, developed circuit-switched data networks

[7]Provision of international service involved arrangements with international record carriers for international transit service and arrangements with PTTs for local points of presence and/or gateways to local data networks.

that mimicked the model of the telex network, thereby displaying the extent to which they remained "locked into" the traditional commercial vision associated with the architecture of the basic telephone system.

Only in the early 1980s did the already-existing telephone organizations move to packet-switching technologies. PTTs tended to select the non-proprietary protocol standard, X.25, which was associated with the International Organization for Standardization's (ISO) Open Systems Interconnection (OSI) reference model; X.25 was approved in 1984 by the International Telecommunication Union (ITU, through what is known as the ITU-T, the telecommunications standards-setting arm).[8] As noted above, most of the private corporate networks at this time relied on proprietary protocols, such as the IBM Corporation's Systems Network Architecture (SNA) or the Digital Equipment Corporation's DECNET standards. The packet-switching mode in the proprietary as well as in the X.25 networks relied on a hierarchical network architecture, which conformed to traditional management notions of the manner in which information should optimally flow and be controlled within the large corporate organization.

This, as shall be seen, was very different from the architecture of the Internet. Outside the United States, this public-utility approach to packet switching was associated with country-specific public data networks (PDNs), some of which involved country-to-country gateways (based on the sister protocol standard, X.75, also used for connections to VANs). Similar to telephony charging, PDN and VAN pricing tended to involve connection-time and traffic (e.g., "kilo-packet") charges.

Early commercial data-communications networks and services—corporate and VAN plus PDN—provided crucial experience that shaped the development of the global telecommunications system and created readiness for the Internet takeoff in the mid-1990s.[9] The context was confused, however. It was an intersection, and occasionally a collision, of the business and engineering orientations that were traditional in the world of the PTTs, and the world of computer vendors and data-processing and data-communications services. Stalemates and acrimony sometimes marked proceedings of technical committees in national and international telecommunications standards organizations during the 1980s.[10]

---

[8]Marvin A. Sirbu and Laurence E. Zwimpfer. 1985. "Standards Setting for Computer Communication: The Case of X.25. A Detailed Examination of the Development of X.25," *IEEE Communications Magazine* 23:35-45.

[9]Marjory S. Blumenthal. 2000. "Architecture and Expectations: Networks of the World-Unite!," *The Promise of Global Networks,* Jorge Reina Schement, ed., 1-52. Washington, D.C.: Aspen Institute. Available online at <http://www. aspeninst.org/publicationsl/bookstore communications-promise.asp>.

[10]U.S. Congress, Office of Technology Assessment. 1992. *Global Standards: Building Blocks for the Future,* TCT-512. Washington, D.C.: U.S. Government Printing Office, March, pp. 12-14.

This discord gave way, by the late 1990s, to broad agreement on many basic principles concerning global networks. These principles include global interoperability (compatibility) and even openness of networks. But the process, unfolding largely in the 1980s but extending into the 1990s, involved complex tussles among ISO, the ITU and its principal constituents, the PTTs, U.S. telephone companies, corporate representatives (notably IBM, with a major stake in SNA), and the heterogeneous supporters of the Internet protocol suite known as TCP/IP. Complicating the picture was telephone-company development of standards for enhancing telephony networks, such as the integrated services digital network (ISDN) and asynchronous transfer mode (ATM) technology. But to simplify discussion, a major focus of international negotiation was on the relative merits of TCP/IP vs. OSI, which the former ultimately dominated.[11]

The OSI Reference Model describes a seven-layer architecture defining functions, services, and interfaces for data-communications systems. There is a related family of OSI protocols, such as X.25 and X.400 for messaging and X.500 for directories, that implement what is described in the reference model and that have been developed through conventional standards-setting processes.[12] Hence, OSI has been described as a "meta-standard" rather than a conventional set of interoperability standards.[13] A critical dimension of OSI is the European prominence in its development, measured by the locus of key engineering activities and ISO's location and environment. In particular, European computer vendors, European governments, and the Commission of the European Union saw the OSI program as an instrument of industrial policy to protect European manufacturers—which already were major vendors of proprietary network solutions—from the predominance of IBM and other U.S. firms. The effort to provide an alternative, or even the *prospect* of one, was intended by some to arrest the widespread deployment of IBM's SNA network standard in Europe.[14]

---

[11]Susanne K. Schmidt and Raymund Werle. 1998. *Coordinating Technology: Studies in the International Standardization of Telecommunications.* Cambridge, MA: The MIT Press.

[12]Todd Shaiman. 1995. *The Political Economy of Anticipatory Standards: The Case of the Open Systems Interconnection Reference Model.* University of Oxford M.Sc. Thesis in Economic and Social History. September.

[13]Paul A. David and Mark Shurmer, 1996, "Formal Standards-setting for Global Telecommunications and Information Services. Towards an Institutional Regime Transformation?," *Telecommunications Policy* 20(10):789-815; Paul A. David, 2000, "The Internet and the Economics of Network Technology Evolution," *Understanding the Impact of Global Networks on Local Social, Political and Cultural Values*, Christoph Engel and Kenneth H. Keller, eds., 40-71, Baden-Baden: Nomos.

[14]In the same way, many in the European telecommunications industry came to regard ISDN not only as the route to providing a seamless means of data communication via tele-

The interplay between OSI and TCP/IP was not straightforward;[15] recollections of those involved reveal a fair amount of acrimony there as well. Yet experience and familiarity with TCP/IP, the development of which had been documented publicly since 1969 through Requests for Comments (RFCs), clearly contributed to OSI.[16] The articulation of seven layers, for example, is an elaboration of the traditional four layers ascribed to basic Internet technology. That description, plus specific references to layers 1 through 7, is widely used in discussing internetworking today, though otherwise the terminology tends to be different.

In the end, however, some of the concrete engineering design work of OSI standards committees was acknowledged or absorbed by the Internet Engineering Task Force (IETF). In 1989, for example, the IETF Open PDN Routing Working Groups addressed internetworking involving X.25-based PDNs using X.121 addressing, and the Network Working Group even proposed experimentation with OSI network layer protocols over the Internet and the creation of an experimental OSI Internet (RFC 1070).

As these examples illustrate, there were individuals who were "bilingual" in these standards environments, people who attempted to work on some kind of coordination, if not integration, of approach. But they were not in the mainstream of Internet technology development.[17] Although TCP/IP was adopted as a U.S. military standard (around 1980), the contention with OSI in the United States came to a head in the late 1980s when the National Institute of Standards and Technology promulgated a

---

phone lines, but also as the means of stabilizing the PTT monopolies on the eve of deregulation and liberalization. The peculiar combination of abstract principles and concrete economic interests may be one reason why neither OSI-based networks nor ISDN was ever translated into an integrated system diffused widely within national networks, let alone on a global scale. See Paul A. David and W. Edward Steinmueller, 1990, "The ISDN Bandwagon Is Coming, But Who Will Be There to Climb Aboard?," *Quandaries in the Economics of Data Communication Networks, Economics of Innovation and New Technology,* 1:43-62.

[15]T.M. Egyedi. 1999. "Tension Between Standardisation and Flexibility Revisited: A Critique," *Standardisation and Innovation in Information Technology SLIT 1999, Proceedings of the Ist IEEE Conference on Standardisation and Innovation in Information Technology (SIIT 99),* Aachen, Germany, September 15-17, 1999, Kai Jakobs and Robin Williams, eds., 65-74. Piscataway, NJ: IEEE.

[16]David M. Piscitello and A. Lyman Chapin, 1993, *Open Systems Networking: TCP/IP and* OSI. Addison-Wesley Professional Computing Series; T.M. Egyedi, 1999, "Tension Between Standardisation and Flexibility Revisited: A Critique," *Standardisation and Innovation in Information Technology SLIT '99. Proceedings of the Ist IEEE Conference on Standardisation and Innovation in Information Technology (SIIT 99),* Kai Jakobs and Robin Williams, eds., 65-74, Piscataway, NJ: IEEE.

[17]This social attitude and discrimination were evident in the criticism lobbed occasionally at the original executive director of the Internet Society, who had a history of involvement in standards setting both at U.S. and international organizations.

Federal Information Processing Standard that related OSI to U.S. government needs—the climax of the Government Open Systems Interconnection Protocol (GOSIP) initiative. GOSIP crystallized evolving concerns with OSI in the technical and business communities, and its demise in 1994 (through a finessing that offered a choice between it and TCP/IP in government procurement) marked the end of serious U.S. consideration of OSI.[18]

By the mid-1990s, the market preference for TCP/IP was clearly established, in part because of its comparative simplicity, which facilitated development of commercially viable products across a range of computing platforms.[19] By the late 1990s, the penetration of TCP/IP technology into private (e.g., corporate) networks was reflected in the use of the term "intranets," an obvious play on "Internet."

Tensions and misunderstandings among OSI and TCP/IP proponents had as much to do with attitudes toward standards-setting as about technology or even international competition. People in the Internet community have historically looked askance at telephony standards-setting, associating it with the slow progress that helped to occasion their own work and with highly bureaucratic and time-consuming procedures. By contrast, the Internet standards-setting process focused on working implementations. The philosophy was articulated by MIT's David Clark (the original Internet architect and architecture board leader), who had been involved in protocol development since the 1970s: "We reject kings, presidents, and voting. We believe in rough consensus and running code." This widely repeated characterization, voiced at a 1992 meeting, has been echoed as a motto by many and codified in official documentation of the Internet's architectural principles—themselves embodied in the TCP/IP protocol suite—and of the IETF's approach to their implementation.[20]

The IETF's roots date back to the ARPANET. Its RFCs were initiated to facilitate quick dissemination and discussion of the ideas and technical specifications that had been suggested by members of what was then a small but geographically dispersed networking community, funded by the Advanced Research Projects Agency (ARPA).[21] If a suggested proto-

---

[18]Shirley M. Radack. 1994. "The Federal Government and Information Technology Standards: Building the National Information Infrastructure," *Government Information Quarterly* 11(4):373-385.

[19]It has been observed that standards can benefit from a bandwagon effect, and this was the case with TCP/IP, for which software and product development grew steadily. See Martin C. Libicki. 1995. *Standards: The Rough Road to the Common Byte.* Washington, D.C.: Center for Advanced Concepts and Technology, National Defense University.

[20]Brian Carpenter, ed. 1996. "Architectural Principles of the Internet," Internet Engineering Task Force RFC 1958. Available online at <http://info.intemet.isi.edu:80/in-notes/rfc/files/rfcl958.txt>.

[21]Janet Ellen Abbate. 1999. *Inventing the Internet.* Cambridge MA: The MIT Press, pp. 73-74.

col seemed interesting, it was likely that someone would implement and test it. Implementations that proved useful were copied to similar systems on the Net.

In this way, the number of technical specifications and the number of people involved in "standardization" grew. Everyone who was interested and had access to the ARPANET could participate, and the results were available free of charge. With more and more people getting involved in Internet standardization, however, the IETF procedures and the standards-approval procedure became somewhat formalized. Only since 1992 has the term "standard" been officially used for technical specifications that have completed the full process of standardization (RFC 1311).

The IETF is now split into more than 100 working groups covering eight to ten functional areas. Working groups can be easily created, and most of them are dissolved after they have finished their task. In contrast with most standardization organizations, participation in the IETF and its working groups is open to anyone. A formal membership is not required. Broad and unrestricted discussion of the proposals via electronic discussion groups and mailing lists is possible. Before Internet standards are approved, at least two independent implementations must have been completed. They must work and must be interoperable.

The success of TCP/IP does not imply that the way it developed could be emulated. By the mid-1990s, the IETF was under strain, reflecting growth in the number of participants and a diversification of interests in developing and implementing the technology. New users, service providers, and network operators make it much more difficult to use the same informal consensus mechanism as before to coordinate further technical changes in the system. Development of the protocols for the Web, for example, has proceeded under the auspices of the World Wide Web Consortium, which coordinates with the IETF but is a membership organization. And a variety of industry-based consortia have emerged to address specific kinds of technology and expedite the standards-development process.

The difficulties encountered in attempting to move to a new generation of the TCP/IP protocol stack, which would enlarge the address space significantly and add other features, illustrates the problem.[22] Although the new protocol (IP Version 6) was adopted by the IETF, and although backwards compatibility with IP Version 4, now widely in use, is guaranteed, not many are ready to migrate from a good to a better technical standard; they hesitate to incur switching costs because no authority can guarantee that everyone else will also switch. In the old NSFNET days, the decision to switch to a new protocol would have been comparatively easy

[22]See CSTB, *The Internet's Coming of Age*, 2001.

because the National Science Foundation (NSF) could stipulate it as a condition for those who wanted connection to this attractive network. As another committee of the Computer Science and Telecommunications Board observed, "[f]or the Internet, . . . the explicit government directive to set standards [in the early ARPANET period, the beginning of the Internet] has been replaced by a process driven by vendor and market pressures, with essentially no top-down control. . . . Currently, the Internet community seems to make short-range decisions with some success, but long-range decisions, which reflect not only immediate commercial interests but also broader societal goals, may not get an effective hearing."[23]

Virtually the only public global data network open to corporate and personal use is the Internet. The fact that the Internet comprises thousands of technically distinct networks is a direct result of the design of the TCP/IP protocol suite, which allows Internet services to be run on top of networks based on other protocols, such as X.25, SNA, and Ethernet. The Internet's architecture and standards separate applications (from the Web to Internet telephony) from the underlying infrastructure, whereas conventional telephony grew as an application that was tightly coupled to its infrastructure. In telephony, the "intelligence" that made applications possible was based in equipment inside the network; in the Internet, that intelligence is largely in the software running on equipment attached by users at the "ends" of the network.[24]

That the Internet standards were developed in an open process facilitated their diffusion; broad participation was possible and use of the standards was unencumbered. Meanwhile, implementations by hardware and software vendors could be proprietary, contributing to the profitability of many businesses built on this technology.[25] There has also been openness of a sort in the business of Internet service provision: No single network operator or service provider owns or controls "the Net," and this network of networks essentially constitutes an "unmanaged" system.

That characterization is a mixed blessing. As a union of different networks, the experience of a user communicating across multiple networks may devolve to a lowest common denominator—one slow-speed or low-quality segment can degrade the whole experience. This problem is of

---

[23]See CSTB, *Realizing the Information Future*, 1994, p. x.

[24]For a fuller explanation of the Internet's generality, flexibility, and architecture, see CSTB, *Realizing the Information Future* (Chapter 2) and *The Internet's Coming of Age*.

[25]Ironically, despite the openness and bottom-up character of Internet standardization, it is not easily accessible to outsiders. Only insiders understand what is being negotiated in Requests for Comments and discussed in developers' meetings. A meritocracy, the IETF pioneers believed that there were technical solutions for every problem, and that a solution can't be the optimal one if it needs to be voted on.

particular concern for users (a minority today) with applications that demand high speed or minimal delay. Thus, the Internet's technology and architecture do not make it a uniform experience—one reason why large providers such as America Online or UUNET have been trying to grow larger and provide complete end-to-end communications, much as the VANs did.[26]

As competition for customers has grown among ISPs, and concern about service quality along with it, connections among networks have become problematic; ISPs tend to discriminate among networks in making judgments about whether and on what terms to effect interconnections.[27] Although the technology makes interconnection—internetworking—easy in principle, business decisions have made it complicated in practice since the mid-1990s. At the same time, the growing use of the Internet increases its value as infrastructure for a growing body of users and uses. This, in turn, will increase pressures for some kind of management and/or coordination system, as well as for mechanisms to support enhancements to quality of service (which might minimize delay for critical applications, for example).[28]

In its early commercial period, the Internet architecture has promoted a horizontal pattern of organizations, in contrast to the more vertical, hierarchical, and controlled world of telephony. The ease of user attachment to the Internet makes it comparatively easy now to set up links to a variety of sources of information and entertainment—and to exchange information and communicate with other users—all without being tied to a single service provider. Even the smallest enterprise thus has the potential to achieve a global market presence. But this potential can be misleading, as new issues are arising now that a growing number of enterprises and individuals have figured this out. How, for example, can all these players compete for attention, or even be *found*, in an increasingly crowded Internet marketplace? And how do small enterprises thrive in the face of an economics that continues, as time progresses, to promote consolidation in markets for both suppliers and users of Internet technology? Chapter 7 on commerce has a related discussion.

---

[26]See CSTB, *The Internet's Coming of Age*, 2001.

[27]See CSTB, *The Internet's Coming of Age*, 2001.

[28]See Blumenthal, "Architecture and Expectations: Networks of the World-Unite!," 2000.

2.3 THE VALUE DIMENSION OF NETWORKS

Different social values and goals have influenced the evolution of data networks. Systems engineers, military leaders, business executives, policymakers, and private users—whether consciously or otherwise—shape the technical characteristics of these communications systems through technical proposals and practical decisions that reflect their individual needs, preferences, and world views. Once these values become "embedded" in the implementation of a particular network, they become latent, not only in the technical standards themselves but in the operating procedures, social conventions, and behavioral norms that develop among the technology's users.

These phenomena are not unique to the Internet; they are evident across a wide range of technologies, such as various forms of manufacturing automation, and reflect the very human processes of technology design and use. They arise because standards affect the architecture of information. As Libicki notes, standards promote different patterns regarding who is connected to whom and what is expressed easily or not; social relations vary, depending on whether a communications protocol is top-down or bottom-up; and the choice of programming language affects the relationship of programmers to their managers.[29]

Like protocol standards, many nontechnical norms facilitate compatibility and interoperability among users. Because they, too, have "positive network externalities" that promote their de facto acceptance, this larger structure of technological and social practices acquires considerable inertia and hence becomes difficult to change.[30] Moreover, the stronger the complementarities among the component elements of the resulting structure, the more likely it is to undergo gradual adaptations through incremental modification rather than radical change.

This is the sense in which one may speak of particular features of the systems' software components, or of certain conventions among network users, as having become "locked in." But it is important to emphasize that the extent of "lock-in" depends on the degree of complementarity among components. TCP/IP illustrates the point. Because the Internet, compared to other communications networks, can tolerate great heterogeneity among the components that may be interconnected, it permits a greater diversity of practices and associated values among its users, facilitating the inclusion of a broad range of systems in the overall network. This

---

[29]See Libicki, *Standards: The Rough Road to the Common Byte*, 1995.

[30]Karl Wameryd. 1990. "Conventions: An Evolutionary Approach," *Constitutional Political Economy*, 1:83-107.

inclusiveness can inhibit radical modification of the system's underlying technologies. This is another face on the Internet as infrastructure: broad dependence can slow evolution.

Interconnection—inter-networking—is thus the most obvious value in the Internet, though just one stage in a complex evolution. It embodies one possible technical solution—albeit a solution that was reinforced by its comparative generality and flexibility—to interconnecting host computers of different kinds of networks based on different technologies. The Internet's principal forerunner, the ARPANET, developed while alternative solutions were being worked on or were already available. They included the efforts of computer vendors such as the PARC XNS protocol from Xerox and the Unix-to-Unix copy protocol (UUCP), originally developed in the Bell Labs of AT&T and licensed out at very low cost. These efforts reflected a perceived need among researchers to interconnect the technically diverse networks that had already come into existence, at least in the United States.[31]

An intentional expansion of networking into the research community—a broadening of interconnection—was enabled by NSF's mid-1980s launch of NSFNET, a network that connected six research supercomputer centers and became a backbone (along with networks established by the Department of Energy and the National Aeronautics and Space Administration) for the larger network of networks.[32] A crucial early decision of NSF, after intense internal negotiations, was to base NSFNET on TCP/IP.[33] Another important decision led NSF to foster development of regional networks, which aggregated traffic from and provided technical support to smaller networks such as campuses.[34]

These regional networks evolved in the second half of the 1980s, and many of them were cosponsored by business organizations that, within certain limits, were allowed to use the networks for commercial purposes. Thus, a new type of hybrid network appeared on the landscape of data networks, and with a very different set of users. Some of the regional

---

[31]Katie Hafner and Matthew Lyon, 1996, *Where Wizards Stay Up Late: The Origins of the Internet,* New York: Simon & Schuster; John S. Quarterman, 1990, *The Matrix. Computer Networks and Conferencing Systems Worldwide,* Bedford, MA: Digital Press; Peter H. Salus, 1995, *Casting the Net. From ARPANET to INTERNET and Beyond,* Reading, MA/ Menlo Park, CA: Addison-Wesley.

[32]See Computer Science and Telecommunications Board, National Research Council, 1988, *Toward a National Research Network.* Washington, D.C.: National Academy Press.

[33]Juan D. Rogers. 1998. "Internetworking and the Politics of Science: NSFNET in Internet History," *The Information Society* 14:213-228.

[34]See CSTB, *Realizing the Information Future,* 1994.

networks spun off commercial networks—for example, NYSERNET in the New York area produced PSI—but most of the original regional networks faded away after the removal of NSF support (prompted by the commercialization of the backbone), the decommissioning of NSFNET in 1995, and the rise of commercial ISPs. During their heyday, however, these regional networks and their local tributaries—based on local area network (LAN) technology, X.25, SNA, DECNET, and other systems—were heterogeneous both socially and technically.

Interconnection was only one dimension; just as important was the motivation behind it. This included not only the need for communication per se but the sharing of information and computational resources. These factors were illustrated—and explored—in the expansion of LANs. As the number of workstations and personal computers in businesses and universities began to grow, vendors began to develop network technology to interconnect the computers and make it possible for users to share information and move files.[35]

Many organizations adopted Ethernet, token ring, or token bus technology and built their own (isolated) networks, which were used for internal purposes and initially not designed for connection to external networks. But in the second half of the 1980s, more and more LANs, including many campus networks, were linked to the Internet, while corporate LANs were linked to private wide-area networks. These developments, and their influence on how and where people did their work, stimulated business executives to rethink strategies of vertical integration. They began to consider technology-based alternatives—such as decentralization, outsourcing via inter-organizational networks, and the creation of the networked firm—to the traditional model of the corporation.

As networks evolved outside the business domain, the interplay of values and technology was even more apparent. Most of the noncommercial networks interconnected universities, governmental and non-governmental organizations, and eventually private households, self-help groups, and the like. These noncommercial networks grew up among user communities with similar interests—initially, people who were active users of particular computer systems or software and who wanted to communicate with kindred spirits. Such systems could be called "cooperative networks," because users or user organizations were involved in setting up the network and coordinating its functions, even though a traditional network provider sometimes operated it.

[35]Computer Science and Telecommunications Board, National Research Council. 1999. *Funding a Revolution: Government Support for Computing Research.* Washington D.C.: National Academy Press, pp. 169-183.

Notable cooperative networks that evolved in the research and education communities were the Computer Science Network (CSNET) and BITNET. E-mail communication, which unexpectedly had proved to be the most popular application of ARPANET, was the dominant service in CSNET and BITNET as well. Supported with limited funds from the National Science Foundation, CSNET connected computer science departments that had no access to the ARPANET and therefore lacked sophisticated facilities to communicate, collaborate, and share ideas.

Early on, computer scientists formed a kind of community, initially built around the time-shared computer and later around programming languages, operating systems, and computer networks.[36] Their sense of being pioneers in a revolutionary change of information-processing shaped the spirit of collaboration, informality, and even social responsibility behind the values and rules that guided these researchers' use of networks in the late 1970s and early 1980s.[37] However, by the late 1980s, the increase in NSF support for networking by other kinds of scientists led to concern among computer scientists that their own support could be eroded. Here, sharing collided with competition for resources.[38]

BITNET was an extragovernmental effort. Based on IBM technology, this completely decentralized network was set up by universities and research centers to facilitate information exchange between faculty, students, and administrative staff. BITNET extended the computer-communications infrastructure beyond CSNET, both in terms of the number and kind of people connected—that is, it involved a much wider range of researchers than computer scientists alone. BITNET was associated with EDUCOM, a nonprofit consortium of higher-education institutions that facilitated access to information resources in teaching, learning, scholarship, and research.

All the early academic and research networks fostered e-mail discussion vehicles. Most remarkable was the UUCP-based USENET, a system of newsgroups (bulletin boards) that was originally designed as a forum in which UNIX users could discuss their problems and assist each other. Very soon, USENET grew into a platform for a broad variety of newsgroups, including anti-authoritarian student groups and hacker com-

---

[36]Arthur L. Norberg and Judy E. O'Neill. 1996. *Transforming Computer Technology. Information Processing for the Pentagon, 1962-1986*. Baltimore: Johns Hopkins University Press. See also CSTB, *Funding a Revolution*, 1999.

[37]Volker Leib and Raymund Werle. 1998. "Computernetze als Infrastrukturen und Kommunikationsmedien der Wissenschaft," *Rundfunk and Fernsehen* 46(2-3):254-273.

[38]See CSTB, *Funding a Revolution*, 1999.

munities.[39] USENET relied on self-organization and also on self-restraint. Many of its rules and norms gave rise to an informal code of conduct for Internet users—such as "never disturb the flow of information" and "every user has the right to say anything and to ignore anything"—that is sometimes referred to as Netiquette. This code was viewed by those who adopted it as a natural extension of the fundamental values of American society, such as freedom of speech.

As the complex of research and education networks grew, federal program managers became concerned about the ways in which government-funded infrastructure would be used. The result was an effort, at least by the program managers, to limit usage of the early Internet components, and notably of NSFNET, by means of an "acceptable use policy" (AUP). In practice, enforcing an AUP was difficult; it depended on an honor system. And it effected a distinction between those with legitimate access and those—typically, parties seeking commercial gain—without it.

Practically, though, the more people experienced the communications capability and information access afforded by the Internet, the more they wanted to use it; differentiating sanctioned research and education activities from other uses seemed increasingly arbitrary and artificial. Avoiding the effect of the AUP, in fact, was one reason for the commercialization of the Internet backbone and the decommissioning of NSFNET in 1995. To enable that transition, NSF provided seed funding for public—as opposed to the intragovernmental—network-traffic exchange points (network access points), at which multiple providers of private backbones could interconnect. This step promoted interconnection and the prospect of multiple ISPs; commercial ISPs, meanwhile, had banded together to underwrite their own exchange facilities, the Commercial Internet Exchange (CIX).[40]

In contrast to the multifaceted growth of computer networks in the United States, progress was slower overseas. Although both the CSNET and BITNET networks, as well as the ARPANET,[41] had links to Europe, the long-lasting European aversion to TCP/IP appears to have been a crucial reason why research and education networks developed slowly there

---

[39]Michael Hauben and Ronda Hauben. 1997. *Netizens. On the History and Impact of Usenet and the Internet.* Los Alamitos, CA: IEEE Computer Society Press.

[40]See CSTB, *Realizing the Information Future,* 1994. Also see Juan D. Rogers, 1998, Internetworking and the Politics of Science: NSFNET in Internet History, *The Information Society* 14:213-222; Carl Malamud, 1993, *Exploring the Internet. A Technical Travelogue,* Englewood Cliffs, NJ: Prentice-Hall.

[41]The Joint Academic Network (JANET) was set-up in Britain and used by universities, the Ministry of Defense, and research organizations. See Malamud, *Exploring the Internet. A Technical Travelogue,* 1993.

and never transformed themselves into commercially viable networks. It took TCP/IP and its supporters another half decade to achieve acceptance in continental Europe.[42] The German example may be the best illustration of policy failure in this respect; industrial policy goals, a commitment to "open standards," and the conviction that it could catch up with the technology leader by a solo effort more or less ensured this failure.

IBM's initiative to launch and sponsor the European Academic and Research Network (EARN, an extension of BITNET) in the early 1980s was welcomed by the research community. Within 6 months after EARN started operation, 75 mainframes had been interconnected in Germany. By the mid-1980s, more than 500 computers in the research organizations of 19 countries were linked to EARN. This system required permission from the European telecommunications monopolies, which up to that time had never agreed to allow data to be transmitted across national borders through private lines. The EARN board of directors had to struggle hard to get that permission. There were also problems with governments. They were concerned that EARN might be part of IBM's strategy to expand market dominance—not least because initially only IBM mainframes and Digital Equipment's VAXes could be linked via EARN. Although some governments had no objection to the project, others, among them the Germans, were only willing to give the green light on the condition that EARN evolve into an OSI-based system. This was agreed to, but it never actually materialized.

The German government reacted to EARN by initiating the Wissenschaftsnetz (Science Network). This was consistent with government programs to support the German computer industry and its most prominent corporation, Siemens. Technical standards played a significant role in this strategy. In a concerted action, most European governments had declared support for open, nonproprietary standards based on the OSI frame of reference. Germany thus insisted that the Wissenschaftsnetz be based on OSI standards as well. It was managed by the Verein Deutsches Forschungsnetz (German Research Network Association), whose members were drawn mainly from universities and large nonacademic research institutions.

In contrast with the United States or the United Kingdom, where dedicated organizations were charged with operating the network, in Germany the PTT—the Bundespost (Telekom)—was regarded as the "natural" candidate to provide this service. The Bundespost had the monopoly right for networks but extremely little experience with packet-switched

---

[42]Malamud, *Exploring the Internet. A Technical Travelogue*, 1993.

data communications.[43] Like practically all of its European partners, the Bundespost was committed to OSI. Thus the Wissenschaftsnetz was embedded in an institutional structure controlled by people who were not only *not* open to alternatives to OSI but rigorously rejected applications from computer scientists and software engineers to support TCP/IP-related R&D.

Although—or because—OSI was shielded from competition, it took years until products based on OSI standards were available that had any appeal for users X.400-based e-mail software, for instance, did not appear on the market until TCP/IP-based products were well established.[44] That lack of competition, together with its reliance on an official and rather slow OSI standardization process and its failure to involve users in the development of products and services, greatly limited the German research and education network's evolutionary dynamics. Thus the Wissenschaftsnetz did not attract many users.

Today, Internet service providers, telephone companies, cable-television companies, wireless device and service companies, computer hardware and software vendors, media companies, and all kinds of firms engaged in e-commerce use the Internet as an infrastructure and a business channel. This has again changed the character of the Internet, but it has not done away with its fundamental characteristics: decentralization, user involvement, openness, and self-organization (by which is meant a network infrastructure designed to allow groups to organize themselves to use it). It would be misleading, however, to infer that today's "community" of Internet users is homogeneous, cohesive, collegial, or has values, objectives, and skills similar to those of the early Internet pioneers. But this only means that, from a culture and values perspective, the Internet has become even more heterogeneous than it was a decade ago.

2.4 GLOBAL NETWORKS AND CHANGING VALUES: TOWARD CONVERGENCE OR DIVERGENCE?

What has been emphasized in the preceding sections of this chapter is how the characteristics of the Internet derive from its development path, how users have influenced that path of development, and how the resulting network has and will continue to influence the users. An important further question to consider is how a system with these technical and social

---

[43]Raymund Werle. 2000. "The Impact of Information Networks on the Structure of Political Systems," *Understanding the Impact of Global Networks on Local Social, Political and Cultural Values,* Christoph Engel and Kenneth H. Keller, eds., 167-192, Baden-Baden: Nomos.

[44]Schmidt and Werle, *Coordinating Technology,* 1998, pp. 230-243.

characteristics can be "coordinated." Depending on who is addressing the issue, that word may mean managed, governed, or regulated. But each of those terms is value-laden and can generate significant resistance, especially among those most closely associated with the Internet's origins.[45]

It remains to be seen whether the anti-hierarchical culture of information freedom that is so much a part of the Internet's history will survive and continue to animate resistance to local regulation. This history feeds the perception, in some quarters, of the Internet as socio-technologically so distinct from other communication systems that it should be treated as a special case—that it should *not* be brought into the established framework by which sovereign states and local political entities have long sought to control or regulate access to information.

A source of countervailing economic and political pressure—indeed, a countervailing "culture"—has been created by the policy decision to promote this technology as the communications infrastructure for interactive electronic commerce. In many countries, the Internet is seen as a positive force for economic development, generating acceptance despite concerns about some of the content that may be communicated or uses that may be supported. As a consequence, the efforts of technologists, entrepreneurs, and international-business-law specialists to facilitate greater use of the Internet for conducting public business are being widely hailed today as socially beneficial innovations.

Among the likely consequences of these developments is reinforcement of the dual trend toward, on the one hand, adapting the Internet for more secure and private point-to-point communications, and, on the other, using it as a medium for mass broadcasting of video, music, and text. The alignment of business interests with the first of these would seem to favor technologies that weaken the abilities of government to monitor and control content in interactive communications, an area that sovereign states have traditionally been less disposed to regulate.[46] Still, business organizations have long ago learned to accommodate themselves to the greater sensitivities of governments regarding unregulated broadcasts that might carry unwelcome news or disruptive messages.

Meanwhile, at the international level, the ITU (like other nongovernmental organizations) has been assessing how it could respond to the upheaval in telecommunications and related activities, from standards set-

[45]See Blumenthal, "Architecture and Expectations: Networks of the World-Unite!," 2000.

[46]Ithiel de Sola Pool. 1990. *Technologies Without Boundaries: On Telecommunications in a Global Age.* Cambridge, MA: Harvard University Press, Chapter 7.

ting to broader policymaking, associated with the Internet. The failure of OSI to achieve commercial success and the success of TCP/IP commercially sent clear signals about process problems. An indication of the potential for change, or at least a willingness to consider different approaches, is a 1998 ITU document that observes: "Competition in telecommunications is rapidly becoming a true market force whose evolution cannot be planned by policymakers, a force which increasingly is seen as best regulated on the basis of principles that are not specific to telecommunications but derived from a broader economic, social and cultural perspective."[47]

Some of the concerns posed by the Internet relate to its technologies for distributing information, which affect private parties with property interest in certain content as well as governments interested not only in protecting those private-property rights but also in meeting their own mission needs (which may be expressed in differing degrees of support for distribution of different kinds of content to different segments of the population). The Internet presents "the culture of sovereign control" with technical challenges that are not present when information comes embodied in conventional, tangible media such as newspapers, books, films, phonograph records, and audiocassette tapes or when signals are transmitted through physical channels, as is the case with telegraph, telex, and telephone messages. Even with regard to the broadcast media, domestic regulations and international conventions that restrict broadcasters to particular frequencies also serve to make it more feasible to identify, and interfere with, transmission and reception of particular sources of radio and TV messages.

Nevertheless, increasing commercial use of the Internet is driving both technical changes and consideration of nontechnical interventions. As Lessig has put it, the "changes that make commerce possible will also be changes that will make regulation easy."[48] For example, company interests in understanding customer behavior have driven the design of mechanisms for collecting personal information; this has led to increased privacy concerns, and to experimentation with technologies to permit anonymous interactions. Large organizations that use the Internet have developed firewalls, which can limit traffic coming into and going out of the organization's network, as well as software—e.g., e-mail filters—to monitor the kinds of communications that network users send. Mean-

---

[47]International Telecommunications Union, Draft Strategic Plan for the Union 1999-2003, dated 1998. Available online at <http://www.itu.int/newsroom/press/PP98/Documents/StratPlan9903.html>.

[48]Lawrence Lessig. 1999. *Code and Other Laws of Cyberspace.* New York: Basic Books, p. 30.

while, governments are contemplating use of the Internet for criminal purposes and the feasibility of eavesdropping or otherwise intervening in communications. All of these developments raise questions about whether the fundamental Internet architecture principles can be preserved.[49]

Do these developments pose a threat to local values? The analysis in this chapter suggests that the increasing dominance of a commercial culture on the Internet will be likely to produce a situation in which local jurisdictions will have considerable autonomy as well as greater technical capabilities to restrict local consumption of Internet content, at least as long as they do not use that power in blatant efforts to protect local commercial enterprises from the competition of politically powerful international media organizations. The implication is that the variations in local cultural norms are unlikely to be swept aside by the future spread and penetration of Internet-based services.

---

[49]See David D. Clark and Marjory S. Blumenthal, 2000, "Rethinking the Design of the Internet: The End to End Arguments vs. the Brave New World," presented at TPRC, September 24; available online at <http://www.tprc.org/AgendaOO.htm>.

3

Understanding Local Values and How They Are Affected by Global Networks

3.1 INTRODUCTION

Some value judgments, like the objection to child pornography, are essentially universal. But even nations as culturally close as the United States and Germany are divided on many value issues. For example, in the light of its history, Germany has actually banned right-wing publications that would be allowed, even if not admired, in the United States. On the other hand, Americans in large numbers deem certain materials pornographic that most Germans would find inoffensive (see Box 3.1 for these and other examples). These kinds of contrasts would seem to lead to the stark and simplistic assertion that global networks threaten local values. But the reality is much more complex. The purpose of this background chapter is to lay the conceptual foundation for understanding what values are, so that the interaction of global networks with the particular value-driven issues addressed in later chapters can be better understood.

There is no universal agreement on what the term '"value"' means. The dictionary definition ("a principle, standard, or quality considered worthwhile or desirable"[1]) has a question-begging quality to it. Although almost all behavioral and social scientists deal with values in one way or another, they tend to avoid the term and replace it with more specific concepts. Economists, for example, typically focus on behavioral responses to incentives, with the assumption that they are a measure of

[1] *The American Heritage Dictionary of the English Language*, Third Edition. New York: Houghton Mifflin Company.

BOX 3.1 Public Views of Internet Risks

A study commissioned by the Bertelsmann Foundation[1] posed two questions to people 18 years and older in the two countries. The first question concerned risks that they associate with the Internet. Each interviewee could name as many risks as he or she wished. The responses were as follows:

Risk	USA	Germany
Data protection	22%	24%
Pornography	13%	17%
Protection of minors[a]	21%	6%
Fraud, Manipulation	8%	3%
Presentation of violence	2%	3%

[a]The distinction between pornography and protection of minors is one of perception, not necessarily of substance, by the persons who responded to the interviewers of the Bertelsmann Foundation. The same caveat applies to the distinction between pornography and nudity in the second table.

The second question addressed attitudes toward censorship. Each interviewee was allowed to name the kinds of content that he or she would like to see banned from the Internet. This yielded the following:

Content Type	USA	Germany
Racist speech	63%	79%
Violence	39%	61%
Pornography	59%	60%
Politically radical speech	26%	58%
Nudity	43%	13%

These responses are striking in number of aspects. First, although similar percentages of respondents in the two countries felt that risks were associated with Internet content, German respondents were much more likely to endorse banning such content. Second, the distinctions made between pornography and nudity suggest very different perceptions in the two countries of what constitutes pornography. Third, the similar percentages of people judging pornography to be a risk, compared to the divergence among those judging possible injury to minors to be a risk, also suggest a difference in perception. Finally, the wide range of reactions to different kinds of objectionable speech in the United States compared with Germany appears noteworthy.

[1]Bertelsmann Foundation, ed., 2000, "Risk Assessment and Opinions Concerning the Control of Misuse on the Internet. Results of representative surveys conducted in the United States, Australia and the Federal Republic of Germany." A project by the Bertelsmann Foundation, Germany, in conjunction with the Australian Broadcasting Authority (ABA), Allensbach archives, IfD-survey 3296, available online at <http://www.stiftung.bertelsmann.de/internetcontent/english/frameset. htm content/c2000.htm> (30.03.00); printed version in Jens Waltermann and Marcel Machill, eds., *Protecting Our Children on the Internet: Towards a New Culture of Responsibility*, Gütersloh: Bertelsmann Foundation Publishers.

(and do not themselves affect) values. Nevertheless, analysis of values has increased—and improved in quality—with the recognition that values can change; they can be affected by public policy, and they influence how people respond to public policy.[2]

This study aims specifically at understanding the influence of global networks on local values, and the public unease to which it gives rise, in order to provide advice to political actors on how—and whether—to take action. Under the circumstances, it is difficult to avoid the general question of what values are, what function they have for the individual, society, and government, and what makes them local. The following sections take up these issues and their implications.

3.2 ARE VALUES ALWAYS THE ISSUE?

Although public concern with the impact of global networks is often cast in terms of the effect on local values, in some instances the perceived threat to a value is a proxy for a more tangible threat. Thus, if people ask to be shielded from inadvertent access to depictions of brutal violence, they may well be driven by a fear of the trauma—that is, the mental injury—that exposure to such scenes might produce rather than a principled objection to the exposure itself. Some forms of crude pornography might fall into the same category. Thus, the objection could be based both on a normative conviction concerning graphic violence and a self-preserving concern for one's mental health.

There is a subtle, but real, difference here. Measures aimed at promoting a normative conviction, or value, are intended to encourage conformity among those who might not be inclined to accept it, though a single violation would not challenge its validity or lead to any great harm. A trauma, on the other hand, hits those whose normative conviction may be quite firm. And a single exposure can be enough to cause unacceptable harm.[3]

In fact, although there are some differences in how they are manifested in the United States and Germany, arguments to limit access to pornography or portrayals of violence are frequently justified in terms of the need to protect minors rather than as a question of morality. To some extent, the approach may be disingenuous in that adults who object to depictions of nudity might simply find it more convenient and effective

[2]Henry J. Aaron et al., eds. 1994. *Values and Public Policy*. Washington, D.C.: Brookings Institution.

[3]J. Douglas Bremner and Charles R. Marmar, eds. 1998. *Trauma, Memory, and Dissociation*. Washington, D.C.: American Psychiatric Press.

to use the child-protection argument than to have to defend the value in the abstract. Of course, this strategy could lead policymakers and designers to develop legal tools and technical approaches specifically directed at minors, which would do little to deal with the actual concerns that prompted the outcry.[4]

The German treatment of Nazi speech illustrates still another distinction (Box 3.2). The use of Nazi symbols, open adherence to Nazi ideology, or the distribution of Nazi publications without a strong disclaimer is a taboo—a very strong form of protecting and enforcing a value judgement. Anyone openly breaking the taboo, even once, is alienated from the community. Yet, the violation does not necessarily threaten the taboo. In fact, occasional breaches can even help a society enforce the tabooed value; it can be argued that the common and visible defense of the taboo can serve as a powerful social bond. At the limit, a society may even define itself by its shared taboos.[5] To some extent, these same arguments might also apply to values that are part of what has been called political correctness.

Finally, there are the circumstances in which the potential harm is not the content itself, but its use in the outside, non-virtual world. The most obvious case is the publication of bomb-building instructions. The concern in that instance does not arise because the communication challenges the principle that it is wrong to kill people. The value itself is not in danger, though people's lives might be.

In these examples, the issue is less a threat to a local value than it is a broader social or political problem. But there are also instances in which global networks may serve to promote local values that have been undermined by political considerations. For example, global networks give German citizens access to environmental information that the German government holds but has been hesitant to release, despite its legal obligation to do so. And the very fact that information of that kind is made available in other countries through the Internet may pressure German administrators to move toward more open policies.[6]

Compared to the situation in Germany, the issue of government openness has been less problematic in the United States. Moreover, global networks serve to multiply sources of information there at a time when consolidation in other media has raised concern that the diversity of viewpoints made available to the public—also a clear local value—might be reduced.

---

[4]See Chapter 5 ("Free Speech and the Internet") for more discussion.

[5]Horst Reimann. 1989. "Tabu," *Staatslexikon*. Freiburg: Recht Wirtschaft Gesellschaft, 420.

[6]See Chapter 6 ("Privacy and Freedom of Information") for more discussion.

BOX 3.2 The Nazi Taboo: Germany Versus Amazon.com

In the summer of 1999, German Minister of Justice Dr. Herta Däubler-Gmelin called on amazon.com and barnesandnoble.com to stop selling and distributing the English translation of Hitler's book *Mein Kampf* to Germany. Däubler-Gmelin also urged German media giant Bertelsmann to influence barnesandnoble.com, in which it has a 40 percent interest. Furthermore, a speaker of the German Ministry of Justice suggested that it was possible to prosecute managers of barnesandnoble.com and amazon.com when traveling in Germany. In initial discussions, the companies were resistant; a spokeswoman from amazon.com said: "We are a U.S. store. We view this as though a German was on vacation here and went into a physical bookstore and bought the books." But amazon.com and barnesandnoble.com later decided to stop shipping *Mein Kampf* to customers located in Germany.

The issue came up when a German-based researcher for the Wiesenthal Center ordered *Mein Kampf* and other books from the two online booksellers. The researcher who ordered the Hitler book from amazon.com received an e-mail suggesting that he might also be interested in *White Power,* by the American Nazi leader George Lincoln Rockwell. In 1999, the numbers of orders of *Mein Kampf* reached a Top Ten list for German buyers, a fact that the company displayed on its Web site. However, as the displayed statistics showed, many of the German buyers bought the books not for racial motives but for historical and academic interests. They also bought inoffensive biographies of Hitler, historical studies, and even books by Karl Marx.

It is illegal in Germany to distribute writings like *Mein Kampf,* designed to incite racial hatred, at least in the German language (Para 86 and 130 German Penal Code). Foreign exporters to Germany must heed these prohibitions, although the case with respect to English translations is not unequivocal. In 1995, German authorities successfully prosecuted and jailed an American citizen, Gary Lauck, for distributing illegal propaganda and for encouraging racial hatred. He served a four-year sentence.

In most countries the publication of *Mein Kampf* can be prevented by refusing to license the copyright, which is held by the state of Bavaria as the legal successor to Hitler's publisher. That is not possible, however, in the United States and in the United Kingdom. The rights to publish *Mein Kampf* in these countries were sold in 1933.

SOURCES: John Burgess, "Amazon Reverses on Hitler Book," *Washington Post,* November 18, 1999; Michael Hanfeld, "Hitler lesen," *Frankfurter Allgemeine Zeitung,* August 11, 1999.

Amy Harmon, "Technology: Internet Sale of Nazi Books in Germany Is Assailed," *New York Times,* August 9, 1999.

Stefan Ulrich, "Machtlos gegen *Mein Kampf,*" *Süddeutsche Zeitung,* August 11, 1999.

3.3 THE FUNCTION OF VALUES

To understand a concept as complex as that of values, one needs to be able to interpret and apply it. For purposes of the present study, that can best be achieved by delineating their function for the individual, for society, and for government. In this way, one needn't be wedded to a particular set of values. In fact, by being clear about the functions that values serve, their "evolutionary potential" becomes clear as well.

3.3.1 Understanding Is Interpreting

Although philosophers have put considerable effort into making sense out of the question, "What is a chair?", most of us are satisfied that we know one when we see one. For the semantically identical question, "What is a local value?", the common-sense answer does not work as well. What a value is depends on how we look at it, and the framework for analyzing the question is not neutral. The way the problem is framed is inherently normative, and it inevitably has an impact on whatever answer is given.

Nearly all the behavioral and social sciences have their own view of what values are. Ethics is obviously about values, but philosophers also rely on values when they insist that understanding is interpreting. They argue that reality cannot be understood without some attempt to interpret what its purpose is and what it does.[7] Some philosophers go even further. They conceive of humans as social animals and see normativity (or values) as the precondition for passing from the isolated individual to a society.[8]

Rational-choice analysis starts from the premise that each individual maximizes his or her own utility. Rationality, rather than a morality of group obligation, guides decisions. This view is predominant in economics, but also has its adherents in political science and sociology. The distinction between preferences and restrictions is fundamental in rational-choice models. Values become institutions that restrict choice. Bad conscience is considered to be a psychic cost. Commonly shared values are modeled as social norms. These restrictions are interpreted as tools that facilitate the coordination of behavior and, in that sense, as goods not provided by the market.[9]

---

[7]Hans Albert. 1978. *Traktat über rationale Praxis.* Tübingen: Mohr.

[8]Günther Jakobs. 1999. *Norm, Person, Gesellschaft.* Berlin: Duncker & Humblot.

[9]Gary S. Becker. 1976. *The Economic Approach to Human Behavior.* Chicago: University of Chicago Press.

On the other hand, second-generation models of rationality incorporate values into a more nuanced understanding of preferences. In this perspective, preferences are no longer taken for granted; values are key to the formation of preference.[10] A third view starts from the observation that two or more persons may share a given value. This is a way of adding context, or history, and leads to rational choices and behaviors that optimize values involving more than one individual.[11]

Sociology is concerned with the society-building function of values. Integration theory views values as a sort of a social glue. In the approach of systems theory, each subsystem—for example, the economy, the law, or politics—is held together by its particular formal code, such as price, legality, or power. The formality of the code opens subsystems up to flexible principles, or values, that may differ from society to society.[12] Sociology also provides a way to interpret or measure how more general descriptions of a society—such as its closed or open nature—manifest themselves in particular value sets.[13]

In psychology, which is concerned with explaining behavior, values arise in at least three different ways. They help the individual understand the social environment to which he or she reacts. They manifest themselves as attitudes that help the individual choose between competing courses of action. And they *motivate* behavior, inducing the individual to translate attitude into action.[14]

The study and practice of law are about formal institutions. The interpretation of statutes or the identification of analogous cases in law is inevitably shaped by values.[15] In legal methodology, this is called teleo-

---

[10]Elinor Ostrom. 1998. "A Behavioral Approach to the Rational Choice Theory of Collective Action," Presidential Address of the American Political Science Association 1997, in *American Political Science Review* 92(1; March) 1-22.

[11]Mark Granovetter. 1995. "Economic Action and Social Structure: The Problem of Embeddedness," *American Journal of Sociology* 91(3; November): 481-510.

[12]Dirk Baecker. 2000. "Networking the Web," in Christoph Engel and Kenneth H. Keller, eds., *Understanding the Impact of Global Networks on Local Social, Political and Cultural Values,* Law and Economics of International Telecommunications, Vol. 42, 93-111, Baden-Baden: Nomos.

[13]Gabriel A. Almond and Sidney Verba. 1965. *The Civic Culture: Political Attitudes and Democracy in Five Nations: An Analytic Study.* Boston: Little.

[14]John Robert Anderson, 1999, "*Cognitive Psychology and Its Implications,*" New York: Freeman; Nicola Döring, 1999, *Sozialpsychologie des Internet. Die Bedeutung des Internet für Kommunikationsprozesse, Identitäten, soziale Beziehungen und Gruppen,* Göttingen: Hogrefe; Sara Kiesler, Jane Siegel, and Timothy W. McGuire, 1984, "Social Psychological Aspects of Computer-Mediated Communication," *American Psychologist* 39:1123-1134; Sherry Turkle, 1996, "Constructions and Reconstructions of Self in Virtual Reality: Playing in the MUD's," *The American Prospect* 24 (Winter), available online at <http://www.prospect.org/archives/24/24turk.html>.

[15]Josef Esser. 1970. *Vorverständnis und Methodenwahl in der Rechtsfindung.* Frankfurt: Athenäum.

logical construction. In the modern world, where neither history nor divine authority establishes law, the legitimacy of the legal code is, itself, a normative question. In other words, laws need to be legitimated by values.[16] And the law adds a helpful methodological distinction between rules and principles. Rules can be expressed in conditional terms: If A, then B. Principles are characterized by their finality. Those bound by a principle seek to realize it in each situation to which it might apply.[17] Values are more like principles than rules.

Finally, cultural theory adds relativity to the picture. In this perspective, value A is not only liable to be replaced by value B over a period of time. They might command attention at the same time, even though they may promote entirely different perspectives or even be somewhat contradictory. Cultural theory deliberately foregoes intellectual neatness and, on the contrary, investigates how societies manage to balance different solidarities, or value orientations. It thereby also helps us understand why and how values change.[18]

This rapid tour is obviously not meant to be an exhaustive discussion of the meaning of the term "values."[19] Indeed, our understanding of what values are, and what makes them "local," will always be tenuous and subject to change. However, the framework is useful in reminding policymakers of the many dimensions of the issue that must be considered when examining the influences of global networks. Policymakers must also be aware of the functions that values serve as they consider where and when action is called for. The following sections address that question.

---

[16]It should be noted that a number of legal scholars, particularly in the United States, would argue that law and values are not quite as separable and values are not quite as arbitrary as is suggested in this paragraph. And Americans would not necessarily link law and formal institutions in the ways that Germans would. However, this formulation allows both German and American systems to be placed in the same framework and still allows for arguments that societal laws should conform to or reflect natural law—which, in a sense, is an argument for how the legal code is legitimized.

[17]Robert Alexy. 1996. *Theorie der Grundrechte.* Frankfurt am Main: Suhrkamp.

[18]Michael Thompson. 2000. "Global Networks and Local Cultures; What Are the Mismatches and What Can Be Done about Them?" *Understanding the Impact of Global Networks on Local Social, Political and Cultural Values* (*Law and Economics of International Telecommunications* 42), Christoph Engel and Kenneth H. Keller, eds., Baden-Baden: Nomos, 113-129.

[19]Further material elucidating the function of values for individuals, society, and government is to be found in Elkhart Scilicet, 1998, *On Custom in the Economy,* Oxford, England: Clarendon Press; and Bruno S. Frey, 1999, *Economics as a Science of Human Behaviour*, Boston: Kluwer Academic Publications.

3.3.2 Function for the Individual

Values endow the individual with yardsticks—a normative language that allows him or her to distinguish. They provide guidance on whether certain behaviors are desirable or not, and to what extent. They provide a basis for deciding on one's own behavior. But understanding, judging, and deciding are normally a balancing exercise, with several values coming into play, and not all of one's actions are actually guided by such a deliberate decision process.[20] Nevertheless, it provides both comfort and assurance to have a set of values, and the capacity to apply them in a deliberate process of decision making, when faced with new circumstances.

The normative grammar of personal values also helps to form hypotheses of what the behavior of other individuals means. And it helps predict how others are likely to react to a person's actions. In both ways, values serve as a cognitive tool to guide social behavior.

Finally, an individual needs values for self-evaluation. Human beings require self-esteem, which comes from a sense of achievement. Personal values tell the individual which achievements are worthy of self-esteem. Indeed, one can argue that values are a key to consciousness itself; many argue that consciousness presupposes the ability to look at oneself from the outside, and values are an instrument for doing so. By adopting a set of values, the individual effectively gains access to an external reference that, in effect, provides the independent point of observation that is necessary for consciousness.[21]

3.3.3 Function for Society

From a practical point of view, individuals are always part of some society. They may move from one society or social grouping to another throughout their lives, but each one contributes to shaping a person's values and, in turn, displays values shaped by the individuals who comprise it. Some argue that the very notion of reality is socially constructed, and that individual values are socially pre-formed.[22] Others go further, argu-

---

[20]For greater detail see Gird Gigerenzer and Peter M. Todd, eds., 1997, *Simple Heuristics That Make Us Smart,* Oxford: Oxford University Press.

[21]Wolfgang Kersting, 2000, "Global Networks and Local Values. Some Philosophical Remarks from an Individualist Point of View," in Christoph Engel and Kenneth H. Keller, eds., *Understanding the Impact of Global Networks on Local Social, Political and Cultural Values,* 9-27, Baden-Baden: Nomos; Döring (supra note 14).

[22]Gebhardt Rusch and Siegfried Schmidt, eds. 1992. *Konstruktivismus. Geschichte und Anwendung*. Frankfurt am Main: Suhrkamp.

ing that only by defining himself or herself as a member of a normatively constructed society can an individual become a person, conscious and distinct from other animal species.[23]

Nevertheless, it makes sense to distinguish between the role that values play for the individual and the related but distinct role that values play for society. Unlike the state, society is not a clear-cut concept and does not have precise boundaries. Each social interaction, from the most transient to the most permanent, from two individuals in a business transaction to the citizens who make up a nation, is a manifestation of some form of society. Individuals may be part of a narrowly defined social group, such as a profession. They may view themselves as being part of a much more loosely knit network like the community of workers. The only link may be a territorial one, as for the inhabitants of a region. Or the social nexus may be the factual overlay of a legal condition, such as citizenship. The voluntary and virtual community of the Internet and its many epistemic (specialized) subgroups are, in this respect, merely a somewhat modified societal form.

From the viewpoint of society, values basically serve three purposes. They convey information, they facilitate coordination, and they give the group an identity. Society is first and foremost an informational community. Precisely because they share values, members can interpret the behavior of other members and establish expectations about it. This is particularly important in judging the credibility of what one person says to another about his or her intentions or commitments—that is, the individual's behavior in the future. The greater the extent to which the intended or promised behavior conforms to a common value, the more credible is the transmitted information.

The communication of information is key to the coordination of behavior, as game theory shows. If two individuals can't talk to each other before they act and share no common values, neither has a basis for making an educated guess as to how the other will behave. And if they talk to each other but do not understand each other's values, neither can predict whether the other will keep any promises made.

Finally, some common value acceptance is the bedrock of group identity. All members of the group must actually adhere to the value, and all members want to be sure that all others do so as well. Normative values form a cognitive framework for allowing individuals to understand social reality. Moreover, society organizes itself around shared values. Thus the function of society is to help individuals by guaranteeing values, and the function of these same values is to give cohesion and identity to the

[23]Jakobs (supra note 8).

society. Common values, in other words, are a key ingredient in societal integration.[24] And integration reflects how society and the state are tied together.

If a single local value is challenged or eroded, social cohesion and integration are unlikely to be deeply affected. Indeed, a society's set of values has never been totally stable over time. Traditional values have been challenged whenever a sufficiently large stratum of society has been exposed to different cultures. But society is an adaptive organism; it adjusts to the new values, rebalances the old ones, and usually bends without breaking. However, all societies have certain values that are fundamental for the self-definition of the group and that weaken group cohesion if challenged. When several such values are challenged simultaneously, rapid adaptation can be highly threatening.

These, then, become important analytical benchmarks against which to judge the effects of global networks. But it is not easy to isolate the influence of global networks—and in particular the Internet—from other factors that affect local values. For example, in both Europe and the United States, post-World War II affluence and the application of many kinds of technology have promoted similar patterns of changes in values—albeit with differing trajectories.[25] By altering people's perceptions of their nation's well-being and of their own well-being, affluence can indirectly alter local values and, across nations similarly situated, promote some convergence of values. That convergence may either strengthen or weaken efforts to preserve remaining differences, as is evident in the conflicts within the United States over multiculturalism and the implications of an increasingly heterogeneous, pluralistic society within with a single nation.[26]

3.3.4 Function for Government and Formal Institutions

Legal formality distinguishes state and society. The state is what it is because its constitution defines it to be so. But such a formally constructed state can take almost any form. At one extreme, it is little more than a fiction—the assertion, for example, of an exile group that controls no ter-

[24]Klaus G. Grunert. 1994. "Cognition and Economic Psychology," in Hermann Brandstätter and Werner Güth, eds., *Essays on Economic Psychology*, 91-108.

[25]Daniel Yankelovich. 1994. "How Changes in the Economy Are Reshaping American Values," in Henry J. Aaron et al., eds., *Values and Public Policy*. Washington, D.C.: Brookings Institution.

[26]See Yankelovich, ibid; also Nathan Glaser, 1994, "Multiculturalism and Public Policy," in Henry J. Aaron et al., eds., *Values and Public Policy*, Washington, D.C.: Brookings Institution.

ritory, provides no services, and has earned no recognition. At the other extreme, it may exist as an absolute dictatorship, with great power but no legitimacy. In neither case is there a need for values. Real-world states fall in-between. They are connected with their citizenry and related to their society by shared values. These values serve three purposes. They provide a basis for the development of statutes to which people are inclined to adhere. Conversely, they give legitimacy to a government whose actions and laws conform to the shared values. And finally, commonly shared and protected values are as important an instrument for building a national identity as they are for building a social identity.

3.3.5 The Dynamics of Values

It is important to remember that time itself alters the relations between individuals, society, and the state. Individual life has a defined beginning and an equally defined end. Since no one is born with a set of values, each person has to learn them. States can also begin and end. A new state is founded by secession, unification, or revolution. And in the same way, an old state can perish. Such events change values over time for people and the states of which they are a part.[27] This is equally true of societies or social groups. Local values may have their origins in a blurred past that is seldom completely abandoned. However, the set of values evolves over time, triggered by events in the world, a changed composition of the population, or fresh ideas. Indeed, one may argue that this is a healthy dynamic, responsive to changing circumstances, producing more open societies, and recognizing the fundamental relativity of values.

The evolutionary perspective draws attention to the salutary effects of a value system that can adapt to change over time. This is analogous to the value of biodiversity in providing a gene pool that, through selection, can adapt life on the planet to changed conditions. Anthropologists have long drawn a parallel between genes and memes (characteristics of a culture that allow it to develop and change).[28] The parallel suggests that cultural diversity and the maintenance of marginal cultures is more than the nostalgic protection of a living museum.[29]

---

[27]States do not always recognize this reality. Uncovering old statutes, still on the books, that reflect the sexual mores of a previous era is a favorite pastime of the U.S. media, and British courts are still willing to rely on cases or statutes from the Middle Ages.

[28]Robert Boyd and Peter J. Richerson. 1994. "The Evolution of Norms. An Anthropological View," *Journal of Institutional and Theoretical Economics* 150:72-87.

[29]Paul A. David. 2000. "The Internet and the Economics of Network Technology Evolution," *Understanding the Impact of Global Networks on Local Social, Political and Cultural Values*, Christoph Engel and Kenneth H. Keller, eds., Baden-Baden: Nomos, 39-71.

3.4 THE LOCALITY OF VALUES

Some values are essentially universal, such as the revulsion to child pornography, while other values are nearly so, stretching over large parts of the world. The developed world, for example, is such a community, sharing a commitment to concepts such as human rights. Still other values are connected with language zones, for language can provide a common understanding of a concept or, alternatively, can reflect the existence of such an understanding. Consider the English word "reasonable." There is no accurate German equivalent. And, indeed, Germans, in general, value reasonableness less highly than, say, the English.

Many values do not spread beyond national borders. However, this does not mean that local values are merely those that underlie a given legal order. It is true that governing is easier when constituencies share values, but in democratic states it is at least debatable whether government has a mandate to form the values of its citizens. Many lawyers go even further. They argue that government may only *ask* its citizens to obey the law, not to believe that statutes are morally binding. Consequently, penal law may protect the prevailing values only insofar as their violation yields socially destructive results. It is the action that is penalized, not the intention. If government oversteps the borderline between legal and moral obligation, it risks becoming totalitarian.[30]

The appropriate link between locality and values is thus not government, but society. For the last hundred years or so, there was little practical difference between the two; in the era of the nation-state, the territorial reaches of government and society were more or less the same. But whether culture and state will continue to be so closely linked is by no means assured; many ask whether globalization will leave cultural boundaries unaffected. After all, the connection between the national economy and the national state already appears to be fading.[31]

Historically, culture has not always been linked to territory; it has frequently been more closely connected to ethnic groups. That is equally true today, particularly as global networks have made it rather easy to maintain close connections across long distances, and as significant migrations have brought new diversity to the ethnic makeup of many countries. It may therefore be more appropriate to define the locality of values by their link to a specific culture.[32]

---

[30]A classic on totalitarianism is Frank Neumann, 1983, *Behemoth:The Structure and Practice of National Socialism, 1933-1944*, New York: Octagon Books.

[31]See Fritz W. Scharpf. 1999. *Governing in Europe: Effective and Democratic?* Oxford: Oxford University Press.

[32]Anthony Giddens. 1984. *The Constitution of Society: Outline of the Theory of Structuration.* Cambridge: Polity Press.

Finally, not all values spread homogeneously over an entire nation. Regional differences are often quite robust, having been recognized and preserved by well-entrenched regional cultures. In this respect, too, the connection of values to culture is apparent.

In describing the locality of values, one needs to distinguish a value that is locally practiced from one that is locally embedded. Since no value is adhered to without exception, embeddedness seems to be the more appropriate measure. It is also analytically easier to handle. Embeddedness is achieved through institutions, both formal and informal, and institutions are easier to discern than mere practice or belief. Even more importantly, institutions can be more easily connected to a social or legal entity. That allows us to determine how far the value reaches and to identify locality, even where more than one institution protects the same substantive value.

At first blush, this ambiguity looks like an analytical drawback, not an advantage. But locality is more related to a value *system* than to a particular value. Because modern societies do not really live in accordance with a hierarchical, rigid, and totally coherent order of values, there will be overlaps and even inconsistencies among the values promoted by various institutions. What makes one society distinct from another is the specific balance of values.

3.5 THE LEGITIMACY OF VALUES

Although we cannot do without values, this doesn't mean that the protection of values should be treated as the highest obligation of a society. Too many values, the wrong values, or an improper balance of them can even be dysfunctional. Even if a set of values served well in the past, it may be a mistake to maintain it as the social environment changes.

The link between values and institutions is instructive in this respect. Institutions provide the means for dealing practically with social dilemmas, but there is almost always more than one institution that can do the job. The choice between the options is normally not exclusively guided by the expected efficacy of the institution or the costs associated with it, but also by group interest. To do something that serves the common good has always been a much easier way to extract rents from others than by openly asking for the redistribution of wealth.[33] For example, Thomas Jefferson, in pressing for the creation of publicly supported universities, argued that they were necessary "to avail the state of those talents, sown

[33]Jack Knight. 1994. *Institutions and Social Conflict.* Cambridge: Cambridge University Press.

equally among the poor as the rich, which perish without use if not sought for and cultivated."

The legitimacy of a set of values depends on the function they have to fulfill. For family life, or for behavior toward old friends, different values are appropriate than for buying a book from an Internet bookseller. Although the result thus depends on the context, the categories can be generalized. A first distinction is the one between formal and substantive values.[34] The archetypal formal value is tolerance. It deliberately leaves open which substantive values another person may adopt, and asks us to respect that decision.

Other formal values are, for example, the moral obligation to keep one's promises, to abide by legitimate statutes, or to pay taxes. Obviously, a person needs greater specificity than that. To make decisions about behavior or to understand the social environment, he or she requires substantive values. But formal values provide the means for leading a fairly consistent life. The distinction between the formal and the

---

[34]See, for example, Kersting (supra note 21). The formal/substantive distinction made here and in other parts of this report is not intended as a legal description, but as a brief recapitulation of a philosophical taxonomy. Formal values are, to a first approximation, those associated with social processes—rules of behavior that facilitate discourse and, indeed, can be a key element in making a community possible—while substantive values come closer to moral convictions or beliefs. We recognize, as many political philosophers have, that the distinction is not crisp. Nevertheless, we believe it is useful. An important question is the relationship of these values to the legal system, a question made difficult for two reasons: first, the terms themselves cause confusion because, although they are familiar in the European context, they are not used as commonly in the U.S.; and, second, the relationship between values and law is viewed differently in Anglo-American and European jurisprudential thought. With respect to the first issue, in legal terms, the formal-substantive distinction maps roughly onto distinctions drawn in American jurisprudence regarding neutrality and non-neutrality of law. In the context of First Amendment law, for example, it corresponds to the difference between content-neutral regulation and content-based regulation. More generally, the European concept of formal values in the legal system would appear to correspond to the liberal rule of law, which is often said to rest upon the state's commitment to neutrality or neutral principles, such as equality before the law and the avoidance of preference for one value choice over another. With respect to the second issue, the idea that there are clearly distinguishable non-neutral and neutral choices in law and that neutrality is a key element in a liberal rule of law seems to be more controversial in Anglo-American jurisprudential and political thought than the formal/substantive distinction is in European thought. Some liberal thinkers deny that neutrality is a principle of liberalism; see, e.g., Donald Herzog, 1989, *Happy Slaves*, Chicago: University of Chicago Press. Furthermore, there is significant school of thought denying that neutrality is either analytically coherent or possible in practice. In this view, liberalism involves particular values that the state prefers over other particular values; see, e.g., Joseph Raz, 1986, *The Morality of Freedom*, Oxford University Press. The latter view is supported in part by the influential writings of John Dewey in the early twentieth century; see, e.g., *Liberalism and Social Action*, Prometheus Books, 1935.

substantive is analogous to that of government and society. In public education, for example, there is a continuing debate as to whether the value content of the curriculum should be limited to the formal, or whether the government should use the institution to instill more substantive values. Many believe that governments and society alike should stay away from actively promoting substantive values. But as a practical matter, it is hard to imagine how any societal cohesion could be maintained without actively promoting at least some commonly shared values.

A useful way to promote societal cohesion without imposing excessive rigidity might be to emphasize sets of values rather than any single value. As suggested above, such a local set of values is more than the juxtaposition of a number of values and less than a strict hierarchical order. It is a web of values, with knots of greater and lesser importance for the network. Some may be untied or loosened, on the basis of individual preference. Others need to be strongly fixed and could be challenged only by a broad and long-term movement originating in a significant stratum of society.

The notion of a web of values sheds light on a related phenomenon. The isolated individual is not only a member of society at large, but also of smaller social groups. The more coherent these groups, the stronger they are tied by substantive, rather than formal, values. They form epistemic communities,[35] a phenomenon made both easier and more widespread by the advent of global networks. If society at large is not to disintegrate into a constellation of such epistemic communities, substantive group values must be outweighed by equally strong formal values at the level of society at large. This places a heavy burden on the institutions that protect these formal values.

3.6 THE IMPACT OF GLOBAL NETWORKS ON VALUES

3.6.1 Caveats

As the discussion in this chapter should make clear, casting light on the impact of global networks on local values is not a straightforward task. The complexities of values and value sets—the different functions they serve for different levels of social aggregation, as well as their dynamic change—mean that well-defined cause-and-effect relationships may not exist.

Global networks are themselves a moving target and thus provide an

---

[35]On epistemic communities see Peter M. Haas, 1992, "Introduction: Epistemic Communities and International Policy Coordination," *International Organization* 46(1):1-35.

uncertain starting point for the analysis. The degree of technical standardization has been consciously kept to a minimum. The Internet, as a network of networks, is open to new networks and to qualitative change. The rapid commercialization of the Internet introduces further uncertainties—for example, how much will e-commerce change the traditional egalitarian Internet culture? Equally uncertain is the extent to which global networks will be split into language and culture zones.[36]

Furthermore, global networks are not the only challenge to local values. An older and no less powerful challenge stems from transnational broadcasting. Migration and tourism bring people from different cultural backgrounds together. Even international trade in goods is not always value-neutral. How goods are designed and marketed is influenced by the culture at their place of origin.

Finally, the impact of global networks on local values is not one of strict cause and effect. Technology does not determine social development. At most, it impedes traditional paths for the development of local values, and opens up new paths. More often, it does no more than change relative costs and opportunities among alternatives. Therefore, the relationship between global networks and local values is not unidirectional. Global networks may have the potential to change the evolution of the local set of values, but the process can also work the other way round. Local values can alter the development path of global networks. An obvious example is the demand to design Internet portals in a way that distinguishes between the physical locations of users. If this became reality, global networks would be effectively renationalized, in order to limit the incursion of foreign values.

The effect of global networks on local values and their balance is likely to be indirect. Faced with new opportunities and risks, the individual is likely to reshape his or her preferences in a way that better fits the changed environment.[37] This is often done unconsciously.[38] Sociologists point out that restrictions and, more specifically, institutions tend to reshape preferences. In practical terms, global networks can thus affect local values by changing social and political structures (see Chapter 4), or ways of doing business (see Chapter 7).

What follows—an attempt to identify specific ways in which global networks have the potential to alter local values—is thus only one cut through a very complex relationship.

---

[36]On the technological background and its development, see Chapter 2.

[37]Michael Domjan. 1998. *The Principles of Learning and Behaviour*, Pacific Grove.

[38]See, for example, Leon Festinger, 1962, *A Theory of Cognitive Dissonance*, Stanford, CA.: Stanford University Press.

3.6.2 The Effect of Global Networks on Value Orientations

Although some advocates of cyber-culture argue otherwise, global networks do not themselves represent an entirely new form of society or a new state. At most, they give birth to new transnational social groups. Normally, they are no more than a new communication medium for persons who remain members of social groups that are rooted in real life. Global networks do sometimes make it easier to "leave" an original social group, or even a state, and become a member of a new group, society, or state. But the individual can not help but remain a member of his or her original group and state. The question, however, is whether the regular contact with global networks changes the relationship between the member and that original group or state. More specifically: does the use of global networks potentially change the individual's set of values in a way that alienates him or her more profoundly than before from the set of values embedded in local institutions?[39]

The answer to that question depends on how global networks affect value orientations. One can envision four possibilities: global networks are potentially globalizers, pluralizers, convergers, or de-contextualizers.

That global networks potentially are globalizers sounds much like a truism. But with respect to values, it can mean two different things. The first interpretation is closely related to what economists call systems competition.[40] An individual, who dislikes a specific value in the local set, or the composition of that set more generally, uses global networks to exit from the local environment. This could occur if and when global networks actually allow a person to leave the social group entirely. More likely, global networks might allow a person to split his or her activities in such a way that the activities viewed unfavorably by the local value system are out of the reach of those local institutions that enforce the system.[41]

In contrast to this rather passive role of global networks, one can also envision circumstances in which the networks serve to globalize a value. For example, Western societies, to a greater or lesser degree, endorse open and wide political discourse in which people can participate regardless of

---

[39]More from Richard Münch, 1998, *Globale Dynamik, lokale Lebenswelten. Der schwierige Weg in die Weltgesellschaft*, Frankfurt am Main: Suhrkamp; Ronald Robertson, 1992, *Globalization*, London: Sage; Benno Werlen, 1993, *Society, Action and Space: An Alternative Human Geography*, London: Routledge.

[40]Lüder Gerken, ed. 1995. *Competition Among Institutions.* Basingstole: Macmillan.

[41]Christoph Engel. 2000. "The Internet and the Nation State," in Christoph Engel and Kenneth H. Keller, eds., *Understanding the Impact of Global Networks on Local Social, Political and Cultural Values* (*Law and Economics of International Telecommunications* 42). Baden-Baden: Nomos, 201-260.

gender or class. Networks promote a globalization of that value, which can lead to conflict with some traditional local values. Even in this instance, the global value may not replace the local one. It may only reach a segment of the local society or it may govern Internet activities alone while other local life is still governed by the traditional values. Or the new global value may simply offer an alternative—another option from which members of the local society may choose (though not without risk).

Although the globalization of values is not very frequent, the pluralizing effect of global networks is ubiquitous. Through global networks, an individual comes easily and frequently into contact with entirely unknown foreign values or with differently balanced sets of values. In that way, global networks force the individual to confront the fact that value systems are fundamentally relative, and that one lives in a pluralistic world.[42] In later chapters, this is illustrated by the very different views that Germans and Americans have about such issues as nudity, privacy, and the balance between the right of free speech and protection against libel.

On the other hand, there are those who fear that global networks, rather than exhibiting and celebrating pluralism, may actually promote an unhealthy convergence of values.[43] Those who hold this view point to the fact that most global networks, and the Internet in particular, originated in the United States. Even today, more than two-thirds of Internet traffic links American users and suppliers. Because of this history, these critics charge, most global networks are deeply influenced by U.S. value systems. The predominance of English, the preoccupation of most providers with the U.S. political climate, and, above all, the democratic vitality of the traditional egalitarian Internet culture all contribute to what some outside observers characterize as U.S. cultural hegemony.[44]

Some convergence of values, of course, may be a necessary precondition for truly global networks, or at least might facilitate their functioning. To the extent that it promotes formal values (and not just a set of conventions, such as the national agreement to drive on the right or the left side of the street), Netiquette is a case in point.[45]

---

[42]William Alton Kelso, 1978, *American Democratic Theory: Pluralism and Its Critics*, Westport, Conn.: Greenwood Press; Roman Herzog, 1987, "Pluralismus, pluralistische Gesellschaft," *Evangelisches Staatslexikon*, Vol. 2, Roman Herzog et al., eds., 2539-2547, Stuttgart: Kreuz-Verlag.

[43]Benjamin B. Barber. 1998. "Pangloss, Pandora or Jefferson? Three Scenarios for the Future of Technology and Democracy," in Raymond Plant, Frank Gregory, and Alan Brier, eds., *Information Technology: The Public Issues*, Manchester, England: Manchester University Press, 177-191.

[44]See Chapter 4.

[45]Its contents are repeated by Sally Hambridge, "Netiquette Guidelines," available online at <http://www.cybernothing.org/cno/docs/rfc1855.html> (31.03.00).

Finally, global networks are de-contextualizers.[46] Global networks promote social interaction, but these interactions are more context-free than any known before. The typical use of global networks is to retrieve information. There is no direct social contact between the person offering the content and the person accessing it; in most cases, the content provider does little more than count the number of hits. In mailing lists, news groups, or chat rooms, the user has the option to respond, but the response is in writing, and only chat rooms allow real-time exchange. Meanwhile, the social exchange that occurs in global networks is largely unnoticed by third parties. If the individuals in communication are concerned about privacy, they can even encrypt the message. If they seek anonymity, they can use pseudonyms or remailers. But even if they take none of these precautions, the sheer amount of communication over global networks makes it impractical to control or even observe it.

All this may threaten local values, as they must be embedded in and protected by formal and informal institutions. And insofar as these institutions rely on third-party scrutiny and enforcement, it is hard to apply them within global networks. Even where local values have been implanted in the conscience of the individual, they are not Internet-proof. For example, psychological research indicates that people pay less attention to social mores and conventions when they communicate electronically than in communicating face-to-face. Other work suggests that the more the situation isolates someone from the individuals that he or she affects, the more the person is comfortable in seeking a short-term advantage.[47]

3.6.3 Potential Impacts on the Local Set of Values

The foregoing discussion provides a starting point for assessing how real the danger is that global networks will erode current local values. If the globalization of a value actually occurs, it obviously replaces a local value that differs from it. For example, it is likely that the proscription of all forms of child pornography will, over time, extend to all societies. If value-pluralizing influences are at work, the legal and social institutions protecting local values will be subject to competitive pressures, which may also result in forcing change. For example, the European commitment to

---

[46]Starr Roxanne Hiltz and Murray Turoff, 1993, *The Network Nation: Human Communication via Computer*, Cambridge, MA: MIT Press; Kiesler, Siegel and McGuire (supra note 14); Turkle (supra note 14).

[47]Joachim Weiman, 1997, "Individual Behavior in a Free Riding Experiment," *Journal of Public Economics* 54:185-200; Iris Bohnet, 1997, *Kooperation und Kommunikation*, Tübingen: Mohr.

protecting individuals' private information from corporate misuse is putting pressure on U.S. institutions to conform. In both instances, if an influential part of the population no longer believes that the traditional set of values should be upheld, a political process can be triggered that leads to their abolition or change.

The privacy example above illustrates two forces at work in effecting change. Making the U.S. population, or influential segments of it, aware of the greater protection for individual privacy provided in Europe can lead people to press for similar protections in the United States. At the same time, U.S. commercial interests may be moved to encourage the prescribed institutional change in order to open European markets to American e-commerce.

Assessing the local consequences of homogenization—the convergence of Internet values that is driven by the historical and hegemonic influence of the United States on its structure—is somewhat more difficult because it is hard to separate transient influences from longer-term change. In the short run, Internet language and content may be dominated by U.S. interests, and it is certainly conceivable that local patterns of communication and business practices will be affected accordingly. In the long run, however, it is entirely possible that the deeper penetration of global networks into local societies may allow for local adaptation that will enable the preservation of local institutions, and indeed, perhaps even increase their effectiveness.

The erosion of the value orientation of individuals is much more likely than the erosion of institutions. The former depends less on globalization than on pluralization, homogenization, and, above all, decontextualization. These phenomena tend to make a person's value orientation less firm. The individual begins to doubt the legitimacy of a traditional value, and if the alternative value encourages actions that are consistent with personal interest, it might appear more attractive and even guide the person's behavior. But behavior in very specific circumstances is only loosely tied to attitude,[48] and this kind of "transgression" may only occur when the person is protected by the anonymity of the Internet.

However, it is also possible that the network influence will be much stronger. The values of an individual are the result of a learning process. His or her contact with different value systems encountered in using global

[48]Icek Ajzen and Martin Fishbein, 1977, "Attitude-Behavior Relations: A Theoretical Analysis and Review of Empirical Research," *Psychological Bulletin* 84:888-918; Icek Ajzen and Thomas J. Madden, "Prediction of Goal Directed Behavior: Attitudes, Intentions, and Perceived Behavioral Control," *Journal of Experimental Social Psychology* 22:453-474.

networks may start a new learning process, at the end of which the traditional value is strongly diminished in the individual's own value system.

Global networks can also have the opposite effect—strengthening one's original values. This is obvious where global networks allow territorially scattered groups to maintain social ties. Community without propinquity becomes a viable option.[49] And global networks are not only pluralizers and de-contextualizers; they also give individuals new options for participation in social life and political decisionmaking.[50] Advocacy coalitions have never before been so easy to build, and global networks make it much easier for the average citizen to gain access to government information.[51] All this helps create a greater sense of responsibility.

The impact of global networks on local values need not be reduced to the simple dichotomy of erosion or corroboration. The use of these networks can also lead to the modification of values or to the rebalancing of the set of values. Although this involves a complicated process of unlearning and relearning, it is an attractive possibility from a political point of view in that it can provide an evolutionary path to a more appropriate or legitimate set.

The problem, of course, is that there is no guarantee that the new set of substantive values will be either more appropriate or more legitimate. During their histories, both U.S. and German society and state have managed to promote coexistence and cooperation within their societies with a small set of substantial values and a highly developed set of formal values. Unlike traditional societies that rely on strong ties among their members, modern societies such as these two achieve cohesion among a large number of persons with ties that are deliberately weak rather than strong.[52] In such societies, one does not expect an occasional business partner to help if one's family is in distress—it is enough if the person pays his or her bills. Strong ties are limited to very small groupings: the

---

[49]Saskia Sassen, 2000, "The Impact of the Internet on Sovereignty: Unfounded and Real Worries," in Christoph Engel and Kenneth H. Keller eds., *Understanding the Impact of Global Networks on Local Social, Political and Cultural Values,* Baden-Baden: Nomos, pp. 197-200; Thompson (supra note 18).

[50]Anthony Downs, 1991, "Social Values and Democracy," in Kristen R. Monroe, ed., *The Economic Approach to Politics: A Critical Reassesment of the Theory of Rational Action,* New York: Harper Collins, pp. 143-170; Miles Kahler, 2000, "Information Networks and Global Politics," in Christoph Engel and Kenneth H. Keller eds., *Understanding the Impact of Global Networks on Local Social, Political and Cultural Values,* Baden-Baden: Nomos, pp. 141-157.

[51]See Chapter 4.

[52]Siegwart Lindenberg. 1988. "Contractual Relations and Weak Solidarity," *Journal of Institutional and Theoretical Economics* 144:39-58.

core family, one's closest friends, sometimes one's closest colleagues at work.

Precisely because global networks confront a person with the relativity of value systems, and the disconcerting effects of de-contextualization, there is a danger that individuals will react by seeking the comfort of a more structured, if simplistic, value system. They might be lured into replacing apparently eroded and weak ties with ones that are newly built and strong, although often unidimensional. The danger is all the more real if it is linked to institutions that typically redistribute wealth or power. Political opportunists might well exploit the situation by denouncing as a vacuum in values what is actually no more than a characteristic of modern life.

3.6.4 Types of Contact with Foreign Sets of Values

The pluralizing and homogenizing effects of global networks depend on the nature of the contact between individual and foreign sets of values. In principle, global networks are weaker in this respect than the traditional media. Because the technology of global networks (e.g., search engines) allows users to specify the information they want to retrieve, there is less likelihood they will be exposed to information that does not fit the specification. Although it is true that today's users may be exposed to information (and hence to values) they did not seek when they follow a link, subscribe to a mailing list, or participate in a news group, technological trends toward greater specificity and precision in information retrieval suggest that inadvertent exposure will be less likely as time goes on. Thus, such exposure will be sporadic rather than systematic.

Furthermore, Internet users need not be passive. If they dislike what they see, they are not only theoretically free to turn away but probably inclined to do so. Technically, an information provider may be able to use "push" technologies to force messages onto a subscriber's screen, but there is still a long way to go before global networks are transformed into propaganda machines.

Still, the exposure to other values does have effects. For example, exposure to a different set of values can be significant for someone whose commitment to traditional values has been weakened. In this case, the different set may be attractive simply as a replacement. In such circumstances, the Internet becomes the medium for a conscious learning process. Global networks also help that process gain social momentum, as they make it easy and inexpensive to spread information challenging traditional values among others who are doubtful.

There is another situation in which the impact of exposure to unfamiliar ideas is subtler: A person may not realize the extent to which the lessons of a different value system have been absorbed. Only later will the individual come to recognize the contradictions between the implicit network value system and his or her traditional system. Such learning without attention is typical if values are embedded in apparently neutral contents—such as in the goods and services shaped by foreign value systems.

For instance, the cookies set by amazon.com to trace customer purchasing patterns give rise to a convenient service through which customers logging onto the site are made aware of new books that might interest them. It was certainly easier for a service based on this technology to develop in the United States, where the protection of privacy is not as high a priority as it is in Germany. However, once they have enjoyed the convenience of the service, people in societies that may be more conscious of privacy as an important value may nevertheless view it in less absolute terms and come to believe that it is a tradable right, well worth relinquishing in particular circumstances.

Although the possibility of eroding traditional values should not be overstated, learning a new value system does not lead inexorably to the replacement of traditional values. The real change brought about by global networks may be the realization that modern life encourages, and often requires, living with multiple value systems.

3.6.5 Three Illustrative Examples

Three examples may serve to illustrate the points made in this chapter. The first is consumer protection. In general, the German legislature and courts have been more active in protecting consumers against unethical entrepreneurs than their U.S. counterparts. A consumer has a week to withdraw from a contract that has not been concluded in the premises of the provider or that the consumer has not solicited, and standard terms come under the close scrutiny of the courts. Marketing material is illegal if even a small fraction of those exposed to it are misled by its statements. These rules are an attempt to balance freedom of contract with protection of naïve consumers—to balance autonomy and paternalism. But in a globalized Internet-based market, when German customers buy goods and services over the Internet they can no longer be sure that a German court will be able or willing to protect them in the same way.

A second example relates to the limitations of copyright protection. As long as hard copies were the only meaningful way to distribute intellectual or artistic works, a compromise between the interests of the author and of the public could be achieved: once a hard copy was sold, its owner was generally free to use it and to hand it over to third parties, and "fair use" exceptions allowed individuals to make copies or quote lengthy passages of works. As more works begin to appear in electronic form, the

BOX 3.3 Bavaria Versus CompuServe

In November 1995, the Bavarian criminal-investigation authorities informed Felix Somm, head of CompuServe Germany GmbH, that five newsgroups with child-pornography content were being carried on the servers of CompuServe Inc. A month later, the prosecuting authorities delivered a list of another 282 newsgroups that, the state contended, displayed sexually oriented content on the Internet that was morally harmful to youth. Somm informed the parent company, which reacted promptly and blocked all the identified newsgroups immediately.

While the child-pornography newsgroups remained permanently blocked, the newsgroups containing "soft" sexual content were deblocked after CompuServe Inc. and CompuServe Germany GmbH provided their members with "child safeguard software" that enabled parents to block such content. In the months following, however, the investigating authorities retrieved individual news articles with hard-pornographic content from the news servers of CompuServe Inc.

In May 1998, a Munich Municipal Court sentenced Felix Somm to 2 years' probation and fined him DM 100,000 ($56,000) for distributing pornographic materials—pursuant to sect. 184 para. 3 of the German Penal Code—on the Internet. Despite expert testimony during the trial that it was not feasible technically to screen Internet material, the judge ruled that CompuServe should have deleted material known to be offensive.

The prosecutors who originally filed the charges later reversed themselves and argued for acquittal. A state court overturned the conviction in November 1999 after both the defense and the prosecution argued that the original court's verdict was flawed. In the meantime, the "Somm Case" was cited in the U.S. State Department's 1998 human rights report, provoking a national uproar. In San Francisco, demonstrations were organized during which participants poured out German beer to show their displeasure.

SOURCES: (1) Gunnar Bender. 1998. "Bavaria vs. Felix Somm: The Pornography Conviction of the Former CompuServe Manager," case note in *International Journal of Communications Law and Policy* 1: 1-4. Available online at <http://www.digital-law.net/papers/index.html>.

(2) The CompuServe Judgement of the Local Court Munich dated May 28, 1998: Summary of the facts of the judgement, *MultiMedia und Recht* 8: 430, available online at <http://www.jura.uni-wuerzburg.de/sieber/article/article.htm>.

technical limitations that made the old compromise workable disappear. On one hand, a single digital copy can be multiplied and distributed at will, without any loss in quality, thus making practical almost any level of copyright violation. On the other hand, the ease of tracing or limiting the use of electronically published material at the source makes it practical to drastically reduce the scope of public use of the work. Thus technical changes are forcing legal institutions to forge a new balance between the rights of author and public.[53]

A third example is provided by new technologies that offer a stronger means of enforcement for local values. Take the desire of many Americans to ban nudity and sexually explicit material from the Internet, or the desire of many Germans to do the same with the portrayal of violence. At first glance, from a local viewpoint, there appears to be no rebalancing of interests at issue. Social norms already strongly limit broadcasting of nudity and sexually explicit material in the United States and of violence in Germany. To a considerable extent, these norms are even embedded in civil and criminal codes. Internet technology makes access to foreign sites with the locally restricted content easy, but there are some tools that can help localities deny or restrict access; hosts and Internet Service Providers can be compelled to prevent their customers from accessing sites with the locally banned content.

Box 3.3 and Box 3.4 provide examples of governments seeking to regulate content of foreign origin. Box 3.5 describes some of the tools that might be used to do so.

But a closer look suggests that, as a practical matter, there has been a real change. In the past, practical limitations on enforcing the majority's norms provided a certain latitude for local minorities—those who chose not to conform to the norms—to evade detection. This led, de facto, to a balance between majority and minority rights that was not necessarily provided for de jure. The new technologies tend to reduce that leeway because they allow for more effective monitoring and control. Given that the balance between majority and minority rights was not explicit to begin with, it is not easy to restore when technological advances upset it. We have yet to see whether a networked world can find acceptable ways of achieving such a balance without appearing to compromise the values that gave rise to the original norms and legal structures.

---

[53]See for example, Computer Science and Telecommunications Board, National Research Council, 2000, *The Digital Dilemma: Intellectual Property in the Information Age,* Washington, D.C.: National Academy Press.

BOX 3.4 Transnational Jurisdictional Issues in Cyberspace

In December 2000, the German Supreme Court upheld the conviction of a German-born Australian citizen, Frederick Toben, who had been found guilty of denying the existence of the Holocaust on a Web site that he operated in Australia. The court held further that German law can apply to foreigners who post Web content in other countries if that content can be accessed in Germany. However, while Toben could face extradition to Germany, to date it has not made such a request.[1]

An Italian prosecutor sought criminal action for libel and defamation against an unknown person for postings on a Web site based in Israel. Following an Italian divorce involving a couple with two children, the mother moved to Israel with their daughters (without the father's consent) and married another man. The daughters were eventually located and returned to Italy, after which statements and images related to the incident began appearing on a Web site in Israel. In the words of the court, this Web site contained "extremely negative opinions on [the father]'s character and actions (as well as on the work of the Italian judicial authorities) and were accompanied by messages inviting Jews to 'free' the two underage girls, 'held captive' by their father, who prevented them from professing Judaism."

While a lower court dismissed the prosecution's case on the grounds that it lacked jurisdiction because of the extraterritorial publication of the material in question, a higher court disagreed, reasoning that defamation is an event in which there exists an action (the posting of the comments) and an outcome (somebody reading them). Since the outcome in this case (viewing the Web site) occurred in Italy, the court concluded that there was sufficient jurisdiction to hear the prosecutor's case.

[1]See <http://www.wired.com/news/politics/0,1283,40669,00.html>.

SOURCE: Matt Gallaway, "International Jurisdiction Soup," February 27, 2001. Available online at <http://www.ecompany.com/articles/web/print/0,1650,9579,FF.html>.

BOX 3.5 Automated Tools to Deny Access to Forbidden Internet Content

Software systems commonly known as filters are designed to block user access to particular Internet material while allowing all other material to pass. In general, filters can employ any of a number of techniques, singly or in combination.

One technique is to block material-specific domain names (e.g., everything that might otherwise be accessible from the domain "example.com") or selected pages within a given domain but not other pages within that domain. Lists of inappropriate sites and Web pages are pre-compiled. A filter checks a request for a certain Web page against such a list, and if the requested page is on the list, it is blocked. In addition, sites to which a suspect site links may also be blocked.

A second technique is for a filter to examine the content of material that has been requested in real time ("on-the-fly") for judgments of inappropriateness. If that content is deemed inappropriate by the program that analyzes it, its display is blocked. The content may be examined for certain keywords that are deemed inappropriate (e.g., if the requested page contains the word "bomb-making"), or an image can be processed by an image-recognition program that checks for naked people or for Nazi swastikas. (A related variant of this technique is to block the use of certain terms in search engines.)

A third technique is to accept or reject material based on the content of a "tag" that is associated with a given Web page. Such a tag is analogous to the rating on a TV show that indicates if it contains sexual activity, nudity, or violence. Depending on the setting on the filter, the viewer may or may not gain access to material that is tagged in certain ways.

Note that the effectiveness of this technique depends on a large volume of Internet content being labeled. If a large volume of Internet material is untagged, and the filter is set to pass all untagged material, the user will see a great deal of objectionable material, and hence the filter is relatively useless. If the filter is set to block all untagged material, the user will be blocked from a great deal of unobjectionable material, and hence the filter is overly restrictive.

The vast majority of filters act to block access to specific Web sites (though these sites may be specified as a class). In addition, some filters provide the capability to block the access of an individual (e.g., a minor) to other common Internet services, such as interactive services (e.g., e-mail, chat rooms), newsgroups, file downloading, or even e-commerce with credit card usage.

For a more detailed discussion of filters, see CSTB, National Research Council, *Youth, Pornography, and the Internet: Can We Provide Sound Choices for a Safe Environment?*, forthcoming.

4

Democracy and Political Institutions

4.1 DEMOCRACY, POLITICAL INSTITUTIONS, AND POWER

For those worried about the impact of global networks on local values, political institutions are a tool for coping with the problem. But the existing political institutions are themselves affected by the networks. Understanding how and why this is so is the aim of this chapter.

Some definitions are useful as a starting point. Power is the ability to impose a solution on others. It applies both within and outside existing political institutions, with or without a legitimate basis and balanced or not by the power of other actors or interests. By contrast, a political institution is an instrumental notion. The creation of political institutions presumes that there are problems to be solved by a consciously created government—a polity—rather than by social institutions or processes. And it further presumes that the institutions act as agents for a collective entity with defined geographical and subject-matter jurisdiction. In this context, democracy comprises a specific set of publicly determined political institutions, in contrast to technocratic government or despotism.

Democracy can also be understood as a normative indicator of the political legitimacy of a system or process. But legitimacy is a complex concept that requires a balance between effectiveness and openness of governance. This balance depends on the size and shape of the polity and on the character of the political problems to be solved.[1] Because any given

---

[1]Seyla Benhabib, ed. 1996. "Toward a Deliberative Model of Democratic Legitimacy," *Democracy and Difference. Contesting the Boundaries of the Political*, 68-94, 69. Princeton, N.J.

arrangement of political institutions has implications for power and democracy, this chapter addresses the three notions jointly.

4.2 THE IMPACT OF THE INTERNET ON DEMOCRACY, POLITICAL INSTITUTIONS, AND POWER

The impact of the Internet on democracy, political institutions, and power is complex. Moreover, it is a work in progress. Clearly, global networks have the potential to change political arenas, the actors within them, the processes of politics, and the tools of governance. They may even change the character of political conflicts and the cognitive frameworks or normative beliefs that drive those conflicts. To be sure, not all institutions, actors, and processes are equally affected, but that fact in itself is a motivation for examining the nature of these impacts in some detail.

4.2.1 Complexity and Uncertainty

As discussed in Chapter 2, global networks are themselves still in a state of continual development. In addition, a variety of organizations are experimenting with different ways of interacting through networks and exploring a variety of (as yet unproven) business models. Many Internet services are still struggling to achieve profitable status, so their future is uncertain. The optimal technical and economic strategies for broadband transmissions at the local level—the so-called "last mile" problem—are also unsettled.[2] Such dynamism and uncertainty make large-scale outcomes difficult to predict. For example, how completely will the Internet penetrate each society? At what points will e-commerce activities saturate their U.S. markets? How quickly will Germany catch up to the United States? These factors, in turn, will affect how political institutions and power relationships evolve.

There are larger issues and conflicts as well, as evidenced by the continuing battle between those who believe the Internet should be privatized and those who believe it should be managed in an open and egalitarian manner. Furthermore, it is hard to predict whether the attempts to re-nationalize the Internet—that is, to reverse the globalizing trend using technical or legal tools in order to serve national cultural, social, and economic needs—will succeed in some or any countries. It is reasonable to expect, however, that political actors will try to influence Internet development—precisely because political institutions are affected by it.

[2]See for example, Computer Science and Telecommunications Board, National Research Council, 2002, *Broadband: Bringing Home the Bits*, in press.

These reciprocal influences are clearly very important, as pointed out in Chapter 1. Global networks create and constrain opportunities for policymakers, who respond by trying to shape the changes to their advantage. In the United States and Germany, the historical and technological starting points are very different, so global networks can easily trigger very different structural change in each of the two countries. An analysis is useful here not so much as a way of predicting the outcome in either country but as a way of describing the potential of global networks to change the political process in *any* polity (while acknowledging the unique characteristics of the United States and Germany).

4.2.2 Political Arenas

The term "political arena" refers to a set of formal and informal institutions that serves as a framework for policymaking and to which both public and private actors have access. The traditional political arena is the nation state, which can be affected by many characteristics of the Internet. Because the Internet is global in reach, it can bring citizens of many nations into contact with one another. Because the costs of Internet access are low (and getting lower over time), more people within each nation have access to it. Because its architecture supports a myriad of applications, there are strong incentives for many parties to access it. Because its management is decentralized, operational control from a central organization is essentially impossible to achieve. And because of technical advances, Internet communications can be conducted in ways that are more secure, secret, and anonymous than other communications have been in the past.

Individually and jointly, these characteristics challenge some of the traditional roles and powers of the nation state. Global networks are a medium for and a factor in globalization. They induce change in the political arena, and can bring it about as well.

If the changes render a particular political arena—a locality, region, or even a nation-state—less able to deal with some issues, policymakers may choose to transfer those issues to another political arena that seems better adapted to the task. The development of public international law is an early example of this kind of globalization of the political arena. Sovereign states react to a new challenge by negotiating an international treaty or setting up an international organization, thereby creating—at least for the issues at hand—a global political arena.[3] In fact, there are a number of

[3]Klaus W. Grewlich. 2000. "Conflict and Good Governance in 'Cyberspace,'" in Christoph Engel and Kenneth Keller, eds., *Governance of Global Networks in the Light of Differing Local Values*, Law and Economics of International Telecommunications, Vol. 43. Baden-Baden: Nomos, 237-264, 239.

examples of global institutions created in the past, under somewhat different stimuli, that can be adapted to address some of the current problems arising from global networks. As early as 1910, for example, a treaty was concluded to combat the distribution of "illicit papers, drawings, pictures or objects that have an international character";[4] today the treaty applies to electronic dissemination as well.

International treaties have not generally been so readily adapted, however. The World Intellectual Property Organization (WIPO), for example, found it necessary in 1996 to propose a new treaty that would address the special problems of protecting copyright on the Internet. Interestingly, this was a case in which the instruments provided in the international political arena effectively finessed the national political process. Those interested in extended copyright protection lost the battle in the U.S. Congress. But they basically succeeded in the WIPO, and Congress ratified the outcome when it was presented to that body in the form of an international treaty.

But international political arenas encompass more than public international law. Government agencies (e.g., the U.S. Trade Representative) promote international trade. The United Nations (UN) provides a forum for high-level international discussions and the application of political pressure. And non-public entities play important roles as well. For example, industry associations from many industrialized countries have negotiated an international uniform commercial code for electronic trade. A second example is the Internet Corporation for Assigned Names and Numbers (ICANN), whose role is to make decisions about top-level domain names; this entity may become a nucleus for Internet regulation at a much broader scale in the future.[5]

Global networks not only spur the development of global political arenas but simultaneously give *local* political arenas more leverage. Local community networks, such as the Cleveland Free-Net and the Amsterdam City Web, were the forerunners of digital communities that serve local (physical) communities (Box 4.1).

---

[4]Treaty of 04.05.1910, RGBl. 1911, 209, as well as protocol of 04.05.1949, UNTS 30, 3 consolidated edition UNTS 47, 159. The Federal Republic has not yet signed the changed treaty, however.

[5]For details, see Klaus W. Grewlich, 1999, "Governance in Cyberspace. Access and Public Interest in Global Communications," *Law and Electronic Commerce* 9: 193-216, The Hague; and, critically, Milton Mueller, 1999, "ICANN and Internet Governance. Sorting Through the Debris of Self-Regulation," *Info* 1:497-520; and Laurence R. Helfer and Graeme B. Dinwoodie, 2001, "Designing Non-National Systems: The Case of the Uniform Domain Name Dispute Resolution Policy," *William & Mary Law Review* 43, October.

BOX 4.1 Participation in the Local Community—The Cleveland Free-Net, Boulder Community Network, and Digital City Amsterdam

As the Internet has become more widely used by private households in the United States and elsewhere in the world, community information systems based in cities and regions have been established to serve them. Such "Free-Nets" are typically text-oriented and use a limited low-tech approach for individuals' free access from home.

The first such system was the Cleveland Free-Net, which went online on July 16, 1986. It was rooted in the Case Western Reserve University's Faculty of Medicine, where doctors, students, and patients successfully experimented with electronic bulletin boards that gave them the opportunity to enter into a continuing dialogue on issues of health. As the date indicates, the Free-Net was launched long before the World Wide Web took over after 1991, turning the Internet into an easy accessible information and entertainment tool.

Free-Nets were, in the American tradition of community organizing, a first ambitious attempt to bring networks to the public; they are open computer systems that give free access to community news and information, as well as basic entry to the Internet. They have elements of an "electronic town," as they usually sport post offices for e-mail, libraries for research, and bulletin boards for community events, all set up in cooperation with city administrations, community counsels, private interest groups, churches, and others. Free-Nets have not always lived up to their envisioned character as new public spaces, however. Contrary to the hopes of many community activists, discussion groups all too often do not deal with local affairs but are centered on private interests such as computers and hobbies. In addition, technical problems such as inadequate bandwidth and storage capacity have led many interest groups to leave the Free-Nets and sign up with commercial online services.

With the advent of the World Wide Web, networks like the Boulder Community Network and the Digital City Amsterdam (*De Degetale Stedeling*) have emerged. Their aim is not to provide basic access to a network but to select and aggregate local information for people who are already connected to the Internet. Typically, they contain job offers or information on spare-time activities and upcoming social events. Additionally, they feature links to institutions that promote civic participation—e.g., nonprofit groups—and such institutions are actively encouraged to post relevant information on the local network site.

Usually, these newer forms of city nets do not provide the means for individuals to communicate via newsgroups. That is seen by many as a major obstacle to their active promotion of community spirit. Thus, at least at present, no more than about 1 percent of the U.S. population seems to be reached by community nets. More and more, commercial services like America Online (AOL) have taken over the task of managing city nets by incorporating local windows into their content.

Moreover, the easy and inexpensive price of entry into the Internet allows community without propinquity.[6] It has become easier to create political groupings—political arenas—along substantive rather than geographical lines. What has generally been available for professional groups is now spreading into other kinds of affinity groups based on particular political issues, ethnic identities, avocations, and casual interests or hobbies. USENET newsgroups were the first manifestation of this trend, and the proliferation of such groups continues unabated.

This trend raises some concerns, however: if these groups isolate themselves from the larger community, the domain of traditional politics might shrink drastically; or, if the groups become dominant actors in the national political arena, the political process could be reduced to little more than a battle of single interests. A further concern is that these groups, by their reach and technical capacity to gather, organize, and use information, may create de facto challenges to government by assuming some roles that are usually associated with government actors. For example, organizations like the Cyber Angels function as a kind of private attorney general. Credit-card organizations replace legal consumer protection through their commercial charge-back systems. Credit-rating agencies assume de facto regulatory power over the management of credit risk.

Sometimes the nation-state has found it wise to ignore these developments or, more to the point, has allowed them to take over the roles they have assumed by not challenging them. Yet typically these groups do not entirely replace existing institutions. Together they create a fractionated system that provides neither equal protection nor efficient service; in some instances, when several such groups emerge simultaneously, they present competitive structures whose authority and responsibility are not well defined. A challenge for the future will be to sort out these relationships in much the same way as the member states of the European Community, and the state and federal governments in the United States, have had to do.

4.2.3 Political Actors

Political arenas are populated by political actors who may function in several arenas at the same time,[7] and global networks have made such multiple opportunities increasingly possible. But the networks have also expanded the opportunities for *new* political actors. They have made it

---

[6]Michael Thompson. 2000. "Global Networks and Local Cultures: What Are the Mismatches and What Can Be Done about Them?," in Christoph Engel and Kenneth H. Keller, eds., *Understanding the Impact of Global Networks on Local Social, Political and Cultural Values,* 2000, 113-129, 123.

[7]Fritz W. Scharpf. 1997. "Games Real Actors Play." *Actor-Centered Institutionalism in Policy Research* 51.

more productive for organizations—such as the currently ubiquitous "nongovernmental organizations"—to participate as well. Thus, the term "actors" encompasses both individuals—citizens, members of organizations, ad hoc participants in movements—and organizations that promote an agenda or participate in a political process as a coherent entity. Like Russian *matryoshka* dolls-within-dolls, these organizational actors can function as whole entities or as a collection of constituents—individual actors—each potentially acting as they see fit.

These organizations—political parties, trade unions, and more loosely tied collectives such as issue-based movements—must now deal with individual-member actors who are increasingly empowered by technology. Since it is technically and economically so easy, constituencies of various organizations can insist on being better and more quickly informed, and then use that information to increase their influence in the management of the organization. On the other hand, the very same information technologies that increase the effective power of an organization's membership also make it easier for members to leave the organization and re-form around more narrowly defined issues and interests; ironically, however, the more credible the threat to exit, the more influential one's voice may become within the organization.[8] Individuals, whether members or not, can also refocus the strength of the large group by forming ad hoc coalitions or loosely knit networks of actors. (See, for example, Box 4.2.)

Of course, the leaders of either traditional organizations or the newer Internet-spawned groups (whether part of formal management structures or an informal leadership hierarchy) need not be passive either. The new technologies give them more ways to respond to their constituencies by allowing voices to be heard and to earn credibility with their constituencies through better communication of their positions and ideas. How these factors ultimately play out, and whether they lead to a strengthening or weakening of established organizations, is likely to be determined on a case-by-case basis. For example, established organizations tend to have easier access to power and money. On the other hand, they are frequently less flexible in addressing new challenges. Which of these two factors dominates will vary from one situation to another.

The number of organizations that count as new political actors is also growing.[9] Once global networks spread over a country, the transaction costs for setting up any new group fall dramatically. A mailing list is

---

[8]Albert O. Hirschman. 1970. *Exit, Voice, and Loyalty. Responses to Decline in Firms, Organizations, and States.* Cambridge: Harvard University Press.

[9]Klaus W. Grewlich. 2000. "Conflict and Good Governance in 'Cyberspace," in Christoph Engel and Kenneth Keller, eds., *Governance of Global Networks in the Light of Differing Local Values,* Baden-Baden: Nomos, 237-264, 251.

BOX 4.2 The Multilateral Agreement on Investment Struck Down

In 1995, the members of the Organization for Economic Cooperation and Development (OECD), together with eight nonmember states, began negotiating the Multilateral Agreement on Investment (MAI). They were driven by the expectation that adherence to international rules would allow for greater efficiency and more stable investment flows.

The MAI was meant to go beyond the scope of the existing World Trade Organization rules and be open to nonmembers as a stand-alone agreement. It would eliminate barriers to international investment-related trade by opening most economic sectors and natural resources to foreign ownership on a nondiscriminatory basis. It also contained a uniform set of rights by which individual firms could sue foreign governments before an international mediation panel in order to protect their investments from volatility or widely defined "expropriation." In addition, no exemption for governmental procurement policies or provincial jurisdiction was conceived.

Over the course of the negotiations a number of concerns emerged in public debate, put forward by nongovernmental organizations (NGOs) such as Friends of the Earth International, Peoples' Global Action, Public Citizen Trade Watch, World Economy, the Ecology and Development Association, and the World Wide Fund for Nature International. They argued that by acknowledging the right of firms to sue over expropriation, the MAI put serious constraints on state and local governments' ability to enforce environmental laws. In the same vein, countries would be pressured to reduce protection of natural resources in order to attract capital in globalized markets, resulting in a "race to the bottom" with respect to environmental standards.

This international coalition of environment, development, and consumer groups took advantage of the political instability of the situation while the final outcome of the negotiations was still open and exploited the speed of online communication to wage a global campaign against the MAI. It was largely carried out over the Internet, although it was coupled with influential traditional mass-media coverage. Seminal newspaper articles appeared in *Le Monde* and *Le Monde Diplomatique* as well as in the *Tageszeitung* in Germany. Web sites opposed to MAI and regularly looked at by journalists, were established. They listed trustworthy NGOs and provided in-depth (though partisan) coverage of the progress of the negotiations as well as suggestions—complete with samples of letters to send to elected officials or newspaper editors—on how to effectively express opposition.

The coalition met with OECD negotiators to present them with resolutions to abandon the MAI, which the government representatives initially rejected. This resulted in even greater organized resistance, backed by worldwide support over the Internet. After a three-year period, the negotiations stalled in 1998 and were no longer pursued by the OECD.

enough for a start, and a quite-professional home page can be prepared on a personal computer. The political effectiveness of even the most modest effort can be impressive, as evidenced by the successful International Campaign to Ban Landmines, a project organized almost entirely through the Internet and spearheaded by an individual without a power base in established organizations.

Until relatively recent times, the difference between political actors and the public in representative democracies has been fairly well understood and accepted. Political actors made decisions for the general public. Government officials or members of parliament were, of course, directly or indirectly elected by the public. However, between elections these officials relied, for the most part, on intermediaries—the media, political organizations, even spokespersons and publicists—to keep in touch with the public.

In an information age, global networks have the potential to reduce (or at least change) the role of intermediaries in the political arena.[10] Broadcasting is being supplemented and sometimes replaced by narrowcasting. Networks make it easier to access information directly and can also make available tailor-made tools for selecting and interpreting information. Thus, with respect to both the provision and the interpretation of information, the trend appears to be one in which traditional intermediaries are becoming less important.[11] As a result, people will be less willing to pay for their services, with the consequence that they will be less visible and used still less.

On the other hand, networks also facilitate the creation of new intermediaries to help people find and evaluate information or express political preferences. Therefore, at the same time, technology creates the potential for direct action (plebiscites) and for new brokers or new political intermediaries (and the bypassing of old ones) in the political arena.

In a world of enormous information surplus, finding reliable information that is directly related to one's interests presents huge difficulties for an individual. Today's search engines (e.g., Google, Yahoo!) are one obvious manifestation of new intermediaries that help people find information. But there is every reason to expect that more sophisticated search engines and other intermediary services will help people identify the kinds of information they need and to evaluate the quality of information

---

[10]Christoph Engel. 2000. "The Internet and the Nation State," in Christoph Engel and Kenneth H. Keller, eds., *Understanding the Impact of Global Networks on Local Social, Political and Cultural Values*, 201-260, 222. Note also that the situation is quite different in e-commerce, where the Internet, and information technology more generally, are increasing the opportunities for intermediation. See Chapter 7 of this volume.

[11]Stephen Coleman. 1999. "Cutting Out the Middle Man: From Virtual Representation to Direct Deliberation," in Barry N. Hague and Brian D. Loader, eds., *Digital Democracy*, 195-210.

that they receive. This should not be surprising, given that these editorial functions are being performed today by the editors of newspapers and magazines and books. (Of course, new information intermediaries have an important commercial dimension as well, and to the extent that new intermediaries are used to support political activity, politics and commerce are not mutually exclusive.)

The emergence of powerful nongovernmental organizations (NGOs) has been aided in large part by the presence of global networks. NGOs too can be viewed as a new kind of intermediary, and networks have increased their power relative to that of governments. First, networks enable NGOs to rapidly assemble large political constituencies that can bring significant pressure to bear on elected governments. And second, networks provide NGOs with rapid access to enormous amounts of relevant information, much of which was previously in the hands of governments alone. (Some have noted that networks similarly enhance the power of governments to assemble and analyze information. But since governments had most of the power prior to the wide availability of global networks, the result is that the *relative* powers of governments and NGOs have shifted in favor of the latter.)

As these changes occur, the public has the opportunity to become much more active, either as individuals or through NGOs. Moreover, the value of delegating authority to elected representatives or "experts" is neither as clear nor as accepted. The technical feasibility of receiving information from a seemingly unlimited variety of sources in real time, and being able to express one's view on any issue, also in real time, leads an increasing number of people to believe that they can understand virtually any public-policy issue and that direct, popular decisionmaking is a real option. Whether this confidence is in fact justified is a different matter entirely, but such perceptions have a strong effect on the legitimacy granted by the public to the "experts."

Changes of this magnitude can affect not only constitutional structures for policymaking; they can also alter the more subtle and informal structures that are part of a nuanced and unwritten balance in society. The boundaries become blurred between public and private roles, between policymaking and the accountability for policy decisions, between political and social structures. In Germany, the informal but strong corporatist structure of politics might certainly be affected, as has the cohesion of party politics in the United States.

The question, difficult to answer at this time, is whether the disappearance of traditional intermediaries will lead to the kind of populist, or direct, democracy described above, or whether it will instead give rise to different kinds of intermediation more appropriate to a networked world. One vision of the future is described in Box 4.3.

BOX 4.3 Noopolitik and Policy in the Noosphere

With a vast and growing global information infrastructure—including not only the Internet, but also cable systems, direct broadcast satellites, cellular phones, and so on—and a proliferation of organizations that focus on information and communications issues, the new concept of "noopolitik" has arisen. Noopolitik is foreign policy for an Information Age. It emphasizes the primacy of ideas, values, norms, laws, and ethics that would be implemented through "soft" rather than "hard" power.

Those who promote noopolitik say it is guided by the conviction that right makes might, rather than the reverse. It would take into account both state and non-state actors and the need for them to work together, but it would not be state-centric. Although national interests would be recognized in noopolitik, they would be defined as one aspect of the transnationally networked "fabric" in which all individuals and groups are embedded. While realpolitik tends to empower states, noopolitik will likely empower networks of state and non-state actors. Realpolitik pits one state against another, but noopolitik would encourage states to cooperate in coalitions and other mutually beneficial frameworks.

Few believe that noopolitik will supplant the realpolitik paradigm in the near future. Rather, the two forms are likely to coexist in some rough, edgy balance that, given the uneven penetration of information technologies around the world, will vary by region.

Noopolitik will be pertinent where technologically advanced societies predominate, and less so where societies remain state-centric and hierarchical. Noopolitik will be most effective where the prevalence of all manner of media allow many voices to be heard, where nongovernmental organizations (NGOs) have the capacity to call attention to issues, where the issues themselves go beyond the limited spheres of national economic, political, and military policy, and where government-NGO relations are cordial.

SOURCE: Adapted (primarily) from the Executive Summary of John Arquilla and David F. Ronfeldt, 1999, *The Emergence of Noopolitik: Toward an American Information Strategy*, RAND Corporation, Santa Monica, California.

4.2.4 Political Process

The global networks that affect political actors also have the potential to change the political process. Reduced transaction costs mean that more voices can make themselves heard before a political decision is taken.[12] But having voices heard is not the same thing as engaging in dialogue. At its worst, the former can result in the empowering of narrower and narrower interests, which then makes it increasingly difficult to reach compromises that settle a number of political issues simultaneously.

On the other hand, global networks do make it easier for political issues to surface. Traditional political actors—and those who have traditionally controlled the media—are much less able to control the public agenda when effective, low-cost means of communication are available to all people. Ad hoc groups can quickly unveil an issue, putting government officials and others into a reactive stance (see Box 4.4 as one example). The Seattle WTO protests also illustrated this point, as did the campaign undertaken against CNN by veterans when the network erroneously reported that the nerve gas sarin had been used during the Vietnam War (Box 4.5). Easier access to information and easier access to political arenas thus reinforce each other.

Global networks not only give the governed new opportunities to be heard; they also make it easier to switch political arenas (a phenomenon that Hirschman describes as "exit").[13] Political actors are mobile and can choose the political arena in which to press their case. Nongovernmental organizations promote the protection of Amazon forests by transmitting aerial photographs of burning forests to their offices in the United States, which then distribute the information around the world and encourage other governments to apply pressure on Brazil. Money can be moved across national boundaries to markets and venues with more favorable tax structures. Businesses can cut the value chain into smaller and smaller pieces, coordinating their activities through information networks and optimizing the geographical location of each part. Nation-states find themselves negotiating with multinational corporations rather than regulating them.

Even individuals gain new exit options. Physically moving to another country or changing nationality may be as difficult and costly as before, but "virtual migration" is now possible. Individuals can cut many

---

[12]Raymund Werle. 2000. "The Impact of Information Networks on the Structure of Political Systems," in Christoph Engel and Kenneth H. Keller, eds., *Understanding the Impact of Global Networks on Local Social, Political and Cultural Values*, 159-185, 174.

[13]Albert O. Hirschman. 1970. *Exit, Voice, and Loyalty: Responses to Decline in Firms, Organizations, and States.*

BOX 4.4 Internet and Rebellion: The Case of Chiapas, Mexico

The Internet has played a decisive role in the ongoing fight in Chiapas—a state in southern Mexico close to the Guatemalan border—between a small number of rebels and the Mexican government. Chiapas is one of the poorest regions of the country, with an underdeveloped economic and educational infrastructure; it is inhabited mainly by indigenous Mayan Indians.

In an uprising against the poor living conditions and a host of social, economic, and political issues—including the perceived "neoliberalism" of the 1994 North American Free Trade Agreement—the small Zapatista Army of National Liberation (EZLN) occupied several cities in Chiapas. However, what began as a traditional revolt soon turned into what commentators called a "netwar"—the formation of vast transnational network-mediated coalitions capable of waging an informational war against the Mexican government and in support of the rebels' cause.

When the rebellion started, the Mexican government tried to find a military solution and to block information transfer to the outside world. Because Mexico is a country with a closely controlled public-television system, limiting media coverage was relatively easy to do. Foreign mainstream media, such as American television stations, soon lost interest in what appeared to be a dwindling local conflict after the initial shootings were over. However, for some years before the rebellion and continually over its course, the Zapatistas—who themselves had no direct connection to the Internet—made material available to independent journalists and sympathetic individuals and groups; they did this through interviews, letters, and, most particularly, large numbers of faxes. From there, the information was uploaded to the Internet and rapidly circulated among newsgroups and other forums for informal discussion or professional assessment.

All this outreach finally led to a mass mobilization in support of the EZLN, both on the Internet and in the form of demonstrations in Mexico City and other major cities around the world. Faced with international attention and expressions of solidarity, the Mexican government was forced to abandon its military approach and undertake negotiations with the Zapatistas under the scrutiny of the "Internet eye."

The conflict is still not settled, though the new Mexican government appears to be committed to finding a solution. Today, thousands of Web sites are devoted to the EZLN's struggle and to the larger issues of nonviolence, minority rights, and self-government. Interestingly, the online campaign has stimulated the Mexican government to establish a Web presence to offer its own perspective on the conflict. Various institutions—including, for example, the University of Texas—regularly gather and distribute such information.

BOX 4.5 The Marzullo Incident: The Power of One

In 1998 the Cable News Network (CNN), owned by Time Warner Corp., aired a news-magazine show titled "Newsstand." In one particular program, Newsstand charged that in 1970, during the Vietnam War, the U.S. Army undertook Operation Tailwind to deliberately drop sarin, a nerve gas, in Laos to kill American defectors.

Tom Marzullo, a former member of U.S. Special Operations Forces in Vietnam, had learned of CNN's interest in Operation Tailwind even before the program went on the air. Having been outraged by earlier CNN stories about the work of the Special Forces in Vietnam, he independently researched Operation Tailwind. Using little more than his personal computer and online databases, Marzullo scoured official archives and questioned Special Forces veterans whom he reached via e-mail. Within days of the broadcast, he was on the Internet with a full and telling rebuttal.

A flurry of e-mails and Internet postings persuasively established that the CNN story was highly inaccurate, the product of shoddy research. Within a month, Marzullo's Internet campaign succeeded in humbling a worldwide news organization and Time Warner publicly retracted the story and apologized to the veterans.

Retired Major-General Perry M. Smith, a military adviser to CNN who had not been consulted prior to the show's airing, credited his "Internet advisers" with persuading him to resign his position at CNN to protest the show's inaccuracy. Smith's resignation helped further spread this "Internet uprising" of Special Forces veterans.

of their social ties in the physical environment and replace them with virtual connections to epistemic and affinity groups all over the world. Many commentators have pointed out how this disengagement is taking its toll on civil society and the sense of community.[14]

4.2.5 Governance Tools

Those in power often learn to use new technologies quickly. This is likely to be true with the Internet as well, and indeed there are already signs of it. Driven by initiatives and directives such as the National Performance Review, the Government Performance and Results Act, and OMB Circular A-130 (concerning the management of federal information

[14] See, for example, Robert Putnam, 2001, *Bowling Alone: The Collapse and Revival of American Community*, New York: Touchstone Books.

resources), almost every department of the U.S. government has moved vigorously to develop data banks, mailing lists, and Web pages to facilitate communicating with the public. These efforts, which have generated a great deal of freely available information, build on the tradition of openness in U.S. society. But they also serve to create direct links to the public that effectively bypass the traditional media.

Some have argued that if this direct communication with the public displaces or reduces the role of the traditional media, which often serve as watchdog, it may actually reduce government accountability. On the other hand, others argue that media mergers have so concentrated power, and commercial considerations have so limited in-depth reporting and analysis, that the print and broadcast media may themselves have become part of the problem. In any case, it is highly unlikely that the public would endorse or accept a strategy that consciously limited the right of the government to communicate directly with its constituents.

Obviously, government can also use technologies to learn much more about its citizens and their activities, and to try to exercise influence and control over those activities. As an example of the latter, broadcast media have provided a powerful tool for many totalitarian regimes. Networks, by contrast, have thus far proven much more resistant to government efforts to bring them under control.

The factors underlying such resistance are multiple. One is the absence of limitations on signal transmission imposed by distance. Because the range of traditional broadcast media is power-constrained, the number of nodes that must be regulated is limited to those that service a given geographical area; beyond that area, the laws of physics attenuate the signal to negligible levels and hence there is no need for regulation.

A second factor is the many-to-many character of the Internet. In an environment in which the number of suppliers of information can be essentially as large as the number of recipients, suppressing all possible suppliers of a given piece of information is very difficult. Government has thus lost, for all practical purposes, the tool of "pre-publication" censorship. It does retain the power to sanction the transmission of information, but such a power is rather blunt, and its use entails great costs to a government whose polity is sensitive to the rights of individuals. (See also Box 4.6.)

The altered role of government in a networked world should not imply the demise of governments so much as it does the need for new strategies. Unilateral state actions need to give way to strategies of negotiation with various social actors.[15] Sovereign power does not disappear, but it becomes more useful in providing leverage than in conferring abso-

[15]Scharpf (supra note 7) 200.

BOX 4.6 Publius: A Censorship-proof Internet Publishing System

Publius is a Web publishing system, developed by researchers at AT&T and New York University, that is highly resistant to censorship and provides publishers with a high degree of anonymity. In essence, Publius encrypts digital content (say, a document), fragments the result, and distributes it among a number of Web servers in such a way that the content can be reconstructed as long as a certain fraction of the fragments are available. For example, the fragments might be distributed to 100 servers and a person able to recover 35 fragments (any 35) would be able to reconstruct the document. However, if 34 or fewer fragments were recovered, the content of the original document could not be determined.

The cooperating Web servers in this system are totally passive and cannot, by themselves, reconstruct the original document. Therefore any entity that provides publicly accessible storage online for any purpose can be used as a cooperating Web server. But because multiple servers are needed to recreate the document, Publius breaks the one-to-one correspondence between a Web document and a server.

lute authority. In this networked society, governance often involves recognizing and nudging certain network-related social and economic structures. Even in settling political questions, central government is likely to rely more on self-governance by technical, commercial, or societal bodies than on detailed regulatory prescriptions. This is now commonly called "hybrid governance" or "hybrid regulation."[16]

The American system of governance, because it is less hierarchical, already relies on hybrid governance to some extent. However, German authorities tend to see major changes, resulting in an altered and more subsidiary role for government (*Gewährleistungsverantwortung*) in which it no longer is responsible for the direct provision of all public goods. Instead, it ensures that autonomous social systems act to provide those goods. This changed emphasis can be expected to affect the political process and political culture as much as the regulatory framework, but it is an example of a value shift that may be salutary.

These comments should not be seen as implying that governments' reactions to the Internet will necessarily be benign or constructive. It is not beyond belief that they may employ traditional command-and-con-

[16]More on hybrid governance is contained in Chapter 8.

trol regulation, well-suited to the Internet environment or not, to deal with what they may see as Internet-related problems. If and when such actions occur, they may not serve democratic and freedom-preserving interests.[17] For example, the U.S. Congress sought to protect minors from exposure to sexually explicit material on the Internet by passing the Communications Decency Act of 1996, a statute that was subsequently overturned on Constitutional grounds. (See Chapter 5 for a more detailed discussion.) In a nation without judicial review of legislative actions, such a law might have stood—despite its infringements on the free-speech rights of the populace.

4.2.6 Conflicts

Because global networks reduce many of the constraints of distance, different ideas, attitudes, political convictions, customs, and cultures can mix in entirely unexpected ways. The richness and value of this mix is obvious, but so too is the increased opportunity for conflict. Conflict, of course, is possible in any society, but a shared national history and a political system shaped by debates and compromises over hundreds of years help to narrow differences and provide incentives for accommodation. Reopening a debate in an international context, where one nation's hard-won resolution is pitted against another's, is likely to prove difficult, because the representatives from each nation who may be charged with resolving the conflict are necessarily closely tied to the consensus-building process within their own national societies.[18]

Adding to the problems of international conflict-resolution that derive from the historical and cultural baggage of the interested parties—that is, the nation-states—are the shortcomings of international political institutions. First, the administrators and professionals who run international organizations, from UN agencies to the WTO, can make no claim to the legitimacy that comes with election to office; the personnel of such organizations are appointed to their positions. There are no truly international parliaments, and as long as no supranational or even international identity emerges, constitutional reform is not likely to change this state of affairs. The German public, for example, would hardly be willing to accept a European Union political decision just because a majority of deputies from other member states agreed to it.

---

[17]For more discussion on this point, see, for example, part III of A. Michael Froomkin, 1998, "The Empire Strikes Back" ("The Great Looming Internet Irony"), *Chi-Kent L. Rev.* 73:1101.

[18]Miles Kahler. 2000. "Information Networks and Global Politics," in Christoph Engel and Kenneth H. Keller, eds., *Understanding the Impact of Global Networks on Local Social, Political and Cultural Values*, 141-157, 146 and 147.

Second, the European Union notwithstanding, no international body has the power to actually legislate. If an international conflict is to be dealt with by legal rules, these rules must be implemented through each of the sovereign member states, whose parliaments are usually unwilling or constitutionally unable to delegate any part of their jurisdiction to an international body. But the step from international decision to national implementation is a precarious one, as much a matter of politics as legal linkage.

A third weakness of the international political arena is the Balkanized nature of its institutions. The jurisdiction of each rulemaking body is very narrow, and coordination among them is, for all practical purposes, ineffectual. Therefore the possibilities for linking issues in the give-and-take of packaging political compromises is difficult to achieve. For example, Balkanization of authority means that it is hard to link trade and nontrade issues, environment and technology transfer, or programming restrictions and intellectual-property protection. Furthermore, such powers as compensatory tax relief, commonplace within the nation-state, are also unavailable to international bodies.

Finally, it is important to consider the class of conflicts that can arise when old values and traditions are challenged by new ideas.[19] This is the pluralizing, or modernizing, effect of global networks.[20] The user of global networks can be exposed to very different cultures, not merely as an objective abstraction but as an inherent component of the broad range of activities and information exchanges that occur through the Net. To a great extent, the foreign cultures are experienced rather than merely observed. One does not need to accept these new values or outlooks in their entirety, but it becomes more difficult to reject them entirely; thus absolute conviction may give way to a more nuanced and relative perspective.

In turn, relativism may present a challenge to one's personal (or group) system of control and accountability. It is conceivable, and often suggested, that a response to this challenge will be to force people into narrowly defined epistemic communities, aided by the technology of networks. Individuals, for example, might customize their own electronic newspapers to receive only information of specific interest to them, avoiding serendipitous exposure to information that might challenge their beliefs.

Such a response may be feasible from a technical point of view, but it is difficult to conceive of it as a successful coping strategy for the future.

---

[19]Sherry Turkle. 1995. *Life on the Screen: Identity in the Age of the Internet*, New York: Simon and Schuster.

[20]Wolfgang Kersting. 2000. "Global Networks and Local Values. Some Philosophical Remarks from an Individualist Point of View," in Christoph Engel and Kenneth H. Keller, eds., *Understanding the Impact of Global Networks on Local Social, Political and Cultural Values*, 9-27, 14 and 21.

In a world in which the separation of the local from the global is increasingly difficult, and the commingling of values and cultures is becoming increasingly evident in the most local of activities, a successful coping strategy necessarily puts a much higher premium on tolerance. This would be not so much because tolerance is a normative value (although it would clearly qualify as one), but because it is a practical strategy for coping politically and even economically with the challenges of a modern world. Managing the transition to this new "modernity" in societies with vastly different structures may become one of the greatest challenges to political systems.

4.2.7 Cognitive Frameworks, Normative Beliefs, and Integration

Normative values allow individuals to give meaning to social reality. Moreover, society organizes itself around shared values. Common values, in other words, are a key ingredient in integration.[21] And integration reflects how society and the state are tied together.

Social cohesion and integration are unlikely to be deeply affected if a single local value is challenged or eroded, since a society's set of values has never been totally stable over time. Traditional values have been challenged whenever a sufficiently large stratum of society has been exposed to different cultures. But society is an adaptive organism; it adjusts to the new values, rebalances the old ones, and bends without breaking.

But global networks can challenge the adaptive capacity of the system. All societies have certain values that are so fundamental for their self-definition that, if challenged, they can weaken group cohesion. And when several such values are challenged simultaneously, the rapid adaptation thus required can be highly threatening. This provides an analytical yardstick against which to measure the threat that global networks might present to a given society.

Global networks also affect social and political integration because they introduce virtual communities and global market opportunities that can compete with nation-states or local communities for the attention and loyalty of individuals. As a result, the nation state's tools for problem solving become more limited and its power to redistribute wealth diminishes. It no longer has a monopoly on its audience's attention, either psychologically or economically.[22]

---

[21]Klaus G. Gruner. 1994. "Cognition and Economic Psychology,"in Hermann Brandstätter and Werner Güth, eds., *Essays on Economic Psychology*, 91-108.

[22]Kahler (supra note 18) 147.

Given this weakened identification with the state, those who are called on to pay the bills to provide a social safety net may not be as easily convinced that it is their moral obligation to do so. Moreover, the legitimacy of formal political institutions within the nation-state is subject to greater skepticism as competing loyalties arise. On the other hand, it is possible that the easier sharing of information and opportunities for participation in governance may strengthen the nation-state in time. And government can avail itself of the new technological possibilities and try to use them to reach, even to manipulate, the citizenry. As with so many other questions concerning the effects of global networks, the possibilities are clearer than the actual outcome.

4.2.8 Global Networks as a Cohesive Force

Global networks do not always threaten values. Indeed, they can reinforce them by providing links to like-minded people who are widely dispersed—community without propinquity. Networks can also provide a mechanism for highly local or specialized groups to organize around highly non-global values.[23] Consider, for example, a neighborhood association that organizes itself via the Internet to block the establishment of a solid-waste incinerator. Not only are political conflicts easier to handle in a local setting, under the umbrella of well-established political structures, but the networks empower local constituencies by putting global voices and global information resources at their disposal.

In such a case, global networks may well strengthen local values to the point that they challenge national values, an ironic reversal in the assumption usually made about the threat of global networks. Box 4.1 and Box 4.7 provide illustrations of how global networks are promoting and building a geographical community.

4.2.9 Pressures for Change

Because political systems differ, the pressure on any given political system to adapt in the face of issues raised by global networks differs greatly from one system to another. This is obvious if one compares totalitarian regimes or fundamentalist states with modern democracies, but it also holds true among industrialized and democratic countries. In particular, Germany has a tradition of fencing political decisions off from public control and influence to a much greater extent than is the case in the United States.

---

[23]Saskia Sassen. 1998. *Globalization and Its Discontents. Essays on the New Mobility of People and Money*.

BOX 4.7 Project Bosnia and Operation Kosovo

Over the last 5 years several dozen law students, engineering students, law professors, and practicing lawyers in the United States and Europe have used the Internet to promote human rights, advance the rule of law, facilitate freedom of the press and open media, and encourage economic development in the Balkans. Launched at Villanova University School of Law in January 1996, the project continues under the direction of Dean Henry H. Perritt, Jr., Assistant Dean Charles S. Rudnick, and Director of Special Projects Harry E. Ashton IV of Chicago-Kent College of Law at the Illinois Institute of Technology in Chicago. Students and others associated with Project Bosnia have connected the Bosnian Constitutional Court and Ombudsman to the Internet, developed a prototype database system for the Bosnian Ministry of Justice, and established an independent media center connected to the Internet in Banja Luka in Bosnia.

Chicago-Kent's Operation Kosovo established an Internet-connected database system for registering refugees and tracking refugee relief before and during the NATO bombing of Yugoslavia. It has now extended the database to keep track of war-crimes evidence provided by refugees in interviews, making use of digital audio recording, encryption, and geographic information modeling technologies. Operation Kosovo participants have used distance-learning technologies to make lectures on judicial procedure available to law students, law professors, and judges in Kosovo. Most recently, Operation Kosovo participants worked with the Interim Government of Kosovo to use Web-based and e-commerce technologies to facilitate foreign investment in start-up enterprises in Kosovo. The project illustrates the power of the Internet to promote democracy, develop commerce, and improve the transparency of legal institutions, while also protecting individuals' privacy.

The low cost of the technologies involved made it possible for a handful of committed people, with only modest funding, to make a difference in a daunting international crisis. And they have been working on their own, albeit in consultation with formal international institutions such as the United Nations, the Organization for Security and Cooperation in Europe, and the World Bank.

For example, Germany ordinarily makes little effort to provide freedom of access to government information, apart from information relating to environmental issues. The German political process affords very few opportunities for public referenda. And in developing new policies, the German government negotiates with only a small number of strongly organized private actors. All of these German political practices have come under pressure from global networks. By contrast, the United States has a much stronger tradition of freedom of information, makes more extensive use of public referenda, and negotiates policy with a wide variety of interest groups. Thus the pressures on the U.S. political system for change are, in this respect, considerably less.

The willingness of nations to respond to pressures created by increasing internationalization also varies. Germany, under these kinds of pressures, has had some success in moving beyond its traditional command-and-control regulation. The United States, on the other hand, is more resistant to international pressures generally; its unwillingness to adapt to global standards when, for example, its social and religious values are involved may prove to be problematical. The dispute between the United States and the European Union over privacy regulations, now resolved in principle, is a case in point. (See Chapter 6 in this report for more detailed discussion.)

All democracies balance individualism, hierarchy, and egalitarian beliefs in some fashion.[24] Normally, political actors take these compromises as a given; indeed, they are embedded in political institutions that restrict the strategy space for political action. The stronger these institutions are, the more difficult it is to challenge the underlying compromises. When global networks do challenge them, the reaction is a confrontational rather than an adaptive process.

How fast change occurs depends on how well the political system is prepared to accommodate it. Neither the United States nor Germany has a formal parliamentary system. In the United States, the President and his administration, and in Germany, the ministerial administration (as well as powerful social actors like the unions), have either de jure or de facto veto power. This makes it somewhat more difficult to coalesce around a strategy for change.

On the other hand, both are federations (Germany, in fact, has three levels of governance, if one includes the European Union), which has given them some experience in coordinating governance across political arenas. Both countries also have powerful and independent constitutional courts, which can enable change by preventing a tyranny of the majority and protecting diverse views and life styles. The courts can also break political deadlocks in which a legislative body is unwilling or unable to act when action is needed.

---

[24] Michael Thompson, Richard Ellis, and Aaron Wildavsky. 1990. *Basic Cultural Theory.* Boulder, Colo.: Westview Press.

4.2.10 Degree of International Conflict Over Democratic Values

The significant differences in the structure of democracy among countries may lead to differences in the reactions of these nations to the pressures for change posed by global networks. For example, nations have different perspectives on how best to ensure order and propriety on the Internet (Box 4.8). However, in contrast to the reaction where issues such as pornography, hate speech, or religious tolerance are concerned,[25] the different forms that democracy takes are not, in themselves, a source of conflict as long as there is little or no overlap in political constituencies.

BOX 4.8 Trust in Politics: Who Should Control the Internet?

The assessment of who can best control misuse of the Internet displays strikingly different national perspectives. Americans clearly look to the users themselves, followed by the online service providers and organizations specializing in child protection or with a special moral authority of some other kind.

In contrast, the German population places trust in politics and law-enforcement authorities to a noticeably greater extent, while it only gives a small amount of responsibility and latitude to the Internet users themselves. Whereas 36 percent of the American population consider the individual Internet user as the best guarantor of an effective control of inappropriate content, barely one-fifth of the German population shares this opinion. In contrast, 28 percent of the German population places trust in politicians, but only 2 percent of the American population does so.

SOURCE: Bertelsmann Foundation: Risk Assessment and Opinions Concerning the Control of Misuse on the Internet. Results of representative surveys conducted in the United States, Australia, and the Federal Republic of Germany. A project by the Bertelsmann Foundation, Germany, in conjunction with the Australian Broadcasting Authority (ABA), Allensbach archives, IfD-survey 3296. Available online at <http://www.stiftung.bertelsmann.de/internetcontent/english/frameset.htm?content/c2000.htm>.

[25]Grewlich (supra note 9) 241-246.

Those differences result from the fact that nation-states are sovereign and therefore free to choose their own political institutions; inevitably, they will make different choices in implementing democratic values. Because there is little or no overlap in political constituencies, most people do not find their own form of democracy threatened merely because it differs from that of another nation-state.

Transnational political arenas would seem to represent a very different case. Here there is very clearly an overlap of constituencies and a possibility for conflict among competing political systems. Fortunately, at least for the issues of concern here, international institutions and governance structures are generally so weak, and so limited in their capacity to compel actions in the member states, that confrontation between national systems seldom occurs.

More serious conflicts arise, however, when political systems become "missionary." For example, those concerned about human rights want to see human rights protected everywhere. In order to join the Council of Europe or the European Community, Eastern European countries have to prove that their constitutions conform to democratic standards in protecting individual rights. For many nations, such an evangelical perspective raises the concern that hegemonic intentions rather than humanitarian considerations may be the real driving force. Some observers question, for instance, the U.S. government's position that the Internet should not be regulated. They wonder whether it is less a manifestation of a First Amendment principle than it is covert industrial policy, aimed at ensuring unconditional access by American e-business to other countries.[26]

This leads to a final concern. Although different national concepts of democracy can, in principle, coexist relatively easily in the era of the Internet, the Internet itself is a global phenomenon. Thus if one nation-state attempts to protect or foster its particular national form of democracy by attempting to shape the Internet in a certain way, the normative differences between states may give rise to a significant international conflict over policy regarding the Internet. Box 4.9 provides an illustration.

4.3 CONSTITUTIONAL POLICY

Global networks have great potential to induce change. They can enhance the effectiveness of some political arenas to the detriment of others, give some political actors power and take it away from others, and

[26]Jacques Arlandis. 2000. "The Clerk, the Merchant and the Politician," in Christoph Engel and Kenneth Keller, eds., *Governance of Global Networks in the Light of Differing Local Values*, 105-117, 109.

BOX 4.9 The French Yahoo! Case

On November 20th, 2000, in *LICRA & French Union of Jewish Students v. Yahoo! Inc.*, the County Court of Paris ordered Yahoo! to comply within 3 months of notification with a May 22 order under which Yahoo! was required to (1) take all necessary measures to "make impossible" access to Nazi merchandise or any other site or service that may be construed "as (apologizing) for Nazism or contesting the reality of Nazi crimes"; (2) warn all Internet surfers before they proceed with searches on yahoo.com of the risks involved in continuing to view such sites; and (3) submit, for deliberation by all the interested parties, the measures it proposes to take to "put an end to the trouble and damage suffered and to prevent any further trouble." If Yahoo! failed to comply, it would be subject to a penalty of 100,000 francs per day of delay following the expiration of the 3-month period. Furthermore, Yahoo! was ordered to make payment of 10,000 francs to each of the plaintiffs.

The court reasoned that even though the "Yahoo! Auctions" site that brought this issue before the court generally targets surfers based in the United States, auctions involving symbols of Nazi ideology "may be of interest to any person." Furthermore, Yahoo!'s claim in the litigation that it was technologically infeasible to identify French users of its site was undercut by its practice of identifying such users so that it could present them with French-language advertising banners. This practice is a clear example of "targeting," which itself is emerging as an acceptable object of transnational jurisdiction.

The court stated that the act of displaying objects of Nazi ideology in France is a violation of Article R645-1 of the Penal Code and thus is a "threat to internal public order." The court also stated that the technical measures and the initiatives at its disposal give Yahoo! an opportunity to satisfy the injunctions of the May 22 order. The two technical procedures identified by the court—geographical identification and user declaration of nationality—would allow Yahoo! to filter out French IP addresses at a success rate of 90 percent.

In December 2000, Yahoo! filed a declaratory relief action in the United States District Court for the Northern District of California (San Jose), seeking to block enforcement of the French order on the grounds that the French court lacked jurisdiction. On November 7, 2001, the Court granted Yahoo!'s request for summary judgment (*Yahoo!, Inc. v. La Ligue Contre Le Racisme et L'Antisemitisme,* F.Supp.2d, 2001 WL 1381157 (N.D. Cal. 2001)), finding that French enforcement of French laws in the United States would chill Yahoo's First Amendment rights in the United States.

The court decision can be found at <http://www.cdt.org/jurisdiction/011107judgement.pdf>.

strengthen some governance tools and weaken others. They can alter political processes, the character of political conflicts, or cognitive frameworks and normative beliefs. They can even change the relationship between the society and the state. It would be naive to expect those who currently hold political power to just let all this happen. This sets the stage for the debates, conflicts, and structural adjustments that are part of the evolution of what might be called "constitutional policy," to which we now turn our attention.

4.3.1 Accommodating Constitutional Policy to Global Networks

Political actors are likely to try to encourage or block a particular effect of global networks on political structures, depending on their assessment of its consequences. But as a practical matter it is really quite difficult to anticipate either the precise way in which the networks will affect each part of the system or all of the consequences that may result from trying to intervene. Given the complex interactions that occur between political and social subsystems,[27] any intervention—whether in the form of new regulations, political co-optation of networks, or even changes in the structure of political institutions—can lead to reactions by each subgroup to preserve the status quo or to maintain the momentum of change. This seems particularly likely when players from the first-generation Internet communities, who tend to blend egalitarian with anarchic elements, are involved.

Although it is beyond the scope of this study to deal with the question of whether there is any compelling reason to encourage one form of democracy over another, the question of how a constitutional change can come about under the influence of global networks is quite appropriate. Democracies deliberately make such change difficult in order to reduce the likelihood that well-organized political interest groups can effect fundamental structural alterations merely to suit their agendas.

The U.S. Supreme Court and the German Constitutional Court play key roles in guarding their respective constitutions against such political manipulation. But global networks can, in a de facto sense, alter constitutional protections or frustrate constitutional goals even without any formal change in the constitution. Given that possibility, a failure to modify the written constitution, or a failure to adjust the informal mechanisms and interpretations that supplement the written provisions of the consti-

[27]For the Internet as a subsystem the argument is made in Dirk Baecker, 2000, "Networking the Web," in Christoph Engel and Kenneth H. Keller, eds., *Understanding the Impact of Global Networks on Local Social, Political and Cultural Values*, 93-111, 96.

tution, may sometimes lead to undesirable changes in a nation's fundamental political structure.

The German constitution might be somewhat better prepared to parry such a challenge. Both countries have constitutionally protected fundamental freedoms, and both empower their respective constitutional courts to interpret them. But the United States's interpretation relies on rights that are explicitly mentioned in or at least implied by the U.S. Constitution, and the U.S. Supreme Court tends to narrow the constitutional issues before it as much as possible, at least by comparison to the German Constitutional Court. The German Constitutional court, on the other hand, has greater leeway for adaptation, thus allowing it to act on the basis of broader considerations. For example, although German Basic Law requires that any governmental interference with freedom or property needs a justification, almost any reasonable policy is accepted as a justification, provided that the proposed restrictions can be shown to be necessary to achieve the desired end.

4.3.2 Internet Policy

Given the reluctance of policymakers to undertake constitutional changes to adjust to the new circumstances presented by global networks, they are likely to focus on policy instruments that would allow control, regulation, or even exclusion of the Internet for the purpose of dealing with the tensions it generates. But none of those approaches is easy to implement. Only two countries in the world have opted for a policy of completely forbidding access to the Internet: North Korea and Myanmar. Singapore and Vietnam have tried to force all Internet traffic in and out of their countries through a few tightly controlled conduits, but they pay a high price for such control: access by their citizens to worldwide information sources is sharply reduced. For countries such as the United States or Germany, such Draconian action has never been proposed.

Short of actually blocking access to the Internet, countries find themselves with options of widely different effectiveness, as illustrated by Germany and the United States. Because of U.S. dominance in the global information technology industry and among large-scale Internet service providers, U.S. policy actions that force change in the Internet-related products and services offered by U.S. companies are likely to affect the development path of the Internet globally. On the other hand, even though German authorities may occasionally sanction a global network (as they did in the CompuServe cases), their influence is limited and can hardly be expected to have a significant effect on the shape of the Internet.

Because of the interconnectedness of the Internet infrastructure (e.g., standards and protocols), if one nation actually effects some change in the structure or operation of the Internet, that change will affect operations everywhere—but not necessarily in the same way or with the same consequences. For example, if the United States forced a technological change to implement its national policy of limiting the distribution of undesirable material, it might well build into the system the technical means for an authoritarian regime to extend its censorship control (a point discussed further in Chapter 5).

It would be simplistic to view Internet policy as entirely a question of regulation or control aimed at preserving traditional political structures, given that global networks offer a new tool for achieving important and very broad political goals. Both the United States and Germany are committed to a political structure that can provide for a range of views to be heard and considered and, at the same time, encourage integration of those views and the people who hold them into a coherent society.

To satisfy the first goal, ideological, political, and ethnic minorities need to have access to the public forum, providing for a kind of cultural biodiversity that introduces fresh insights and makes political innovation possible. This goal has not been easy to meet through traditional electronic media. The radio-frequency spectrum is limited and crowded, and cable channels are expensive, as are broadcasting facilities of significant power. Constitutional courts have tried to overcome these inherent limitations by instituting fairness doctrines, with mixed results.[28] By contrast, the Internet and its related technologies make the goal of access much easier to attain. The spectrum is virtually unlimited, the costs are low, and public policies can easily be put in place to promote Internet literacy, wide availability of terminals in schools and libraries, and help for any group interested in setting up a Web page.

The situation is reversed with respect to the goal of societal integration. With traditional electronic media, the small number of program originators, the high set-up cost, the one-to-many nature of broadcasting, and the typically passive role of the message recipients are all conducive to societal integration. Moreover, the small number of programmers also makes it easy to impose and enforce policy.

The Internet makes societal integration harder to achieve because individuals have much greater autonomy both as transmitters and recipients of messages. Indeed, the technology allows societal atomization to an unprecedented degree. Some technical approaches have been proposed to promote integration in the Internet context—for example, "push" technologies that force users to open a publicly designed or prescribed window before they can get access to any other site. But there are obvious

[28]For an account, see Cass Sunstein, 1995, *Democracy and the Problem of Free Speech*, The Free Press.

objections to such an imposition on personal freedom. For the time being, therefore, it appears more feasible to depend on network-based technologies to serve the goals of access and diversity, and more traditional broadcast media to promote social and political integration.

It should be noted, however, that technological convergence may require a reconsideration in the future of how best to achieve a balance of diversity and integration. Technological developments are gradually blurring the distinctions between various communication media. DSL technology can increase the bandwidth of telephone lines so that they can support motion-picture transmission or other kinds of broadcasting; cable-television lines can now support Internet communication and real-time voice communications; and various kinds of compression technologies are increasing broadcast-channel availability, thus allowing more customized programming. In time this may alter the view of broadcast media as passive and integrative, and Internet media as active and diverse, but for the near and mid-term future the distinction remains useful.

4.3.3 Networks and Representative Versus Direct Democracy

Democracy theorists have been attracted by one feature of global networks in particular: the fact that it is now technically and economically possible to let people decide political issues directly. This reopens the debate over representative versus direct democracy and the desirability of a shift of law-making jurisdiction from a legislature to the electorate.[29]

Different countries have had different experiences with plebiscites. In Switzerland, plebiscites seem to work reasonably well. But many analysts believe that the demise of Germany's Weimar Republic was accelerated by an overly broad use of that instrument. The "electronic town hall" would appear to increase input legitimacy, because it increases participation. On the other hand, it is more difficult to ensure that voters are as fully informed about complex issues as one might hope legislators are, and so output legitimacy may suffer. Voters may be lured into the illusion that access to information through global networks is tantamount to complete understanding. Moreover, legislation by referendum usually requires that the issue at hand be reduced to a simply phrased question. Experience has shown that the outcome of a referendum depends strongly on how the question is phrased,[30] and most experts agree that it is all but impossible to keep a question simple and, at the same time, capture important nuances.

---

[29]See Jeffrey Abramson. 2000. "Democracy and Global Communications," in Christoph Engel and Kenneth Keller, eds., *Governance of Global Networks in the Light of Differing Local Values*, 119-130.

[30]See, for example, R. Nisbett and L. Ross, 1980, *Human Inference*, Prentice-Hall.

Of course, legislative decisions may not be fully informed either, and the traditional political process does not necessarily lead to the most desirable outcome. For example, political actors may be motivated by concerns other than solving the policy problem at hand.[31] The legislative agenda can be shaped by the media, scandal, or a host of other factors rather than by substantive priority, and logrolling or political influence may determine outcomes as much as the needs of the polity.

The fact is that neither popular nor legislative approaches to problem solving are free from risk—or without merit. A larger role for direct democracy could serve three purposes. It could increase the participation of the public in decision making, resulting in a greater sense of ownership and responsibility. It might be an important tool in promoting societal integration. And it could make those in political power more accountable to the public. If the threat of plebiscites, formal or informal, exists, it is more difficult to ignore the public will between elections. In that respect, some opportunities for direct democracy can be part of the system of checks and balances in the political structure.

It may well be that the most important contribution of networks will not be to replace representative democracies with referendum/plebiscite-based direct democracies, but to offer a rich range of intermediate possibilities. Such options could enhance participation in governance, increase the diversity of viewpoints in public debate, and place additional pressure on public officials to be responsive and accountable. The mere potential of global networks to redistribute political power forces decision makers to explain their actions more clearly and thoroughly.

Referenda can be used to express public views without actually shifting formal decision-making power. Even without formal referenda, the ease of network communication makes it possible for many different voices to be heard. And with broader freedom-of-information policies, the new technologies can allow the public to gain increased access to government files.[32] By shedding brighter light on the processes of government, the ability of the public to hold its elected officials accountable for their actions may thus be enhanced.

---

[31]Daniel A. Farber and Philip P. Frickey. 1991. *Law and Public Choice*, 22.

[32]As discussed in Chapter 8, there are significant differences between the United States and Germany in this respect. Freedom of information is already a much more broadly applied principle in the United States than in Germany.

4.3.4 The Impact of Networks on the Evolution of Political Landscapes

Political structures need to be open to change over time, both because new technologies introduce new issues and because the value judgements of those governed may change. Society's formal institutions and political culture need to be prepared for evolution, to be able to respond to fresh ideas and be attentive to new challenges. The healthy society develops mechanisms to adapt in much the same way an ecosystem does, encouraging processes of variation and selection. The analogy has limitations, however. Both variation and selection have dangers for a society. The former promotes fragmentation of the body politic, the latter encourages single-issue politics. Those are dangers that societies need to be aware of but cannot easily avoid.

Global networks affect variation *and* selection, but they do more for the former than the latter. They provide a means for giving people with new ideas wide distribution and a means for people seeking ideas to find them. In doing so, they reshape political arenas, empower political actors, and reconfigure political processes. Their effect on selection is less clear. Do they lead to a more thoughtful process of weighing and implementing ideas, or do they provide an opportunity for special interests or single-issue groups to promote changes that do not serve the broad polity well? If the latter is the case, one might view an appropriate regulatory strategy for global networks as one that promotes globalization and pluralization to increase the range of ideas available, but restricts the role of the networks in the actual process of lawmaking.

Central government policies undertaken to deal with social problems almost always have distributional consequences that affect one group differently than another. If a way cannot be found to compensate a constituency that is negatively affected, the government stands to alienate that group. In the modern world, networking technologies provide opportunities for such groups to leave the polity, virtually or in reality. For single-issue constituencies, the opportunities for government to craft some kind of compensation are quite limited. Thus, the very network that increases a group's power to press its case also decreases its need or willingness to accept a negative decision to serve the greater good.

Although the issues discussed in this section are exacerbated by global networks, they are really part and parcel of the modern world. Even if a country was prepared to cut its population off from global networks, it could not avoid many other forms of globalization. The nation-state is inexorably losing its traditional role as a monopolistic provider of a highly aggregated bundle of public goods. More and more, it is under competitive pressure from other providers—other nation-states, and different structures of formal and informal political organization.[33]

At the same time, national political systems continue to have significant power. The roles and services that governments provide, as well as their authority and effectiveness, may be attenuated, but they will remain vital to their constituents. In that sense, the nation-state may be altered, but it is not threatened. States will still provide social services, education, physical protection, public health, and environmental stability and will fulfill the host of functions that are associated with place and identity. This will give a state the legitimacy and power to retain certain authority and to negotiate with other nations to protect its rights and the rights of its citizens. Most international treaties are examples of the effectiveness of national systems to organize a global order, even in the modern world. One may view this as a practical and acceptable alternative to constitutionalizing the world order,[34] and one that is perhaps more important than ever before precisely because of the advent of global networks.

But given the ad hoc nature of this globalizing process, the future is quite open-ended, in both descriptive and prescriptive terms. Nation-states and their constitutional orders will certainly continue to come under competitive pressure. Those governed will have increasing leeway to move away from a nation-state's regulatory power and, clearly, the more credible the threat to move, the more carefully nation-states will have to listen to their demands. But because one cannot accurately predict which interest groups will mount the most credible threats at any particular time, it is difficult to know what the nature of the competitive pressures is most likely to be or how nations will respond. Will democratic institutions be harmonized? If so, will we see "a race to the bottom," a "race to the top," or an entirely changed governance structure? And if we do see the emergence of a significantly changed structure, on what basis should we judge it to be a good or a bad thing?

[33]Jean-Marie Guéhenno. 1998. "From Territorial Communities to Communities of Choice: Implications for Democracy," in Wolfgang Streeck, ed., *Internationale Wirtschaft, Nationale Demokratie. Herausforderungen für die Demokratietheorie.*

[34]Jochen A. Frowein. 2000. "Konstitutionalisierung des Völkerrechts," *Berichte der Deutschen Gesellschaft für Völkerrecht* 39:427-448.

5

Free Speech and the Internet

5.1 INTRODUCTION

The preceding chapters have sought to provide a framework for understanding how global networks influence local values, political institutions, and ways of doing business, as well as how those networks might be governed. This chapter and the next look more closely at some particular issues—namely, those related to free speech and to the tensions between privacy and freedom of information.

To a certain extent, the selection of these topics is arbitrary. In other chapters, the report has touched on other topics that might reasonably be examined more closely: consumer protection and copyright; the social changes inherent in a networked world; and the shifting boundaries between public and private spaces and the blurring of the line between consumer and producer. Transnational issues could have been added as well: tax policy, customs and tariffs for Internet traffic, and technical standardization are obvious examples.

But free speech and privacy stand out in two respects: they have attracted considerable public interest, and they are characterized by conflict between the two nations that are the focus of this report. Therefore, this chapter and the next will address these issues. The intention is to discuss them as examples of the tensions and challenges that global networks introduce in a society's values, but these are issues with such strong legal overtones that it is impractical to approach them without incorporating legal considerations into the discussion as well.

5.2 THE VALUES INVOLVED IN FREE SPEECH

For both the United States and Germany, freedom of speech is such an important formal value that it is explicitly protected by the First Amendment to the U.S. Constitution and by Article 5 of the German Basic Law. Because of this constitutional protection, legislatures have very little latitude to pass laws that restrict speech. If the legislature, or any other governmental body, moves too far in that direction, individuals in each country can seek relief in the highest court.

This constitutional protection of free speech obligates both government and private parties to tolerate many kinds of expression, regardless of how much it may clash with individual values or with the traditions of the country. Yet, restrictions on speech are common around the world, with many instances of censorship and criminal prosecution for the criticism of government policy. Even in the United States and Germany, policymakers have sought legislation from time to time that would place restrictions on various kinds of speech. Such legislation has usually been struck down as unconstitutional, but the continual efforts made, and the restrictions sometimes allowed, suggest that the right of free speech is not absolute and that some substantive value is being explicitly or implicitly applied to distinguish protected from unprotected speech. This substantive value (or these values) may well be in tension with the formal value of free speech.

Some of those competing values may also be formal ones. For example, the exercise of free speech might directly or almost directly cause physical harm—such as injuries and death resulting from the publication of bomb-building instructions or the psychic trauma of children that might occur as the result of exposure to certain kinds of sexually explicit material. Similarly, one cannot (falsely) shout "Fire!" in a crowded theatre; as Oliver Wendell Holmes noted, "Your freedom ends where my nose begins." Where the connections among formal values are relatively clear and unambiguous—they are not always so—it is relatively easy to make judgments about which one should take precedence. The situation is not so straightforward when substantive values are involved.

Generally speaking, formal values such as free speech establish rights and procedures that enable a society to function effectively and, it is hoped, fairly. But it takes substantive values to provide the glue, the shared outlook that makes a society more than a collection of individuals. If the values under which a society operated were composed exclusively of formal values, normative views of the world, such as the hierarchical, the egalitarian, or the fatalistic, which hold societies together and distinguish them from one another, would be denied any status whatsoever.[1]

In fact, substantive values do come into play. For example, restrictions on free speech may be the result of seeking balance—the formal value of free speech weighed against the competing claims of certain substantive values. Of course, the notion that a balance is involved suggests that the mere existence of a conflicting substantive value is not a sufficient reason to restrict free speech. The critical question is whether the exercise of free speech violates a substantive value to an unacceptable degree; answering this question entails a value judgment that is not only contentious but often rendered differently in different societies, even those as similar as the United States and Germany. The treatment of two such issues—hate speech and protection of children and adolescents—is discussed in the following sections.

5.3 COMMON AND DIFFERENT TRADITIONS AND THE INTERNET

Free speech was an important right long before the advent of the Internet, but there were practical limitations on how well individuals could exercise it to influence their societies. People could find a soapbox in Hyde Park or Union Square, send a letter to the editor, or distribute leaflets.[2] But if they wanted to have an impact on public policy or on society at large, they had to go through intermediaries. The Internet brings society much closer to the ideal of a free market of ideas, in that surfacing a wide range of ideas in a public forum, including those disparaged as fringe, is easier than it has ever been before. Nevertheless, limitations clearly remain, and the availability of ideas on a Web site does not assure that everyone will find them or require that everyone access them.

5.3.1 Hate Speech

Hate speech can be defined as the willful public expression of hatred toward any segment of society distinguished by a characteristic such as

---

[1]Michael Thompson, Richard Ellis, and Aaron Wildavsky, 1990, *Cultural Theory*, Boulder, Colo.: Westview Press; for an application to the topic of this report see Michael Thompson, 2000, "Global Networks and Local Cultures: What Are the Mismatches and What Can be Done About Them?," in Christoph Engel and Kenneth H. Keller, eds., *Understanding the Impact of Global Networks on Local Social, Political and Cultural Values*, Baden-Baden: Nomos 113-130.

[2]Computer Science and Telecommunications Board, National Research Council. 1994. *Rights and Responsibilities of Participants in Networked Communities*. Washington, D.C.: National Academy Press.

color, race, religion, ethnic origin, or sexual orientation. Hate speech can be particularly debilitating to a society because it attacks an entire group. Thus it threatens the peaceful coexistence of different groups within the population and, ultimately, the stability of the community.

Hate speech is more than merely hurtful; it creates a climate that can lead to depriving certain groups of their civil rights. The danger need not be concrete and immediate; sad experience has shown that the verbal stigmatization of particular groups in a community can build up negative attitudes in the population at large, which can lead to discrimination and may even erupt into violence against the group. Despite the near-universal revulsion to hate speech among civilized peoples, there are significant differences between the United States and Germany in how it is handled.

Two cases, widely reported in the media and described here in Chapter 3, demonstrate the problems created by these differences: the online sale of *Mein Kampf* (August 1999) and the CompuServe case (May 1998). The first arose from differences in the laws of the two countries concerning what can be distributed, and the second concerned the responsibility of a service provider for the messages transferred through its network. The CompuServe case attracted particular attention in the American press, with headlines like "Germany's Internet Angst," "A 'cyber-coup' for Germany's cyber-cops," "German Net future questioned," and "Efforts to control the Net abuse liberty."

The United States

In terms of value balance, the United States gives the formal value of free speech more weight than essentially any substantive value and almost all other formal values. Therefore, attempts to proscribe hate speech using legal remedies such as the criminal code or municipal regulations have invariably been struck down by the Supreme Court, based on the idea that such remedies violate the constitutional right to freedom of expression contained in the First Amendment. Indeed, because Article 20 of the International Covenant on Civil and Political Rights[3] required signatory states to agree that "any advocacy of national, racial or religious hatred that constitutes incitement to discrimination, hostility or violence shall be prohibited by law," the United States refused to ratify that part of the Covenant. Furthermore, in ratifying the Genocide Convention, the

[3]The International Covenant on Civil and Political Rights was adopted and opened for signature, ratification, and accession through U.N. General Assembly resolution 2200A (XXI) of 16 December 1966. It entered into force on 23 March 1976.

United States made specific reservations to prevent any impact of the Convention on First Amendment rights in the United States.

A measure of the primacy given to the right to freedom of expression is that the First Amendment does not specify any exceptions, and the Supreme Court has been very cautious in allowing any. Over the years, it has developed a strict set of criteria defining circumstances in which some state abridgement of free speech might reasonably be allowed in order to serve other constitutional goals, but the exceptions have been very few.

Proposed government restrictions that are based on the content of an expression have to be capable of standing up to an intense examination called "strict scrutiny." Under this test, restrictions can be justified only if the state is able to show a compelling public interest in doing so. Even then, it has to choose the least restrictive means for achieving the desired aim. Furthermore, if the proposed measures are too vague or too broad, in all likelihood they will be rejected as unconstitutional. In fact and in practice, the strict scrutiny test is equivalent to the initial assumption that any restriction on free speech is unconstitutional.

Government measures aimed at preventing the purely abstract dangers of hate speech, which would certainly encompass most substantive-value concerns, have always been struck down by the Supreme Court because they have not passed the strict scrutiny test. In 1952, the Court did hold, in *Beauharnais v. Illinois,*[4] that the defamation of a group should not fall within the protection of the First Amendment. But even that decision, though never officially reversed and overruled, has not guided subsequent Court action, particularly following *Collin v. Smith*[5] and *R.A.V. v. City of St. Paul*[6] (Box 5.1).

In *Brandenburg v. Ohio*, 395 U.S. 444 (1969) (per curiam), the Supreme Court held that the First Amendment even protects speech that encourages others to commit violence, unless the speech is capable of "producing imminent lawless action." Thus, arguing that "if the First Amendment protects speech advocating violence, then it must also protect speech that does not advocate violence but still makes it more likely," a three-judge panel of the 9th Circuit Court of Appeals held that a Web site and posters calling abortion doctors "baby butchers" and criminals were protected by the First Amendment. The court stated that "political speech may not be

[4]343 U.S. 250 (1952).
[5]578 F.2d 1197 (7th Cir. 1978); cert. denied 439 U.S. 916 (1978).
[6]505 U.S. 377 (1992).

BOX 5.1 Selected Decisions on Hate Speech

Collin v. Smith is based on the following facts: In 1977 the city of Skokie, north of Chicago, had about 70,000 inhabitants; 40,000 of them were Jewish, including some 5,000 who were survivors of the Holocaust. In March 1977 Frank Collin, "Führer" of the National Socialist Party of America, informed the municipal administration of Skokie that his party was planning to organize a walk through the city and that party members were intending to wear Nazi uniforms. City officials tried to prevent the wearing of such uniforms and the distribution or display of material that could "cause or promote hatred against people of Jewish faith or Jewish origin." The Court of Appeals for the Seventh Circuit decided that the march and the wearing of uniforms were protected expressions of opinion—and the necessary price of freedom in America. "The result," it said, "is dictated by the fundamental proposition that if these civil rights are to remain vital for all, they must protect not only those that society deems acceptable, but also those whose ideas it quite justifiably rejects and despises." The Supreme Court rejected the appeal of the city of Skokie and thus gave its permission for the march. (See *Collin v. Smith,* 578 F.2d 1197 (7th Cir. 1978), cert. denied sub. nom. *Smith v. Collin,* 439 U.S. 916 (1978).)

In *R.A.V. v. City of St. Paul* (505 U.S. 377 (1992)), the accused, Robert Allen Victoria (R.A.V.) had, together with others, burned a cross in the front yard of a black family that had just moved to an all-white area. Their purpose was clearly and avowedly to intimidate the family. Victoria was found guilty according to a municipal criminal statute that penalized as disorderly conduct "the placing on public or private grounds of a symbol or an object . . . including a burning cross . . . if one knows, or should know, that this action causes anger, fright, or fear by making reference to race, skin color, religion, or sex of other people." The Supreme Court decided that the municipal statute was unconstitutional and therefore the verdict was overturned. The statute was deemed contrary to the protection of expression of opinion protected by the First Amendment, since "protected expressions were only penalized on the basis of the choice of the target group of the speech."

punished just because it makes it more likely that someone will be harmed at some unknown time in the future by an unrelated third party."[7]

[7]244 F.3d 1007 (9th Cir. 2001); reh. en banc granted, 268 F.3d 908 (9th Cir, October 3, 2001). The latter citation refers to an order from the court that the case be reheard by the en banc court, with the three-judge panel opinion not being cited as precedent by or to this court or any district court of the Ninth Circuit, except to the extent adopted by the en banc court.

On the other hand, the Supreme Court has allowed exceptions to First Amendment protection when the expression could likely lead to a hate-engendered crime. In such cases, the Court has applied the "Clear and Present Danger Test." Expressions that give rise to a clear and present danger of criminal action, and thus infringe on the rights of some segment of the population, can be forbidden. This exception is called "communications tending to incite lawlessness" or "advocacy of unlawful action."

Germany

The German legal system, in contrast to the American system, generally penalizes hate speech. Given the experience under National Socialism and the former German Democratic Republic, the Federal Republic takes the position that a democracy has to be able to defend itself as a political system. There is a particularly strong feeling that it must be able to stop any attempt to reestablish a National Socialist authority. Interestingly, in addition to the resolve of the post-war German generation to resist National Socialism, other countries that fought the Nazi regime and certain ethnic groups (such as those of Jewish descent, who were victimized by the regime) expect this vigilance of Germany. In addition to measures targeted against hate speech, there are also German laws that prohibit the defamation of victims of National Socialist crimes, denial of the Holocaust, wearing of the swastika, and distribution of National Socialist propaganda.

The compatibility of these laws with the constitution has never seriously been questioned, even though in Germany, as in the United States, freedom of expression is an important value. The Bundesver-fassungsgericht (the German equivalent of the U.S. Supreme Court) says that freedom of expression is simply an inherent aspect of democracy. However, the constitutional right of freedom of expression, as granted in Article 5 Abs. 1 GG, is worded as follows:

> Anybody has the right to freely express his opinion in words, written materials, and pictures and to distribute it and to draw information from generally accessible sources without any interference. The freedom of the press and the freedom of broadcasting and film are guaranteed. There is no censorship.
>
> These rights will find their barriers in the provisions of the general laws, the legal provisions for the protection of the youth and the right to personal honor.

The wording of this article is similar to guarantees in other Western European constitutions (for example, Article 10 of the European Convention on Human Rights). There is a good deal of room for interpretation in the words and, particularly in view of the last sentence, a number of circumstances in which this constitutional right can be restricted. Thus the prohibition against hate speech would fall under the category of a general law. Its provisions are viewed as "not directed against the expression of an opinion as such, but that rather serve the protection of *a worthy legal value*, without consideration of any special opinion (italics added)."[8] Forbidding Holocaust denial has been justified by the Bundesverfassungsgericht as necessary to protect the personal honor of the Holocaust's victims, who might otherwise be viewed as threatened and compromised.[9]

There are efforts, sometimes driven by actions and interpretations of the European Court of Human Rights, to limit the extent to which the right of free speech can be abridged. For example, the Bundesverfassungsgericht requires that the conflicting interests be balanced and that there be a consideration of whether there are any less restrictive means available in order to achieve the intended goal. But, in the face of Germany's recent history, it is not surprising that the prohibition of hate speech is regarded as legitimate and appropriate.

The contrasts between Germany and the United States in regard to free speech are relatively easy to understand. The generally high tolerance in the United States for free speech is generally regarded as critical in a highly heterogeneous society—one with a long history of absorbing wave after wave of immigrant groups—to avoiding pressures that might otherwise arise to conform ideologically and culturally. Indeed, guaranteed individual and political liberties have always been one of the attractions of the United States to those forced to leave their homeland for reasons of political repression. Recent history in Germany, on the other hand, has provided a sad lesson in how fast political propaganda and incitement in a relatively homogeneous society can lead to the separation and murder of whole segments of the population. It has led to a broad consensus on the need to place limits on freedom of expression in order to preserve freedom generally.

This practical explanation raises the question of whether it is fair to characterize the American situation as one in which the formal value of free speech dominates any consideration of substantive values or whether the commitment to diversity, which free speech facilitates, is itself a substantive value. In the latter case, societal cohesion and individual liberty both support the idea of free speech, giving added weight to its protection. In the German situation, there is warranted concern that the shared substantive values—protection of the rights of minorities and the dignity

---

[8]BVerfGE 7, 198, 209 f.

[9]BVerfGE 90, 241, 252.

of individuals—may be threatened by an unequivocal commitment to free speech; so the balance between the two plays out differently.

5.3.2 The Protection of Children and Adolescents

Both the United States and the Federal Republic are deeply concerned with protecting children and adolescents, and both have established laws in that spirit.[10] Those that deal with material in print, film, or electronic media are of two basic kinds. First, there are laws aimed at preventing abuse and maltreatment, which make it illegal to distribute, purchase, or possess written materials, videos, and other items that depict child pornography. The argument is that such material is a stimulus to carrying out the acts depicted, and that it leads producers to abuse children in the course of its production.

It is no surprise, then, that on both sides of the Atlantic, legislatures have proscribed child pornography in every format and venue. The distribution of child pornography through the Internet, as well as its possession, is a criminal offense. Even images that have been created by computer or drawn, where children are obviously not involved in production, may be illegal.[11]

In neither country have constitutional concerns been seriously raised about these laws. In the United States, they meet the strict scrutiny test. In Germany, although the contents of child pornography are, in principle,

---

[10]In Germany it is even at the constitutional level; see Art. 6 Abs. 2 GG or Art. 5 Abs. 2 GG. But in the United States as well, the Supreme Court found, in the decision of *Ginsberg v. New York* (390 U.S. 629 (1968)), that the state had a legitimate interest in protecting the physical and psychological well-being of minors.

[11]In the United States, the Child Pornography Protection Act of 1996 (CPPA) expanded the definition of child pornography to include any visual depictions of individuals that appear to be minors, or visual depictions presented in a manner to convey the impression of a minor, engaging in sexually explicit conduct. (As of this writing [November 2001], this provision of the CPPA is pending before the Supreme Court. It was held unconstitutional by the U.S. Court of Appeals for the Ninth Circuit (*Free Speech Coalition v. Reno,* 222 F.3d 1113 (9th Cir. 2001)), but was upheld by the First, Fourth, Fifth, and Eleventh Circuits (*United States v. Fox,* 248 F.3d 394 (5th Cir. 2001)); United States v. Mento, 231 F.3d 912, (4th Cir. 2000); *United States v. Acheson,* 195 F. 3d 645 (11th Cir. 1999); *United States v. Hilton,* 167 F.3d 61 (1st Cir. 1999), cert. denied, 528 U.S. 844, 120 S. Ct. 115, 145 L. Ed. 2d 98 (2000)). Under the U.S. criminal code, possession, distribution, and transportation of child pornography so defined is a felony. In Germany, Section 184 of the German Criminal Code prohibits the distribution of both "real" and "fictive" child pornography (real with real persons involved; fictive with drawings, computer-produced images, and even written or acoustic material). However, the German Criminal Code does not prohibit the possession of fictive child pornography.

protected by the Constitution, child and adolescent protection has been recognized as a legitimate basis for outlawing it.

The second area of law related to protecting minors aims at preventing them from being exposed to material that might be psychologically traumatic or might adversely affect their development. This is the more difficult area of the two. Much of the material is itself not considered innately harmful and, therefore, is not proscribed; the practical question is how to specifically control only the inappropriate material, and how to accomplish that without interfering with those who have a right to receive it. Here the balancing of rights comes into play more directly, as does the determination of the appropriate roles of government, the private sector, and parents. How, then, have the United States and Germany dealt with this set of issues?

The United States

In February 1996, the Congress adopted the Communications Decency Act (CDA), a sweeping law that held content providers criminally liable if a person under 18 years of age obtained "obscene," "indecent," or "patently offensive" material through any "telecommunications device." There was a so-called "safe harbor" provision, which protected a provider who makes good-faith efforts to deny access to individuals under 18; such efforts would include the use of a credit card, a debit account, an adult access code, or an adult personal-identification number.[12] The Act triggered immediate challenges and was quickly reviewed by the Supreme Court (*Reno v. American Civil Liberties Union*[13]).

The Court found (as had the lower courts) that the so-called Section 223 (47 USC 233) provisions of the CDA were too broad and too vaguely formulated. The vagueness of the expressions "indecent" and "patently offensive" allowed for such a wide range of interpretations that they could not be reconciled with the Court's strict criteria for allowing freedom of speech to be abridged. The chilling effect of the ambiguities in the law would lead producers to be so cautious that it would inhibit legitimate

---

[12]In order to be able to consider technological innovations in this area without a statutory change, every method that is feasible will be treated in the same way. The Federal Communications Commission would have had the task of choosing suitable systems and to qualify them as such. The safe harbor clause has as its aim—similar to the age restriction on youth-endangering publications or visits to establishments in red-light districts—the denial of access to online offers to adolescents only, and not to adults. The complete criminalization of the contents is not intended with this so-called Zoning Approach.

[13]521 U.S. 844 (1997).

freedom of expression and restrict the availability of content that adults might quite legally want to obtain.

Even the safe-harbor clause was regarded as inadequate. It was not clear that the access control systems available would be judged sufficient to trigger the protections of the safe-harbor clause. And even if effective, installing the controls would entail substantial costs beyond the capacity of most noncommercial providers. Therefore the law would discriminate against them. Finally, much of the objectionable content came from abroad, where American law could not easily be enforced.

In response to the Court's action, Congress took a different approach, passing the Child Online Protection Act (COPA) at the end of 1998. COPA had a narrower scope of application than CDA, but its intention was similar and it has often been referred to as "CDA II." The intention of its sponsors was to deal with the Supreme Court's objections by dropping unacceptable terms like "obscene" and "indecent" and substituting a narrower "harmful to minors" standard. Furthermore, COPA dealt only with the commercial distribution of material and only on the World Wide Web. It did not try to regulate other Internet services such as newsgroups. COPA also included a safe-harbor provision that exempted from prosecution parties that take good-faith measures—through any reasonable means feasible under available technology (e.g., the use of a credit card)—to restrict access by minors to material that is harmful to them.

Still, many of the groups that objected to the CDA also found the new statute to be objectionable, and the American Civil Liberties Union (ACLU) and other groups challenged it in court. The United States District Court for the Eastern District of Pennsylvania issued a preliminary injunction against COPA, holding that the law was likely to be found incompatible with the First Amendment for many of the same reasons that the CDA had been rejected.[14] Content providers would be inhibited, by fear of liability as well as by the costs associated with installing access-control software, in what they produced, with the net effect of adults being less able to receive legal material that they might want.

The District Court acknowledged that youth protection was a legitimate reason for restricting freedom of expression, but it argued not only that less restrictive means were available but that the prescribed access-control systems would be of limited effectiveness anyway; they would not apply to foreign Web sites, noncommercial providers, or newsgroups.

---

[14] *American Civil Liberties Union v. Reno,* 31 F. Supp.2d 473 (E.D.Pa. (1999). This decision can be seen online at <http://www.cdt.org/speech/copa/990201ACLUvsRENOdecision.shtml>.

Less restrictive means, such as filtering software (discussed in Chapter 3), might be simpler, cheaper, and no less effective. On April 2, 2000, the U.S. Justice Department appealed the District Court's decision, and on June 22, 2000, the Third Circuit Court of Appeals upheld the decision of the District Court. The U.S. Supreme Court has accepted a further appeal from the U.S. Government for its 2000-2001 term and is expected to hear this case in November 2001.

Another attempt to protect youth was enacted on December 21, 2000—the Children's Internet Protection Act (CIPA).[15] CIPA requires public schools and public libraries that receive discounted service for Internet access through federal funds ("e-rate") to enforce a policy of Internet safety for minors. Such public institutions must use "technology protection measures" that prevent access to visual depictions that are obscene, "harmful to minors," or contain child pornography. CIPA further defines material that is "harmful to minors" as material that if "taken as a whole and with respect to minors, appeals to a prurient interest in nudity, sex, or excretion; depicts, describes or represents, in a patently offensive way with respect to what is suitable for minors, an actual or simulated normal or perverted sexual act, or a lewd exhibition of the genitals, and taken as a whole, lacks serious literary, artistic, political or scientific value to minors."[16] The American Civil Liberties Union and the American Library Association have announced their intention to challenge CIPA on First Amendment grounds.[17]

Germany

In 1997, a comprehensive Internet-specific law for the protection of minors was adopted in Germany that prohibits young people from receiving certain kinds of material. As part of the law's implementation, a list was developed of materials that are inappropriate for minors and that may not be distributed by electronic means or, for that matter, made accessible in any other way. The list includes material that is "immoral, [has] a brutalizing effect, [gives] incentive to violence, crimes, or racial hatred . . . [or glorifies] the war"—categories that clearly go beyond the proposed laws in the United States.

Like the U.S. legislation, the German law places responsibility for limiting access primarily on the provider. The law also has a safe-har-

---

[15]P.L. 106-554, § 1(a)(4), 114 Stat. 2763.

[16]47 U.S.C. § 254(h)(7)(G).

[17]*Multnomah County Library v. United States;* No. 01-CV-1322; <www.aclu.org/features/fo02001a.html> (site visited April 26, 2001).

bor provision, insulating providers from prosecution if they have made a good-faith effort to prevent minors from accessing the inappropriate material. The law describes such an effort as making "technical provisions . . . to restrict the offer or its distribution within [Germany] to adult users." The kind and type of these "technical provisions" have not yet been specified.

Of course, either the provider or the user can do the actual restricting. The German law allows for user-initiated controls when it is the user who initiates access to the inappropriate material. Material is allowed to be distributed this way only "if devices are supplied by the provider or other(s) that allow the user to block these offers." This leaves to parents or guardians the decision of whether or not to use the blocking device. Again, in this case, the legislature didn't say anything about what kinds of blocking devices would be suitable—a not-unreasonable stance given the dynamic nature of the technology.

Although all the arguments used to challenge the CDA and the COPA as unconstitutional in the United States would apply to the German law, no significant objection to the law has been raised in Germany. It is another indication of the difference in attitude toward freedom of speech in the two countries, discussed at length in the previous section. But it also indicates the fact that, in Germany, the public is willing to give administrative authorities the latitude to administer a law that *might* threaten constitutional rights, on the assumption that those rights will be taken into account in actually applying the law's provisions. This difference in attitude toward government appears to be an important distinction between the two countries. The greater trust in government, evident in this as well as other examples, leads German society to look more to government itself, rather than to tightly drawn laws, to protect and balance rights and values.

The safe-harbor provisions in U.S. and German law introduce an incentive for the development of appropriate screening technologies, but it is not clear at this point either how effective these new technologies are likely to be or what new threats to constitutional rights they might introduce. For example, the U.S. courts have viewed filters as a reasonable approach to controlling inappropriate transmissions. But many in Europe (and the United States) worry that the use of these systems, even by private organizations, might amount to precensorship, particularly where the filtering is based on the identification of unacceptable sites rather than specific material.

In Europe, there is also the fear that political or religious zealots might wield control over the site-assessment procedure and that the systems might become oriented too much toward American moral concepts. Some have favored systems that control which users have access to the site of a particular content provider. Similar to age restrictions on the purchase of written material considered harmful to young people, or a visit to an establishment in a red-light district, access to the online offers would be denied to adolescents, but not to adults. Unfortunately, this "zoning approach" also requires content evaluation. Also, it is unclear whether digital age-verification systems or similar access controls can really work in the highly decentralized world of the Internet. Thus, both the technical uncertainties and the different political value judgments in the two societies continue to present serious challenges, which are discussed in greater depth in the following section.

5.4 OPERATIONALIZING THE REGULATORY GOAL

Even if government policymakers decide under what circumstances to restrict freedom of speech for the sake of a competing substantive value, many issues remain. What is the appropriate point of intervention? Is it the content provider, the recipient, or one of the intermediaries between them, such as the Internet service provider? Here the question is not merely one of where it is most practical to interdict inappropriate transmissions, but which party should be made responsible to act, although the two facets of the question may well be related. Furthermore, should the potentially harmful content be prohibited, or is it sufficient to make access more difficult or more costly? The latter approach is exemplified by the "watershed rules" that are typical for television broadcasting in many countries, which restrict the airing of "offensive" material to the late-evening hours. These questions take on great importance because even though an initial value balance may have been made in reaching the decision to restrict free speech, the way it is implemented could profoundly alter the balance.

Given some of the practical difficulties in holding providers or recipients responsible for restricting access to potentially harmful content, a number of efforts have been made to hold intermediaries responsible. Because intermediaries are relatively few in number—at least compared to the number of content providers or recipients—and they generally have a local presence in order to do business, they are an attractive target for regulation.

Yet regulation of intermediaries presents different kinds of difficulties. Access providers connect content producers and users to each other via the Internet. Once the connection to the network has been made, they have no influence either on what material moves through the wires or where it goes. They are much like the postal system in that they don't know the contents of the messages they deliver. In consequence, it is generally agreed in both the United States and Europe that the access provider should not be held responsible for the contents of messages. In Europe, this has been codified in the E-Commerce Directive of the European Union[18] as well as the German Teleservices Act.[19] In the United States, so-called "common carrier" provisions allow certain carriers of communications to carry all manner of traffic without liability (e.g., telephone service providers), and more recently, Congress granted limited immunity to access providers for violations of copyright law in the Digital Millennium Copyright Act.[20]

Host providers, however, are a different story. A host provider may be a portal or a proprietary service that gathers in one place a large amount of third-party content for user access. Being closer to a virtual forum site or bazaar than to a postal system, it provides Web space, helps its subscribers find material more easily, and establishes "bulletin boards" and e-mail services. Generally, the host provider does not have anything to do with the contents placed on the server, but a good deal to do with its organization in the "marketplace."

Because the host provider offers more than a connection service, the question of liability is more complicated. Legal systems have to determine when the value added by the host provider's services begins to make it look less like an access provider and more like a content provider. The task is made all the more difficult as the ground keeps shifting: new technologies create new business opportunities for inventive entrepreneurs, and the services offered by host providers change. It is unlikely that a simple or permanent resolution to this question, or that the resolution of differences in this area between the United States and Europe, is in the offing.

Access providers and host providers are not the only important Internet intermediaries. Search-engine operators, mirror sites, and local hosts all play a role in connecting producers and users. Technological changes that begin to blur the distinction between broadcast and network media will add to this group—and to the problems of sorting out liability. Each will add to the challenge of harmonizing U.S. and Euro-

---

[18]Directive 2000/31/EC of the European Parliament and of the Council on certain legal aspects of information-society services, in particular electronic commerce, in the internal market (Directive on Electronic Commerce), Official Journal of the European Communities L 178/1 (July 17, 2000); available online at <http://europa.eu.int/ISPO/ecommerce/legal/documents/2000_31ec/2000_31ec_en.pdf>.

[19]The German Teleservices Act is part of the Information and Communication Services Act of July 7th 1997, BGBl. I, S. 1870; available online at <http://www.iid.de/iukdg/gesetz/engindex.html>.

[20]17 U.S.C § 512 (limiting liability for persons who transmit, route, provide connections, or provide intermediate and transient storage of material infringing copyright).

pean approaches to these issues, which are already difficult, as the discussion below demonstrates.

5.4.1 The United States

Although the provisions of 47 USC 223 of the CDA, described earlier, quite clearly made providers liable if inappropriate material got into the hands of minors through the Internet, 47 USC 230 of the Act declared that third parties—that is, intermediaries—were not responsible for material they transmitted and were not liable for refusing to transmit material they viewed as "questionable."[21] Congress's position was probably influenced to some degree by contradictory court decisions that had been handed down on the question of host-provider liability.[22] However, the Act's language suggests that Congress was also guided by the belief that interactive computer services should be given strong protection because they "provide a forum for the real variety of political discussion, unique possibilities for cultural development, and a multitude of ways in which intellectual activity can develop." These services had already developed, helping the United States to establish its leadership in the networked world, and the Act's preamble stated that it is the "policy of the United States to keep the lively and competition-shaped open market that now exists for the Internet and other interactive computer services as free as possible from federal or state regulations."

In the court tests thus far, 47 USC 230 has fared very well, with intermediaries held harmless from liability whether or not they have known what they were transmitting, known that it was illegal, or even if they paid the provider for it.[23] The Supreme Court has not yet handed down any rulings on this section, but all indications are that the strong commitment to freedom of expression in the United States will continue to result in support for 47 USC 230. Furthermore, the wording of the Act and the actions of the lower courts are consistent with the American belief that self-regulation is preferable to governmental controls.

---

[21]Through these provisions, referred to as "Good Samaritan" clauses, it should be made clear that no provider is liable because it, in good faith, attempts by the use of computer programs to remove questionable contents from its servers, that is, to block access to these contents.

[22]*Cubby v. CompuServe*, 776 F. Supp. 135 (S.D.N.Y. 1991); *Stratton Oakmont, Inc. v. Prodigy Servs. Co.*, 1995 WL 323710 (N.Y. Sup. Ct. May 24, 1995).

[23]A description of cases involving 47 U.S.C § 230 can be found online at <http://www.techlawjournal.com/courts/zeran/47usc230.htm#cases>.

5.4.2 Germany

The laws of the Federal Republic place much greater responsibility on host providers, although they do not regulate other intermediaries such as search-engine operators or providers of hyperlinks. In Germany, host providers are "responsible for foreign contents that they provide for use if they had knowledge of these contents and it is technically possible, and also reasonable, to prevent their use." This is called "notice liability"; that is, if one knows about the material, one is liable if no action is taken to remove it. Furthermore, under German law, a provider cannot defend itself by arguing that it didn't consider the questionable contents to be illegal. Article 14 of the EU Commission's Directive on Electronic Commerce takes the same approach.

There have been no explicit constitutional objections to this law raised in Germany. It obviously goes in a very different direction from U.S. law. However, many argue that the host provider's liability is actually more limited than it may appear because the provider need only act if it is "technically possible . . . and . . . reasonable" to prevent the distribution of the objectionable material. This allows for some judgment and balancing by the prosecutors and courts in deciding, for example, whether a small provider could "reasonably" be expected to install blocking software so expensive that it might put the company out of business. Moreover, the law does not require that the host provider make an active effort to root out illegal material.

With these factors softening the impact of the liability provisions, there appears to be a broad consensus throughout Europe that the German law and the E-Commerce Directive of the EU Commission represent an appropriate middle path. In the view of most Europeans, these regulations balance the protection of minors with the right to freedom of expression and the economic interests of host providers.

With the laws in the United States and Germany as different as they are in this case, and with the strong consensus and deep, principled conviction that exists in each country for its own law, it is difficult to see how a practical compromise can be achieved and easy to see how the differences will inevitably lead to conflicts. The *Bavaria v. CompuServe* case, mentioned earlier in Chapter 3, certainly demonstrates the problem.

American criticism of the German action in the CompuServe case was based on the strong objection in the United States to any action that would (1) have a chilling effect on freedom of speech and (2) unreasonably or unnecessarily burden a private company with economically debilitating regulations. Germans, for their part, are generally much less concerned than Americans that government regulations might burden industry, if those regulations appear otherwise warranted. Furthermore, most Germans would attach more importance to the protection of minors than to the protection of free speech and would have no compunction about forever blocking a transgressing newsgroup—or even 282 of them—if it were necessary to prevent the distribution of child pornography.

But another source of the tension that arose in this case was the frustration of the German prosecutors, who had very little leverage to take action against CompuServe USA. Because the company is headquartered in the United States and its executives live there, German law could not reach them. The United States would not cooperate in extradition proceedings because the company's actions were not violations of U.S. law.

The Munich prosecutor, anxious to enforce the German law on child pornography, instead charged the executive director of CompuServe Germany, the local affiliate, with violation of the law. The problem, of course, was that the local affiliate had no way of blocking the offending newsgroups. Thus the prosecutor's actions were criticized in Germany as well as in the United States; but the German criticism arose not because of any objection to host-provider liability but because the person charged was not the person responsible. In fact, though the executive director was initially found guilty, the conviction was overturned in November 1999 precisely because the court recognized that he was neither responsible for sponsoring the newsgroups nor able to remove them from the network.

5.5 INTERNET CONTENT REGULATION AS A CHALLENGE TO GOVERNANCE

The difficulties in regulating Internet content epitomize the challenges that global networks present for governance. It therefore does not come as a surprise that almost all the elements discussed in Chapter 9 (on governance) *in abstracto* have a bearing on content regulation.

5.5.1 The Limited Power of Traditional National Regulation

It is useful to keep in mind that the Internet contributes to globalization in two ways. First, it is a global entity that brings together cultural and political influences from many countries and gives rise to a burgeoning new field of commerce. Second, the Internet makes it possible for established businesses to coordinate activities across the globe through various commercial arrangements, freeing them to a certain extent from the constraints of geography and national boundaries.

Globalized business activities are much more difficult for governments to regulate and control, both because they may not be physically located within a country's boundaries and because nations compete to attract businesses.[24] This reduces the feasibility of strong, unilateral command-and-control as well as the reach of penal law. The change is one of degree, and national governments certainly do not lose all their options.[25] For example, a person residing in a country can be held liable for violation of its national law or regulation even if he or she is part of an international business or the illegal action involves transmission of inappropriate material from another country.

Similarly, a nation could enforce its laws extraterritorially by attaching a foreign company's assets that happened to be located within its boundaries or even arresting a visiting company official.[26] Under German law, prosecutors not only would be allowed to take these actions, but are actually required to do so. With respect to Internet sites, some have suggested that nation-states could actually go further. They might attack foreign Web sites that contravene their laws, using such technical means as denial-of-service attacks similar to those mounted by hackers against Yahoo! and amazon.com.[27] There seems little question that such tactics would violate public international law[28] but, perhaps more to the point, they illustrate how the initial value balance involved in a decision to restrict transmission of certain content can be distorted by the means employed to implement the decision.

The ideal situation, of course, would be one in which national laws pertaining to the Internet and other global activities were harmonized. That does not seem to be a realistic expectation for the foreseeable future, however. So the most reasonable hope is for cooperation among governments to help providers and hosts understand the laws and regulations in each jurisdiction. Over time, this kind of transparency might lead toward creative harmonization and compromise.

The practical question is how far one nation can go in imposing laws and regulations in a global economy in which firms have the ability to

---

[24]On the governance of the Internet in greater detail, see Christoph Engel, 2000, "The Internet and the Nation State," in Christoph Engel and Kenneth H. Keller, eds., *Understanding the Impact of Global Networks on Local Social, Political and Cultural Values* (*Law and Economics of International Telecommunications* 42), Baden-Baden: Nomos, 201-260.

[25]This point has been stressed repeatedly by Jack Goldsmith. In the context of this report see in particular Jack Goldsmith, 2000, "The Internet, Conflicts of Regulation, and International Harmonization," in Christoph Engel and Kenneth H. Keller, eds., 2000, *Governance of Global Networks in the Light of Differing Local Values*, Nomos: Baden-Baden, 197-207.

[26]For greater detail, see Werner Meng, 1994, *Extraterritoriale Jurisdiktion im öffentlichen Wirtschaftsrecht*, Berlin.

[27]Cable News Network, "Cyber-attacks Batter Web Heavyweights," February 9, 2000. See <http://www6.cnn.com/2000/TECH/computing/02/09/cyber.attacks.01/index.html>.

[28]Cf., Jamie Frederic, 1997, "Rwandan Genocide and the International Law of Radio Jamming," *American Journal of International Law* 91:628.

withdraw their activities from the nation's territory. Some observers believe that this threat is overstated—that firms are unlikely to abandon a large national market that would be difficult to maintain without some presence in the country. There may also be other reasons for keeping a presence in a country, including the preference of investors or the availability of research-and-development capacity. However, although these considerations may make it impractical for a firm to avoid a nation's laws on illegal Web content or its intellectual-property regulations, it is certainly possible for the firm to move large parts of its operation offshore, to the detriment of the nation's economy.

5.5.2 International Legal Harmonization

International treaties provide one way of creating global order in a world where there is no supranational government. They work reasonably well when there is a common view on the values to be protected, general agreement about what needs to be done, and an obvious advantage in dealing with the issues on a global basis. A number of treaties are in existence today that appear, at least nominally, to deal with matters closely related to some of the content issues that have arisen with regard to the Internet.

For example, the Convention on the Prevention and Punishment of Genocide, dating from 1948,[29] requires the parties to make criminal the "direct and public incitement to commit genocide." The 1966 International Convention on the Avoidance of All Forms of Racial Discrimination[30] proscribes words and acts of racial discrimination. The United Nations' Human Rights Pact of the same year[31] not only deals with human rights, but also bans war propaganda and "every encouragement of nationalistic, racial, or religious hatred [that] incites discrimination, animosity, or violence." In addition, there is a UN International Convention on the International Right of Correction from the year 1953[32] (although neither the Federal Republic nor the United States has adopted it).

One promising approach to internationalizing some aspects of Internet regulation would be to extend existing treaties to the new context. That would require a willingness on the part of each signatory coun-

---

[29]Convention of 09.12.1948, BGBl. 1954 II. 729.

[30]Convention of 07.04.1966, BGBl. 1969 II 961; compare also BTDrs. 13/1883.

[31]International Pact on Civil and Political Rights of 09.12.1966, BGBl. 1973 II 1533.

[32]Convention on the International Right of Correction from 31.03.1953, UNTS 435, 192. The "right of correction" refers to the right of a nation "directly affected" by a private or public report that it considers "false or distorted" to secure "commensurate publicity" for the "corrections" that the nation wishes to publicize.

try to interpret or extrapolate the treaty's provisions to the new environment of the Internet and to amend its own national laws to reflect the new interpretations. Thus far, that has not happened.

For these and other reasons, there continues to be a push for new treaties to achieve international harmonization. Of course, they are easier to negotiate when nations largely agree on the issues. That requires either finding issues on which there is essential unanimity to begin with or defining a set of countries or a region with largely shared values. What should be evident from the discussion in this chapter is that the value agreement must pertain not only to the problem giving rise to the challenge but also to the appropriateness of government roles and regulatory tools for implementing a solution.

At the moment, the one area in which it appears likely that some international harmonization will be achieved, at least in Europe, is the regulation of child pornography. In June 2001, the European Committee on Crime Problems (CDPC) of the Council of Europe approved the Draft Convention on Cybercrime, which was submitted to the full Committee of Ministers for adoption in September 2001. Article 9 of the Draft Convention commits signatories "to adopt such legislative and other measures as may be necessary to establish as criminal offenses under its domestic law, when committed intentionally and without right," acts that relate to child pornography.[33] In addition, a supplement to the Europol agreement is being prepared that gives the European police authorities wider jurisdiction to deal with the production, sale, and distribution of child pornography.

However, the inclusion of content-related offenses other than those related to child pornography (e.g., the "distribution of racist propaganda through computer systems") proved too controversial to include in the Draft Convention. The European Committee on Crime Problems may consider an additional protocol relating to these offenses, but it faces opposition from a number of civil liberties organizations.[34]

The problem with harmonization is that if consensus requires drawing a too-small circle of cooperating nations, violators can find a regulatory haven fairly easily in a nation-state not party to the convention. There

[33]These acts include producing child pornography for the purpose of its distribution through a computer system; offering or making available child pornography through a computer system; distributing or transmitting child pornography through a computer system; procuring child pornography through a computer system for oneself or for another; and possessing child pornography in a computer system or on a computer-data storage medium. See <http://conventions.coe.int/treaty/EN/projets/cybercrime27.htm>.

[34]See <http://www.privacyinternational.org/issues/cybercrime/coe/ngo_letter_601.htm>.

are, of course, political and economic pressures that can be brought to bear on nonsignatory states to bring them into compliance. And for that matter there are carrots as well as sticks, as has been shown in certain aspects of global environmental protection.[35]

There are dangers in this approach, however, where global networks are concerned. The uneven penetration of the Internet (and its benefits) has already created a global sense of "haves" and "have-nots" that might well be exacerbated by unidirectional pressure from the United States or Europe on other nations, regardless of the merit of their position. Beyond that, there is the danger that harmonizing with a particular set of values, or adopting a universal approach to the structure of legal institutions, will reduce the very diversity that the Internet has the useful potential to promote.

5.5.3 Commercial Law

As pointed out elsewhere in this report, there are a number of circumstances in which commercial law—rules that have been developed for resolving business conflicts by coordinating the laws of different nations—could be used to deal with harmful contents accessible through the Internet. Consumer fraud, for example, does not change its legal character just because it is carried out with the aid of a Web page.

Nevertheless, commercial law is a weak foundation for matters such as child pornography and politically tainted hate speech. The major problem in such cases is that the potential harm is to people who are not likely to bring a private legal action for redress, may well not have standing to sue, and might have a difficult time proving damage. Who would sue and how would the case be made if easy access to child pornography increased the risk that more children might be abused? Who would sue and what would be the proof if easy access to Nazi propaganda increased the risk that extreme right-wing political forces might gain on the next Election Day? Even if the law gave standing to the public at large, would enough people have the incentive and the wherewithal to bring such actions?

5.5.4 Self-regulation Without State Intervention

A number of groups, certainly among them the Netizen and e-commerce communities, argue that in most instances the best approach to controlling the diffusion of offensive Internet-based material is self-regu-

---

[35]See Rüdiger Wolfrum, ed., 1996, Enforcing Environmental Standards. Economic Mechanisms as Viable Means, Berlin.

lation. The great attraction of this approach is the flexibility it provides; individuals can make their own judgments about what material they want to avoid (or to access), and the need to force value consensus within a particular country or across the globe is removed. When one nation's nudity is another's pornography, broad consensus is next to impossible. On the other hand, access-control systems, age-verification systems, and various kinds of filtering software can facilitate customized nonstate regulation.

To understand filtering systems, it is important to distinguish between a site's content and the judgment one makes about it. For example, though a site might have an image of a naked woman or a swastika, there may be many judgments about whether or not such content is offensive—one person might think so; another might not.

Many filtering systems are designed by vendors who act both as labeler and judge—they describe the content and also make a judgment about appropriateness (though they may or may not provide the user with an option to override their judgment). A second approach is to separate the functions of labeler and judge. To facilitate content labeling, the World Wide Web Consortium designed the Platform for Internet Content Selection (Box 5.2), which provides a standardized vocabulary and format for labeling content. Once labels have been associated with specific content, the user can deploy a filter that examines the labels associated with incoming content, and based on those labels, makes judgments about whether content with certain labels should or should not be displayed.

Note that that different filters can behave differently with regard to the same content. That is, Filter A may allow content that is labeled as containing "nudity" and reject content that is labeled as containing "swastikas," while Filter B may do exactly the opposite.

A second issue is that the scope and granularity of the labeling are critical. If the labeling vocabulary does not include a category for "swastikas," a filter based on this approach cannot block content containing swastikas. At least one particular vocabulary—of the Internet Content Rating Association—allows labeling of sites that contain certain kinds of language, nudity or sexual content, violence, and information related to gambling, drugs, and alcohol. However, there is no reason in principle that a party concerned about other categories of possible offensiveness cannot create vocabularies that cover them (though in practice, obtaining a broad scope of coverage for such alternatives is difficult).

Though filtering systems can be created by anyone, the required effort may be large. In principle, the organizations responsible for filtering systems must stand behind the judgments they make about offensiveness (and perhaps about content labeling as well), and users of filtering sys-

BOX 5.2 The Platform for Internet Content Selection

The Platform for Internet Content Selection (PICS) is technology that is intended to give users of interactive media, such as the Internet, control over the kinds of material to which they and their children have access. PICS is intended to enable "self–rating" (the ability of content providers to voluntarily label the content they create and distribute) and "third-party rating" (the ability of multiple, independent labeling services to assign additional labels to content created and distributed by others) in an easy-to-use manner that allows individuals to use ratings and labels from a diversity of sources to control the information that they and those under their supervision receive. Using the capability for third-party rating, services may each devise their own labeling systems, and the same content may receive different labels from different services.

The philosophy underlying PICS is one of voluntary use. However, PICS-based technology can be installed anywhere—at the end user's client, at the proxy servers of the user's employer, school, or library, at the servers of the Internet service provider to whom he or she subscribes, or even at the points of Internet entry to a country. Thus, concerns have been widely expressed that PICS is a technology that can greatly facilitate government censorship. Furthermore, to the extent that PICS is used by private parties other than the end user as a tool for censorship, it is not subject to the political processes that can be used in democratic countries to forge compromise and consensus.

SOURCE: Description of PICS adapted from <http://www.w3.org/PICS/principles.html>.

Articles critical of PICS include:

- Simson Garfinkel. 1997. "Good Clean PICS: The Most Effective Censorship Technology the Net Has Ever Seen May Already Be Installed on your Desktop." See <http://hotwired.lycos.com/packet/garfinkel/97/05/index2a.html>.
- Lawrence Lessig. 1997. "Tyranny in the Infrastructure," *Wired* 5.07 (July). Available online at <http://www.wired.com/wired/5.07/cyber_rights.html>.
- Jonathan Weinberg. 1997. "Rating the Net," *Hastings Comm./Ent. L.J.* 19:453.

tems may make their own judgments about the attractiveness of products from different vendors based on how well their own values about offensiveness are reflected in the vendors' judgments. Thus, users not wishing to see pro-racist material might use filters developed by civil-rights organizations, or users not wishing to see anti-religious material might use filters developed by their church.[36]

One of the attractive features of a labeling system is that it is inherently self-policing. The value of the label depends on the reputation it develops for reliability. Each site that receives the label's endorsement has a stake in giving it meaning. The user community itself has an interest in the quality of the label and can also be part of the enforcement process.

As movie- and video-rating organizations in the United States have learned, making judgments about offensiveness is fraught with difficulties. Such groups must tread a fine line between being overly rigid and prescriptive in their classifications and being so ambiguous that no real information is conveyed to the user. Generally speaking, categories or rules that have some flexibility are more likely to be suitable for a rapidly changing world like the Internet.

An important technical issue is the extent to which computer-executable rules for distinguishing between appropriate and inappropriate content can be formulated. Some of the filtering software with which people have experimented thus far has shown how difficult this can be, sometimes leading to absurd results, as when some particular words are coded as unacceptable. Moreover, filtering systems are usually designed with some particular point of view to take advantage of a market, pursue an ideological agenda, or avoid liability on the part of the software provider. This means that, at least until now, there has been little incentive for transparency in how the filters are created[37] and little attempt to take opposing interests or values into account, as one might hope would be the case in a legislative approach to regulation.[38] In that sense, filter systems can

---

[36]A fuller discussion of the advantages, disadvantages, and other realities of filters is contained in CSTB, National Research Council, *Youth, Pornography, and the Internet: Can We Provide Sound Choices in a Safe Environment?*, Washington, D.C.: National Academy Press, forthcoming.

[37]This is not to say that it is impossible or even difficult to increase transparency of filters by making available the lists of Web sites that are blocked or the lists of keywords that might be objectionable. However, vendors of filter products often argue that the creation of their blocked lists or "bad words" is their intellectual property, and that publication of such lists would deprive them of the benefits of their work if others took their work as a starting point to develop other lists.

[38]This has been recently pointed out by Lawrence Lessig, 1999, *Code and Other Laws in Cyberspace*, New York: Basic Books.

work against certain free speech values of a community and, indeed, help to de-integrate the community.

Host providers have a different problem in undertaking self-regulation; the control systems available to content providers or content users are not applicable to them. First, the material that host providers carry is an aggregate from a huge spectrum of content providers; and second, they are not end users, so that filtration software would be inappropriate. Many host providers have adopted their own codes of ethics. They may commit themselves, for example, to checking complaints about sites that come from users or to working cooperatively with legal authorities of particular nation-states to take action against sites involved in illegal activity.

Critics of self-regulation point out that because such codes of ethics are unenforceable, they are primarily symbolic. However, it may be possible to develop a legal framework that would make codes enforceable, even if the host providers themselves determined the details of the code. A more serious criticism is the possible curtailment of free speech; the codes may deprive content providers who are sanctioned or excluded by a host provider of the due process they would have under a more formal legal structure. Such points have not been thoroughly discussed at this early stage in the development of these self-regulatory instruments.

The role of hosts as intermediary between user and content provider suggests that it may be inappropriate to think of them as engaged in regulation per se. Their role in a nongovernmental regulation scheme is to provide a service to users who would like to be shielded from harmful or otherwise unwanted contents. Users could do this for themselves by simply not accessing certain sites or by installing filters on their computers (or using other technologies that may be available in the future), or they could access the Internet via a service provider with a declared access policy. Whether users want to pay for the host's service is something to be determined by the market. In fact, it would appear that, in the future, host providers will compete with each other and with companies producing self-help tools like filters, and users may choose on the basis of convenience, comprehensiveness, and selectivity.

5.5.5 Hybrid Regulation

Self-regulation and intermediation have many attractive features, but if governments do not intervene, the market alone will shape the array of mechanisms actually used to control the distribution of harmful content. These mechanisms, in turn, will largely determine what material is electronically available to whom. Obviously, the outcome may not always conform to the values of the society. It might therefore be useful to consider hybrid forms of regulation, combining public and private controls.

Governments can use both sticks and carrots to influence the operation of self-regulatory schemes.[39] As pointed out earlier, command-and-control regulation of content providers doesn't work very well in the networked world. The CompuServe case indicates that an alternative for governments is to threaten action against host providers. But there are softer options.

Governments can insist on an organizational framework for self-regulation that gives outside interests a voice and ensures that the process of developing and applying a rating system or excluding a provider from a host network is transparent. They can give industry limited antitrust or liability protection to encourage joint rulemaking and vigorous joint action. Or they can set up an authority to check on how well self-regulation is working (a role played by the U.S. Federal Trade Commission with respect to certain privacy issues and other aspects of consumer protection). It is even possible to envision governments supporting or encouraging education and training programs to improve the media competence of users so that they are better able to use the self-help tools that become more and more available as technological advances occur.

It does seem likely that a hybrid regulatory approach will finally emerge, but it is difficult to predict what particular balance of mechanisms will actually obtain in each country. The experimentation now going on appears to be healthy, and if there is a bottleneck, it is the legal system's difficulty in understanding the technical possibilities and reacting quickly and flexibly to them. It may well be that in an area as technologically dynamic as this one and as capable of bringing about major social changes, expert panels similar to those developed under the aegis of the Intergovernmental Panel on Climate Change could play an important role. They might be especially useful in advising governments on the state of the technology and the feasibility of various regulatory approaches.

---

[39]For the theoretical framework, see Fritz W. Scharpf, 1997, *Games Real Actors Play: Actor-Centered Institutionalism in Policy Research*, Boulder, Colo.: Westview Press.

6

Privacy and Freedom of Information

6.1 INTRODUCTION

Chapter 5 discussed how the United States and Germany differed in their approaches to resolving the tensions between formal and substantive values.[1] Both countries subordinated the formal value of free speech to certain substantive values, but in the case of the United States, the trumping substantive value was an aversion to pornography, while for Germany it was an aversion to hate speech and its Nazi overtones.

This chapter examines potential tensions between another substantive value (privacy) and a formal value (transparency in government, as exemplified by notions of "freedom of information," or FOI). The situation is not quite the same as that in the earlier chapter, however. Free speech is more or less understood in the same way in both nations and it enjoys explicit constitutional protection, which can be abridged only in very limited circumstances. Privacy, on the other hand, is not interpreted in the same way in the two countries and, at least in the United States, arguments continue as to whether it enjoys constitutional protection.

Freedom of information is also interpreted in different ways in the United States and Germany, and is not explicitly protected in either constitution. How privacy and freedom of information are actually inter-

[1]Recall (Chapter 3) that formal values can be regarded as general principles by which individuals choose to live, while substantive values relate to specific aspects of one's environment and behavior.

preted in the two countries determines when and how they are in tension as *values*. What kinds of information are explicitly designated as public in the pertinent statutes, and, at least in the United States, what protection of privacy is provided for in statute, determine when and how they are in tension as a legal matter.

Although neither nation protects privacy or freedom of information as strongly as it does free speech, to the extent that they do provide protection Germany puts greater emphasis on privacy and the United States favors transparency. Germany, and Europe more generally, have comprehensive systems of law and regulation in place to protect privacy. The United States, by contrast, has a patchwork of incomplete protections. With respect to freedom of information, the situation is reversed. The United States has a comprehensive system that provides the public with access to an enormous range of information and data, while Germany has a patchwork system.

With respect to freedom of information, both countries rely on ordinary legislation rather than constitutional law to specify which documents should be accessible to the public and under what terms. The situation with respect to privacy is somewhat different, in that German constitutional jurisprudence does recognize the right explicitly and many American scholars argue that privacy protection is implicit in a number of constitutional provisions. Nevertheless, here too legislation plays the more important role in defining the meaning of the right.

A further distinction between the tensions described in this chapter and the one addressed in the preceding chapter is that the threat to privacy does not necessarily come about because of information made available by the government; it often derives from information collected by and/or shared between private parties.[2]

Privacy and freedom of information are not always in tension; in some instances, society's commitment to freedom of information is the *key* to maintaining a person's privacy. That is, if an individual can invoke FOI rights to learn what personal information the government holds about him or her and how it has used the information, the government can be held accountable for any misuse. Thus, the person can effectively exercise some control over abuse of the information, which is one of the important dimensions of privacy.

In many other cases, rights to privacy and FOI rights do not intersect at all—for instance, data on the performance of the economy, on land use,

---

[2]The distinction is not always clear-cut. For example, personal data in a company's possession may enter government records (e.g., through a bankruptcy or other court proceeding). In such a case, information may be subject to FOI disclosure.

or on a host of other issues of importance to governments are not obviously relevant to privacy.[3] In other words, to the extent that privacy refers to keeping personal information private and under the control of the individual with whom it is associated, privacy rights need not conflict with the free disclosure of information relevant to the workings of government. Even in these cases, however, the formal value of transparency of state activities is not necessarily viewed by governments as an unalloyed good. That is, a question arises concerning the extent to which governments need to be able to deliberate in private or to control the release of raw data to prevent public panic (one end of the spectrum) or provide a desired spin (perhaps the other end).

But despite these caveats, privacy rights and FOI rights do, in many instances, come into conflict. In these cases, privacy is in conflict not only with the formal value of transparency of state activities, but also with the public interest (e.g., in the prevention and prosecution of criminal offenses) or commercial interests (e.g., in the collection and exploitation of data).

Global networks such as the Internet have raised the stakes significantly for both privacy and freedom of information. Clearly, they facilitate dissemination of information held by both public and private institutions. But perhaps even more significantly, the capabilities of computers and software to mine, sort, and reorganize data have increased the ability of many institutions to exploit that information. They can more readily put it into useful formats and tease out of disparate databases comprehensive and accessible profiles on private individuals and the actions of governmental bodies.

6.2 PRIVACY

6.2.1 The Values Involved

Privacy is the epitome of a substantive value. It encompasses ideas of autonomy, dignity, and personal freedom and control, and it provides protection for the individual. Box 6.1 describes examples of what might be regarded as violations of privacy.

Privacy is different from secrecy and confidentiality. Secrecy is a functional concept, requiring an agreement on the part of those who are party

[3]The development of new technologies make statements of this kind always subject to caveats. For example, the increasing capacity to mine nominally "anonymous" data to back out information about individuals is often acknowledged. Further, even when data are gathered remotely, low-orbit photoreconnaissance satellites with high resolution (or even photoreconnaissance aircraft) might yield data on the behavior of individuals.

BOX 6.1 Examples of Privacy Violation

A drugstore chain sold customers' medical information to a marketing company that sent consumers coupons for drugs related to their disorders. An outcry over privacy concerns halted the practice.

Veteran U.S. sailor Timothy R. McVeigh (not the Oklahoma City bomber) faced expulsion for homosexuality based on evidence the Navy gathered from America Online. McVeigh, since reinstated, had cited his sexual orientation in an online profile that he thought was confidential. A judge ruled that the Navy violated the law by obtaining confidential information about McVeigh from AOL without a warrant or court order.

Retail salesman Bronti Kelly, 34, couldn't land a job for years and had no idea why. The reason was that a police record sent across the Internet to employers had wrongly labeled him a shoplifter. The company that failed to correct the report was ordered to pay more than $73,000 to Kelly.

State motor vehicle departments in Florida, South Carolina, and Colorado sold drivers' photographs in digital form to a private firm that developed a system to enable clerks at points of sale to verify a customer's identity. Once the public learned about the sale of photos, the reaction in all three states was highly negative, causing the effort to collapse.

SOURCES: Robert Gellman, "Privacy and Harmonization: A Discussion Paper for a Symposium on Global Networks and Local Values," National Academy of Sciences, Woods Hole, Massachusetts, June 3-5, 1999.

David E. Kalish, "Net Privacy Victims Lash Back at Thefts," *The Detroit News*, April 19, 1998.

to some information to not share it with others. It generally does not require (or seek) the sanction of society, merely the commitment of those who share the information. Confidentiality is a more formal and social concept, a set of rules that govern the use of information held by institutions about individuals and the conditions under which that information can be shared. Privacy is quite distinct from both of these concepts; it refers to the right of individuals to control information about themselves—to keep it secret or to share it with others only as they see fit.

Although privacy in essence serves individuals by protecting and empowering them, it also serves society and government. When a person believes that his or her privacy is threatened, that individual may become defensive, minimizing personal exposure by being cautious about expressing views and disengaging from society as much as possible. But because democratic societies rely on full participation and free expression by its citizens, the threat that gives rise to the individual's defensiveness becomes a threat to society as well.

Obviously, privacy is not an absolute right. For example, commitments to maintain privacy may conflict with free expression (if, for example, that free expression might divulge private information). Societies have asserted a need (and therefore a right) to gather and use information about individuals for such purposes as taxation, census, and health; to hold people to their obligations as citizens; to serve them in accordance with their entitlements; and to support law enforcement efforts. Such societal assertions must be balanced against the desirability of the personal right of individuals to know what information about them is being gathered and used; in that way, they can monitor the conformity of such use to law, and control any uses beyond those sanctioned purposes.

Private institutions or other individuals do not have a constitutional right to violate an individual's privacy, although they may gain the privilege of using someone's personal information in certain ways under a contractual arrangement with that person. (On the Web, personal information is often collected under a theory of "implied consent," in which use of a Web site grants the site operator the right to collect certain personal information automatically through "cookies" and the like (Box 6.2).

To illustrate the conflicting pressures, it is instructive to compare disclosure policies for health records with policies for pizza-delivery records. There are many users who can legitimately argue for access to patient health records without the specific authorization of the patient. In order to meet a number of social, economic, and health needs, a society may allow access to some parts of health records by public health authorities, health researchers, fraud and abuse investigators, accreditation firms, and even law-enforcement agencies under some circumstances. Actually, electronic databases may provide for greater privacy protection in these instances than traditional paper records because it is easier to limit access to only certain parts of the patient record. For pizza-delivery records, on the other hand, it may never be appropriate to allow for any nonconsensual disclosures because there are no overriding societal needs that justify it.

The privacy interests of individuals are likely to be greater in their medical records, however, than in their pizza-delivery records. And, the public uproar over unauthorized release of medical records is inevitably much larger than in the case for pizza delivery records. Confidentiality of medical information has also been regarded as a prerequisite for free and candid discussions between health-care professionals and their patients. For these reasons, a culture of resistance to unauthorized disclosure of medical records is common in the health profession.

BOX 6.2 "Cookies" Facilitate Collection of Personal Information Regarding Information Retrieved from Web Sites

A Web server typically cannot link one user's visit to a given site to any other visit by that same user. This limitation is overcome by causing a Web client (i.e., the user's workstation) to submit an identifier with each request for information. The identifier, called a "cookie," can be associated with personal data obtained from the requester on his or her first visit to a particular Web site. Because the individual's cookie is resubmitted with each subsequent visit, the server knows all the information that interested a particular requester before. The server can thus create a profile of the customer. And by combining profiles from multiple Web sites, cooperating providers of information can construct even richer profiles.

6.2.2 German and American Perspectives

In 1983 the German Constitutional Court summarized the underlying value balance as follows:

> The individual . . . has the right to know and to decide on the information being processed about him. At the same time, as a social being the individual cannot avoid becoming the object of information processing. However, limitations to his basic right have only to be accepted when there is an overriding general interest and if that interest is molded into a law that follows the basic requirements of clarity and proportionality. To protect these principles a number of safeguards are required; these safeguards consist of data processing principles (correctness, timeliness, purpose limitation, fairly and lawfully obtained), derived rights (access, correction), and organizational safeguards (independent institutions).[4]

In the United States, the development of privacy policy has been slow and uneven, with the privacy of information collected and held by government receiving much more attention than information collected and held by private companies and organizations. For example, the Privacy Act of 1974 (P.L. 93-579) and the subsequent Privacy Protection Study Commission both focused on information collected and held by the government as the potential misuser of personal information. The Privacy

[4]BVerfGE 65,1 (41 ff).

Act in particular provides a broad policy framework for privacy relevant to such information.

Some specialized privacy protections applicable to nongovernmental entities emerged in the 1970s and 1980s, including the Fair Credit Reporting Act of 1970, the Family Educational Rights and Privacy Act of 1974, the Cable Communications Policy Act of 1984, the Electronic Communications Privacy Act of 1986, and the Video Privacy Protection Act of 1988. The privacy of health information was addressed in the Health Insurance Portability and Accountability Act of 1998 and the Children's Online Privacy Protection Act of 1999. However, U.S. privacy policy remains unsettled, in part because of concerns about the costs (and other burdens) of compliance, ambiguity about the appropriate application of underlying philosophical principles (property and free speech, for example), and unresolved political clashes between those who collect and process data and those who advocate for broad privacy protection.

As the above paragraphs illustrate, the United States and Germany (which is much like the rest of Europe in this respect) approach privacy from very different political and legal traditions. The German approach is rooted in its experience with totalitarian regimes and military occupation, which has given rise in Europe to a strong antipathy toward, even an anxiety about, invasions of privacy or illegal surveillance. On the other hand, Europeans, and Germans in particular, tend to trust their government more than Americans do and turn to it to protect their interests. Thus the first data-protection law in the world, the Hesse Data Protection Act, was passed in Germany in 1970, and it established an enforcement structure that became the model for data protection all over Europe. The act created a governmental structure to preserve each individual's privacy rights, and it stipulated that the data-protection officer established under this act, though formally a public official, would be independent from all other branches of government.[5]

As importantly, the willingness to trust government has made it acceptable for German privacy law to take a comprehensive approach. All record keepers, public and private, have to comply with fair information practices (Box 6.3). Although earlier laws imposed different rules on public and private record keepers, more recent legislation dealing with the Internet largely removes that distinction. The 1997 Teleservices Data Protection Act[6] implementing the European Union directive on the protec-

---

[5]The Federal Data Protection Commissioner's independence is laid down in sect. 22 par. 4 sent. 2 and 3 of the Federal Data Protection Act. He is independent in the performance of his duties and subject to the law only. According to Art. 28 par. 1 subpar. 2 of the European Directive the data protection authorities act with complete independence in exercising the functions entrusted in them.

[6]BGBl. I 1997 S. 1871-1872

BOX 6.3 Fair Information Practices

1. *Openness.* Existence of record-keeping systems and databanks containing data about individuals should be publicly known, along with a description of the main purpose and uses of the data.
2. *Individual participation.* Each individual should have the right to see any data about himself or herself and to correct or remove any data that is not timely, accurate, relevant, or complete.
3. *Collection limitation.* There should be limits to the extent of personal data collection, those data should be collected by lawful and fair means, and they should be collected, where appropriate, with the knowledge or consent of the subject.
4. *Data quality.* Personal data should be relevant to the purposes for which they are to be used, and should be accurate, complete, and timely.
5. *Finality.* There must be limits to the uses and disclosure of personal data. The data should be used only for purposes specified at the time of collection, and it should not be otherwise disclosed without the consent of the data subject or other legal authority.
6. *Security.* Reasonable security safeguards against such risks as loss, unauthorized access, destruction, use, modification, or disclosure should protect personal data.
7. *Accountability.* Record keepers should be accountable for complying with fair information practices.

tion of privacy in the telecommunications sector,[7] and the 2001 amendments to the German Federal Data Privacy Act[8] implementing the 1998 European Union's directive on data protection,[9] apply to private companies and individuals as well as to public authorities. German law does distinguish between privacy (*"Schutz personenbezogener Daten"*) and business secrets, providing less protection for business secrets on the argument that the individual rights at stake are not of the same order.

---

[7]Directive 97/66/EC of the European Parliament and of the Council of 15 December 1997 concerning the processing of personal data and the protection of privacy in the telecommunications sector: Official Journal L 024 , 30/01/1998, p. 0001-0008. Available online at <http://europa.eu.int/eur-lex/en/lif/dat/1997/en_397L0066.html>.

[8]Federal Data Protection Act of December 20, 1990 (BGBl.I 1990 S.2954) as amended by law of May 23, 2001 (BGBl I S. 904).

[9]Council Directive 95/46/EC of 24 October 1995 on the Protection of Individuals with Regard to the Processing of Personal Data and on the Free Movement of Such Data, art. 32, 1995 O.J. (L 281) 31, 49 (requiring member states to adopt legislation conforming to terms of directive) [hereafter European Privacy Directive]. Available online at <http://europa.eu.int/eur-lex/en/lif/dat/1995/en_395L0046.html>.

BOX 6.4 A Patchwork of Privacy Legislation

Credit reports are protected by the Fair Credit Reporting Act.[1]

Medical records have historically been protected by state legislation. However, in late 2000, federal regulations to protect medical records were promulgated by the Clinton administration under the provisions of the Health Insurance Portability and Accountability Act of 1996. These regulations granted individuals new rights with respect to medical privacy.

Bank records are protected by (among other things) 15 USC 6801 (Title V of the Gramm-Leach-Bliley Act of 1999), which requires disclosure of financial institution policies on the sharing of nonpublic personal information. This affords individuals the opportunity in certain cases to decline to allow such sharing.

Records pertaining to videotape rentals are protected by 18 USC 2710 (the Video Privacy Protection Act of 1988), which provides for civil damages against unauthorized disclosure of such records.

[1]15 U.S.C. § 1681a.

By contrast, the United States has a populist mistrust of governmental institutions and a strong tradition of relying on market forces not only to regulate the economy but to serve many social needs as well. Thus while the U.S. Congress has adopted legislation to protect personal privacy from encroachment by federal agencies,[10] the regulation of private industry has moved more slowly and in a piecemeal manner. In practice, the U.S. norm is a patchwork of legislation and court decisions arising from episodic scandals and political pressures from both industry and privacy advocates. Thus, highly specialized solutions have been crafted for different technologies (e.g., statutory regimes specific to the protection of postal mail, telephone communications, e-mail, and other Internet communications) and for different subject areas (Box 6.4).

Finally, in U.S. law, privacy—that is, the control of one's personal data—is basically understood as a property right. Individuals can transfer or sell their property rights to a firm interested in its use or even to government, provided that the transfer is voluntary and the terms and conditions are fair. But the traditional European approach treats individuals' interests in data about themselves as an inalienable liberty right—that is, a right that cannot be given up, even voluntarily.

[10]Federal Privacy Act, 5 U.S.C. § 552a.

Yet despite the differences in legal traditions, both Germany and the United States over the last 25 years have developed what have become known as "fair information principles" that reflect substantial agreement on basic issues. This common ground is summarized in Box 6.3. The question is whether these commonalties—coupled with the strong linking forces introduced by global networks in general as well as the more specific desire to exploit them for commercial uses—will ultimately lead to harmonization, in which the United States moves toward the more comprehensive and integrated approach to privacy that is prevalent in Europe.

If privacy is to be protected by direct legal enforcement, then there are two possible approaches (regardless of whether privacy rights are characterized as property or liberty interests). The first approach is to establish independent governmental data-protection authorities responsible for monitoring and enforcing fair information principles, as is done in the German system. This approach avoids the high transaction costs, and the difficulty of proving cause and establishing injury, that may make individual enforcement illusory. However, as a practical matter, it is difficult for publicly funded enforcement authorities to handle all individual complaints.

The second approach is to allow individuals to bring lawsuits to protect their privacy rights and to recover damages for injuries resulting from violation of those rights. This approach decentralizes enforcement of privacy rights, but it may not be efficacious because it is difficult to prove cause, and the stakes involved in any particular invasion of personal privacy may be so small that individuals are unwilling to pay the costs of litigation (though efficiency can be increased when numerous injury cases are grouped into class actions).

6.2.3 Technology and Privacy

Individuals have many good reasons to want information about themselves to be stored electronically and to be made available over communications networks. The rapid and accurate transfer of electronically stored medical records can improve a person's medical care and might even save a life; stored credit card and address information makes Internet shopping convenient; and user-friendly online banking transactions have attracted millions of customers.

Yet advances in information technology can also threaten privacy. A visitor to a Web site may involuntarily leave behind personal information that the Web site owner can later use for commercial purposes. Seemingly harmless fragments of information left at different sites can be combined into a potentially harmful aggregate. Even easier, cookies can be set in a user's hard drive, creating a built-in history of sites visited, material browsed, and purchases made. Such data can be used for marketing purposes—targeting an individual with ads that are customized to his or her tastes—which may represent a convenience to some and little more than an annoyance to others. However, it is the absence of control over the collection or the use of the information that is the quintessential violation of privacy, and it is not difficult to construct scenarios in which that violation can be harmful to individuals.

Of course, personal information can be collected by Internet service providers as well as by Web site hosts. ISPs can and do record information on user actions for internal purposes or to comply with court orders, and this might include sites visited, the amount of information downloaded, and when such visits occurred.

Databases containing "public" information are another source of privacy concern. Much of such information—e.g., records pertaining to property tax, motor vehicles, drivers' licenses, convictions—was heretofore *not* public because it was hard to access or extract from voluminous databases.[11] Making such information easily available to the general public through the Internet may well be viewed as a violation of an individual's privacy rights because this allows it to be used for purposes other than those for which it was originally collected (together with the individual's implied or explicit consent). In the United States, for example, these databases have been a valuable source of information for telephone-solicitation operations.

Other methods of data collection are possible as well, including records of cellular-telephone location, records of building ingress and egress (created when magnetic cards are used to gain access), and records of credit-card and telephone usage. And the World Wide Web itself is a source of information about individuals. Commercial transactions and political dialogues posted in forums create opportunities to collect information about personal interests and activities.

Today, different structures exist for regulating personal data collection and use in each of these areas of activity from local exchange to long distance telephone companies to cable television companies and Internet service providers. That is certainly a source of confusion and chaos. Technological convergence, however, is leading companies to strive to become sole-source information providers and handlers, and the differing regulatory traditions and customs that characterize each domain may well come to overlap, leading, at least initially, to greater turmoil even within national borders. The technical convergence can also create the opportunity for a kind of regulatory arbitrage that can work to the detriment of pri-

[11]In Germany, third-party access to all these kinds of information is severely controlled by law, so that the term "public" in this discussion is even more properly put in quotation marks.

vacy rights. On the other hand, the turmoil and the obvious regulatory inequities may serve as a stimulus to rationalize the present cacophony of regulatory regimes. In so doing, it could reinforce the fundamental concepts of privacy sometimes lost or distorted in the past as individual sectors developed rules that weighed particular political, commercial, and even technical factors more heavily than privacy per se.

Information technology is not only a threat to privacy; it can also provide the technical means for increasing one's privacy. For example:

- Encryption (Box 6.5) is widely used to ensure privacy and to enable secure commerce. Encryption (at the sending end) and decryption (at the receiving end) provide end-to-end confidentiality when the inter-

BOX 6.5 Secret-key and Public-key Encryption

Classic encryption requires both the sender and receiver to possess a secret key—which is used to encode (encrypt) the message at one end and to decode (decrypt) it at the other. The most common secret-key crypto system in use today is the DES, or Data Encryption Standard, developed in the mid-1970s. It is in widespread use for high-volume commercial/financial transactions.

Of more relevant current interest is "public-key encryption," which makes possible the secure transmission of messages without requiring the sender to have access to a secret key. Public-key systems, also developed in the mid-70s, use two different, but mathematically related, keys—the "public key" and the "private key." Knowledge of the public key allows anyone to encrypt a message, but not to derive from the encrypting key (without enormous computational effort) knowledge of the private, decrypting key. It can take a supercomputer weeks or months to "break" a private key; indeed, if the key is made long enough (e.g., 2048 bits), the task can become, in effect, impossible.[1]

In practice, a person's (or an organization's) public key is published in a trusted public directory. Then, anyone wishing to send a confidential message to that person encrypts the text using the person's public key and transmits it. The intended recipient uses his or her private key to decrypt the message, which, since it is encrypted, cannot be read by anyone else.

[1]Thus "key length" and its effect on secure communications has become an important matter of public-policy debate. The question is what encryption software—that is, what encryption-key length—should private parties be allowed to use or export to other countries? The balance sought is between the right of private parties to secure their transmissions and the need—or right—of governments, with appropriate judicial supervision, to monitor commercial traffic or to maintain an edge in its ability to protect the security of its own messages.

BOX 6.6 Anonymizers

An anonymizing service dissociates the identity of a user from a message that he or she sends. Anonymizing services fall into two categories: true anonymous remailers and pseudonym servers.

A true anonymous remailer is based on a chain of remailers. The user sends a message to the first remailer, which passes it along to the second remailer, and so on, using a protocol that provides anonymity with respect to mailers farther up the chain. Thus, only the first remailer knows the identity of the sender. And, if each remailer discards information about the sources of the messages it receives for forwarding, it is technically very difficult to reconstruct the identity of the original sender. (Note that under such circumstances, replying to a message sent through a true anonymizing remailer is quite difficult.)

A pseudonym server provides a pseudonym for a user and more easily supports replies to a message. The pseudonym owner sends a message to the server, which substitutes an e-mail address such as <johndoe@.alias.net>, and people can send mail to the user without knowing who he or she is. However, in order to route replies back to the user, the server must keep local records that map real e-mail addresses to pseudonyms. This leaves the server open to compromise (e.g., by law-enforcement authorities in that country acting under court order). To reduce the likelihood of compromise, pseudonym servers can be an element in a chain of remailers. In this scenario, the person who owns the pseudonym leaves a set of multiply encrypted instructions on how to route mail to him or her (a "reply block"). Typically, a reply block will contain the address of an anonymous remailer, and then an encrypted block that only the remailer can read. When the remailer decrypts the block, it will contain the address of another remailer, and a block only *that* remailer can decrypt.

Typically, anonymous remailers in the chain are set up in different countries, with different legal traditions. Thus in order to compromise the anonymity of a sender wishing replies, every single remailer would have to be compromised—a difficult and time-consuming task.

Note also that replies can be effected in ways that do not depend on knowledge of a user's return path. For example, a reply can be broadcast to a widely read newsgroup in an encrypted form, using a key known to the sender. Anyone can view the encrypted message, but without the key it shows up as gibberish. However, the sender can read it easily, because he or she knows the decryption key. Another possibility is to send the reply to a Web-based e-mail service such as Hotmail, which the user can check from any location. (And, using an anonymizer that enables anonymous Web surfing, the user can keep his or her identify private.)

mediate communications channels are either public or, if private, subject to malicious intrusion.

• Anonymization enables a user to send (and sometimes to receive) messages anonymously (Box 6.6). Anonymizing services make it very difficult and sometimes impossible to trace the identity of a user.

• Automated privacy-negotiation protocols, such as the Platform for Privacy Preferences Project (P3P), enable Web site operators to express their privacy policies in a standardized machine-readable format that can be interpreted by clients linking to the Web site. Clients "remember" their users' own privacy preferences, which are automatically compared with the policies of the visited Web site. If the two match, the connection is allowed; otherwise, discrepancies are called to the user's attention. Thus, the human user need not read the privacy policies at every site he or she visits, but rather can rely on his client for this task.

Reliance on technical approaches has two major drawbacks. First, technical approaches generally require explicit user action—an individual wanting to protect privacy must take an action to do so (this may change in the future if defaults for encryption are widely built into e-mail or other communications software). Because many individuals do not know that the tools exist or do not have the skills to use them effectively, the privacy interests of those individuals may be compromised.

Second, if privacy protection relies on software that both client and provider must install, such as P3P, then it is viable as a privacy-protection mechanism only if a large number of Web site operators adopt the same software and a critical mass of users install it in some relatively brief initial period. The issue of timing is important because the value of the system grows with numbers of users (an illustration of positive network externalities discussed further in Chapter 7), so that the willingness of operators to invest in such a system depends strongly on how rapidly users can be recruited and a financial return generated.

In any case, although technical tools can offer some degree of data protection, few in the United States or Europe advocate relying on them exclusively. Technical tools per se do not provide a framework for balancing competing values where privacy is involved—or, for that matter, in any other case. The appropriate balance cannot and should not depend on the ever-changing state of technology and the relative power it may confer at any particular moment on those who seek to protect their privacy or on those who seek to invade it. It is the role of communities to come to agreement about the appropriate framework and to use institutional structures to regulate, guide, or stimulate the use of technical and other tools to achieve the desired value balance.

6.2.4 Privacy Protection as a Challenge to Governance

Although, or perhaps because, European and American approaches to privacy differ, together they provide a rich array of tools to help an individual maintain control over personal information. These include not only mandatory legal regulations introduced through laws and enforced by courts and government agencies, but also a variety of self-regulatory procedures and practices.

The Limited Power of Traditional National Regulation

The globalization of information flows makes it much more difficult for a single nation-state to unilaterally protect the privacy of its citizens. Routine consumer transactions can involve players in five or even more countries, given that consumers, merchants, manufacturers, Web site operators, credit-card issuers, and other parties to a single transaction can all be located in different political jurisdictions.

In effect, a nation's data-protection laws are subject to a kind of competitive pressure. In many instances, strict privacy legislation in one nation-state can be circumvented by shifting the collection and use of the data to another nation-state that has less restrictive laws. However, data protection differs from content regulation in the global-networked environment. The businesses collecting personal data during commercial transactions often require a local presence in order to make money. If so, this feature makes an out-of-nation vendor vulnerable to the extraterritorial application of national rules. Even if the actual storing or processing takes place abroad, local data-protection authorities can argue that the local entity representing the operator is subject to local law and, moreover, responsible for the parent company's actions. Thus, the local authorities can take action against the local representative.

Neither the argument nor the threat is merely theoretical. In the well-publicized conflict between the European Union and the United States concerning e-commerce transactions, the European position embodied in the European Privacy Directive—which stated that personal data cannot, in most instances, be transferred out of the European Union to countries that do not provide an "adequate" level of privacy protection[12]—was ef-

[12]Article 26 of the European Privacy Directive provided several exceptions to this general prohibition. In particular, transfers of personal data to third countries that do not ensure an adequate level of protection can take place anyway if (1) the data subject has given his or her consent unambiguously to the proposed transfer, or (2) the transfer is necessary for the performance of a contract between the data subject and the controller or for the implementation of precontractual measures taken in response to the data subject's request, or (3) the

fectively an extraterritorial applicability argument.[13] The fact that U.S. corporations were vulnerable to prosecution through their local offices gave significant negotiating power to the European position, resulting in the "safe harbor" compromise whereby American corporations undertook a contractually enforceable commitment to privacy protection (see discussion below).

International Legal Harmonization

A straightforward solution to harmonizing data protection would be the conclusion of an international treaty on the issue. Within Europe, this is precisely what happened. The Council of Europe prepared its Convention for the Protection of Individuals with Regard to Automated Processing of Personal Data, and the European Union used its power to legislate the Directive on Data Protection. These two legal instruments effectively harmonize the standards and, more to the point, spread and reinforce the substantive value.

Similar approaches have been tried in the broader international arena as well. In September 1980 the Organization for Economic Cooperation and Develoment (OECD) adopted Guidelines on the Protection of Privacy and Transborder Flows of Personal Data,[14] and in December 1990 the General Assembly of the United Nations adopted Guidelines Concerning Computerized Personal Data Files.[15] But neither instrument has the enforceability associated with domestic law. Indeed, as noted elsewhere, substantive international treaties work only when there is such complete

---

transfer is necessary for the conclusion or for the performance of a contract concluded in the interest of the data subject between the controller and a third party, or (4) the transfer is necessary or legally required on important public interest grounds, or for the establishment, exercise or defense of legal claims, or (5) the transfer is necessary in order to protect the vital interests of the data subject, or (6) the transfer is made from a register that according to laws or regulations is intended to provide information to the public and that is open to consultation either by the public in general or by any person who can demonstrate legitimate interest, to the extent that the conditions laid down in law for consultation are fulfilled in the particular case.

[13]Although prohibiting data transfers out of Europe does not, in a formal sense, contravene international-law principles of prescriptive, adjudicative, and enforcement jurisdiction, the practical effect of such a prohibition is to disrupt international commerce. See Henry H. Perritt, Jr. and Margaret G. Stewart, 1999, "False Alarm," *Fed. Commun. L.J.* 51:811.

[14]OECD Document C(80)58 (Final). Available online at <http://www.oecd.org/dsti/sti/it/secur/prod/PRIV-EN.HTM>.

[15]Resolution Number A/RES/45/95. Available online at <http://www.un.org/documents/ga/res/45/a45r095.htm>.

agreement on the values involved that domestic law is, or can easily be made, consistent with the treaty's provisions.

There are in fact sufficient differences between the United States and Europe on defining what privacy does and does not mean with respect to government and commercial institutions that such agreement has proven difficult to obtain. Moreover, both jurisdictions fundamentally differ in their approach to structuring institutions of enforcement. While the Europeans are willing—indeed, prefer—to rely on command-and-control regulation and governmental enforcement authorities, the United States prefers industrial self-regulation and litigation.[16]

Finally, it should be noted that the traditional international treaty process is slow and cumbersome, certainly more so than the process of reaching agreement within the European Union. Few who are familiar with the International Telecommunications Union or the World Trade Organization would view a similar approach to privacy protection as practical, particularly within the context of the rapidly evolving technical environment of the Internet.

Internationally Coordinated Private Law

A second technique for resolving the U.S.–European conflict over data protection involves coordinating legislation with the help of each nation's rules on the application of foreign commercial law to international cases. This technique, called the conflict-of-laws approach, is available because the protection of data among private parties is generally covered by private rather than public law,[17] and privacy issues on the Internet often involve the use of data by private businesses rather than by government.

One obstacle to this approach, however, arises from the distinct difference between the U.S. view of privacy (analogous to a property right) and the traditional European view (which deems individuals' interests in data about themselves as an inalienable liberty right). In a case in which this difference was significant, it is quite possible that Europeans might not regard the U.S. legal provisions as being functionally equivalent to their European counterparts. Under those circumstances, the national conflict rules might require that the European, rather than the U.S. rules, apply.

---

[16]Henry H. Perritt, Jr. 1997. "Regulatory Models for Protecting Privacy in the Internet," in William M. Daley, ed., *Privacy and Self-Regulation in the Information Age*, U.S. Department of Commerce, Washington, D.C., Chapter 3. Available online at <http://www.ntia.doc.gov/reports/privacy/selfreg3.htm>.

[17]Reinhard Ellger. 1990. *Der Datenschutz im grenzüberschreitenden Datenverkehr. Eine rechtsvergleichende und kollisionsrechtliche Untersuchung.* Baden-Baden, 582 s.

There are other complications as well. If a private lawsuit is brought by a foreign customer in the country of origin of the supplier, will the courts be convinced that an Internet transaction between these two parties is properly viewed as having occurred in the home country of the customer (so that the customer's national laws apply)? Furthermore, even though the private-law rules can generally be applied where only private entities are concerned, nation-states have generally been unwilling to apply foreign rules if they are perceived as a hidden regulatory tool. This is likely to be the case with data-protection rules, given the conceptual differences between nations about what should be protected and how.[18] Indeed, the fact that independent public officials have jurisdiction to intervene would signal the inherent public-law character of data protection laws. Finally, from a pragmatic point of view, it seems doubtful that Europeans would accept, for example, a data-protection arrangement under which European nationals would have to sue U.S. firms before U.S. tribunals; nor would Americans be comfortable with the opposite arrangement.

Self-regulation Without Direct State Intervention

Many data users in the United States have expressed a strong preference for self-regulation, and American industry has begun to move in that direction. Whether motivated by the need to respond to consumer pressure or the desire to avoid legislation, American companies acknowledge the pressures that lead to calls for regulation but assert that they can police their own actions. When the Federal Trade Commission (FTC) undertook a series of investigations of online privacy in the mid-1990s and began to develop guidelines for possible regulation, the Direct Marketing Association responded by adopting a code of Fair Information Practices. Since 1998, industry representatives have worked with the Federal Trade Commission to develop credible and effective self-regulatory approaches and accompanying audit and enforcement mechanisms. There are limits to how far the FTC can go. For example, the Children's Online Privacy Protection Act, which was passed in 1999, makes the Commission responsible for rulemaking and requires any Web site or online service that is directed to children to obtain parental consent before collecting personal information from children under the age of 13.

Self-regulatory approaches can be more decentralized and flexible than governmental regulation, and thus more responsive to particular circumstances. On the other hand, they are unlikely to have much credibil-

[18]For greater detail, see Ellger (supra note 17) 597-604.

ity if they comprise no more than broad guidelines. Effective self-regulation needs substantive rules, as well as mechanisms to ensure that consumers *know* the rules—e.g., a requirement that companies publish privacy policies. Furthermore, there must be some sanction for failure to comply with these rules. Among the suggested approaches are the creation of certifying seals or logos, which can be withdrawn for noncompliance; publishing the names of noncompliant companies on a "bad actor" list; or making a company liable under fraud laws. Other possibilities are audits of compliance with established fair information practices or independent authorities with power to resolve complaints.

None of these self-regulatory approaches, including the publication of codes of good practice, are acceptable to most privacy advocates, who view them as toothless and therefore not truly protective of individual interests. However, some of these advocates are willing to agree to a system with "opt-in" provisions, which requires individuals to agree explicitly to the collection or use of personal information. (Industry usually argues for "opt-out" provisions that permit collection or use of personal information unless individuals explicitly object.)

Self-regulation has been strongly opposed on the European side for many of the same reasons advanced by the privacy advocates. Many, perhaps even most, Europeans do not trust the mechanism, suspecting that self-regulation is merely a cover for lowering the standards of data protection, or ignoring them entirely.

Hybrid Regulation

Thus there is a growing interest in new forms of governance, which might be characterized as "hybrid" in character, that feature flexible international public-law frameworks within which private self-regulation is used to work out the details. Private self-regulation within a public international law framework may not only provide solutions to the inherently international character of traffic in personal data; they also may avoid some of the problems of the fragmented regulatory structures currently in place. Some precedent for such an approach can be found in a German-U.S. contract between the Berlin Data Protection Commissioner and Citibank (Box 6.7).

A more contemporary example, and one that has received a great deal of attention, is the hybrid regulatory scheme developed by the European Commission and the United States government to avoid privacy-related disruptions of transborder data flows and international trade. In 2000, they exchanged letters that articulated a "safe harbor" for U.S. companies and other organizations receiving personal data from the European

BOX 6.7 The German RailwayCard and Citibank

The RailwayCard (BahnCard) is a popular discount card issued by the German railway company, Deutsche Bahn. In November 1994 Deutsche Bahn announced a co-branding agreement with the German subsidiary of Citibank to issue a RailwayCard with a Visa credit-card function as a no-additional-cost option for the customer. Under the agreement, after July 1995 the RailwayCards were no longer produced in Germany but in data centers run by Citibank subsidiaries in South Dakota and Nevada. Huge quantities of sensitive personal data on the creditworthiness of customers of Deutsche Bahn were transmitted to and processed in the United States.

Although the EU Directive on Data Protection was not officially in effect at that time, the Berlin Data Protection Commissioner (the German supervisory authority in this matter) demanded that no transborder data flow to the United States take place unless the requirements of the directive were met. In February 1996 Deutsche Bahn and Citibank signed a specific Data Protection Agreement making the German Data Protection Law applicable to their handling of cardholders' data on both sides of the Atlantic. The Citibank subsidiaries in the United States agreed to on-site audits by the Berlin Data Protection Commissioner or designated agents—e.g., an American consulting or auditing firm acting on the commissioner's behalf.

Whereas the data protection commissioner of Berlin, Hansjürgen Garstka, described the agreement as a useful tool, reactions in the United States were rather skeptical. *Business Week* saw "Europe's privacy cops trek[king] from Berlin all the way to Sioux City, S.D., to Citigroup's giant processing center, where computers store financial information about millions of German credit-card holders." It went on to say that an "ideological rift between Europe and the United States exists with regard to the regulation of privacy. At the root of the battle is a philosophical chasm nearly as wide as the Atlantic. Europeans look to democratic regimes to protect their privacy. Americans, meanwhile, tend at first to leave information flows unregulated. Later, they slap controls on objectionable areas, such as child pornography on the Web." Emanuel Kohnstamm, a Time Warner Inc. vice president in Brussels, was quoted in the article as saying: "In Europe, people don't trust companies, they trust government. In the United States, it's the other way around. Citizens must be protected from actions of the government."

SOURCES: (1) Alexander Dix, "Case Study: North America and the European Directive. The German RailwayCard—A Model Contractual Solution of the 'Adequate Level of Protection' Issue?," Speech at the 8th International Privacy and Data Protection Conference: "Privacy Beyond Borders," Ottawa, Canada, September 18-20, 1996; available online at <http://www.datenschutz-berlin.de/sonstige/konferen/ottawa/alex3.htm> (03.03.00).

(2) Stephen Baker, Marsha Johnston, and William Echikson, 1998, "Europe's Privacy Cops," *Business Week* 2 (November), 49-51.

Union.[19] Organizations receiving personal data transfers from the EU and complying with certain principles (Box 6.8) would be regarded as meeting the "adequacy" requirements for data protection in accordance with the European Union's Directive on Data Protection.

In this instance, hybridization allowed the United States and Europe to organize the coexistence of their diverging regulatory traditions and styles. The Europeans came to the negotiation table with their trust in government, and with an existing framework of independent data-protection officers. The United States, for its part, had neither a strong regulatory framework nor the inclination to impose one. The compromise was self-regulation with public oversight via the Federal Trade Commission—i.e., a hybrid solution.[20]

The actual implementation mechanism is complex, with roles established for both government and nongovernment organizations, the issuance of a "seal of compliance," and the creation of a dispute-resolution body. Noncompliance is penalized by a range of sanctions, including publicity for findings of noncompliance, the requirement to delete data in certain circumstances, suspension and removal of a seal, compensation for individuals for losses incurred, and injunctive orders. In addition, the U.S. Federal Trade Commission has committed itself to reviewing allegations of noncompliance with safe-harbor principles made by privacy self-regulatory organizations; the Commission will be looking to see whether the alleged actions amount to violations of the FTC Act prohibiting unfair or deceptive acts or practices in commerce. In this context, all of the usual tools available to the FTC can be applied, including administrative cease-and-desist orders prohibiting the challenged practices, as well as pursuing complaints in U.S. federal courts to obtain judicial remedies. Persistent failure to comply can be punished by denying the violator the benefits of the safe harbor.

The success of these safe-harbor negotiations between the European Union and the United States does not mean that the agreement is without controversy. For example, the Trans Atlantic Consumer Dialogue (TACD), representing a group of consumer and privacy groups, argued that the safe-harbor agreement ". . . fails to provide adequate privacy protection for consumers in the United States and Europe. It lacks an effective means

---

[19]The U.S. letter can be found online at <http://www.export.gov/safeharbor/larussacovernote717.htm>. The European Commission letter can be found at <http://www.export.gov/safeharbor/EUletter27JulyHeader.htm>. Other related documents can be found at <http://www.export.gov/safeharbor/sh_documents.html>.

[20]Henry Farrell. 2000. "Negotiating Privacy Across Arenas—The EU-US 'Safe Harbor' Discussions," in Adrienne Heritier, ed., *The Provision of Common Goods: Governance Across Multiple Arenas,* Boulder, CO: Rowman and Littlefield.

BOX 6.8 Safe Harbor Privacy Principles

ISSUED BY THE U.S. DEPARTMENT OF COMMERCE ON JULY 21, 2000

"**NOTICE:** An organization must inform individuals about the purposes for which it collects and uses information about them, how to contact the organization with any inquiries or complaints, the types of third parties to which it discloses the information, and the choices and means the organization offers individuals for limiting its use and disclosure. This notice must be provided in clear and conspicuous language when individuals are first asked to provide personal information to the organization or as soon thereafter as is practicable, but in any event before the organization uses such information for a purpose other than that for which it was originally collected or processed by the transferring organization or discloses it for the first time to a third party.

"**CHOICE:** An organization must offer individuals the opportunity to choose (opt out) whether their personal information is (a) to be disclosed to a third party or (b) to be used for a purpose that is incompatible with the purpose(s) for which it was originally collected or subsequently authorized by the individual. Individuals must be provided with clear and conspicuous, readily available, and affordable mechanisms to exercise choice.

"For sensitive information (i.e., personal information specifying medical or health conditions, racial or ethnic origin, political opinions, religious or philosophical beliefs, trade union membership or information specifying the sex life of the individual), they must be given affirmative or explicit (opt-in) choice if the information is to be disclosed to a third party or used for a purpose other than those for which it was originally collected or subsequently authorized by the individual through the exercise of opt-in choice. In any case, an organization should treat as sensitive any information received from a third party where the third party treats and identifies it as sensitive.

"**ONWARD TRANSFER:** To disclose information to a third party, organizations must apply the Notice and Choice Principles. Where an organization wishes to transfer information to a third party that is acting as an agent, . . . , it may do so if it first either ascertains that the third party subscribes to the Principles or is subject to the Directive or another adequacy finding or enters into a written agreement with such third party requiring that the third party provide at least the same level of privacy protection as is required by the relevant Principles. If the organization complies with these requirements, it shall not be held responsible (unless the organization agrees otherwise) when a third party to which it transfers such information processes it in a way contrary to any restrictions or representations, unless the organization knew or should have known the third party would process it in such a contrary way and the organization has not taken reasonable steps to prevent or stop such processing.

"**SECURITY:** Organizations creating, maintaining, using or disseminating personal information must take reasonable precautions to protect it from loss, misuse and unauthorized access, disclosure, alteration and destruction.

"**DATA INTEGRITY:** Consistent with the Principles, personal information must be relevant for the purposes for which it is to be used. An organization may not process personal information in a way that is incompatible with the purposes for which it has been collected or subsequently authorized by the individual. To the extent necessary for those purposes, an organization should take reasonable steps to ensure that data is reliable for its intended use, accurate, complete, and current.

"**ACCESS:** Individuals must have access to personal information about them that an organization holds and be able to correct, amend, or delete that information where it is inaccurate, except where the burden or expense of providing access would be disproportionate to the risks to the individual's privacy in the case in question, or where the rights of persons other than the individual would be violated.

"**ENFORCEMENT:** Effective privacy protection must include mechanisms for assuring compliance with the Principles, recourse for individuals to whom the data relate affected by non-compliance with the Principles, and consequences for the organization when the Principles are not followed. At a minimum, such mechanisms must include (a) readily available and affordable independent recourse mechanisms by which each individual's complaints and disputes are investigated and resolved by reference to the Principles and damages awarded where the applicable law or private sector initiatives so provide; (b) follow-up procedures for verifying that the attestations and assertions businesses make about their privacy practices are true and that privacy practices have been implemented as presented; and (c) obligations to remedy problems arising out of failure to comply with the Principles by organizations announcing their adherence to them and consequences for such organizations. Sanctions must be sufficiently rigorous to ensure compliance by organizations."

SOURCE: Reprinted from <http://www.export.gov/safeharbor/SHPRINCIPLESFINAL.htm>.

of enforcement and redress for privacy violations. It places unreasonable burdens on consumers and unfairly requires European citizens to sacrifice their legal right to pursue privacy complaints through their national authorities. The proposal also fails to ensure that individual consumers will be able to access personal information obtained by businesses."[21]

The controversy illustrates what is bound to be a continuing debate between those who see hybrid regulation as the answer to the conflicting approaches and inconsistent regulations between one country and another, and those who see it as a threat to the existing protections that national regulation provides in at least some countries. Experience gained in these next years with the Safe Harbor agreement may well provide important evidence for future decisions on whether or not to use this approach.

6.3 FREEDOM OF INFORMATION

The term "freedom of information," as used in this report, is not only a legal concept but also a social and political one. In the former sense, it refers to the legally enforceable right of access to information—an individual right. But in the social and political sense, it is a measure of the openness of the society, as discussed below. It is in this context that we may define what kinds of information ought to be accessible and, additionally, begin to understand the associated conflicts in public and private interests.

6.3.1 The Value Involved

As pointed out in the introduction to this chapter, freedom of information is a formal value. Adherence to this value safeguards transparency and accountability of governmental action, and it is closely related to the Western concept of democracy. Access to information gives citizens a sense of ownership of their society, and it creates confidence in the legitimacy and appropriateness of government administration. Freedom of information is a tool for engaging citizens in the work of government, alerting them to any excesses of government, and providing them with the basis to exercise their rights and obligations more knowledgeably. In

[21]Available online at <http://www.epic.org/privacy/intl/TACD_SH_1299.html>.

Thomas Jefferson's words, "The best protection of a democratic society is an informed public."

Technological developments have affected the availability of information in at least two ways. First, the Internet and the World Wide Web have made it increasingly practical for enormous amounts of information to be made available—quickly, easily, and inexpensively—to the public. The complete texts of laws, court records, judicial findings, administrative rules and records, statements of public officials, transcripts or minutes of public meetings, and the like can all be put online for the public to access, copy, or search. This is an extraordinary new tool for implementing freedom of information in societies unambiguously committed to that value. However, it is also a challenge to those who are less than enthusiastic about such total disclosure (and who, in the past, could be shielded from the need to justify restrictions on the distribution of information by simply citing its impracticality).

Second, new computer tools allow the manipulation and reorganization of data and records into much more useful and transparent forms. Tools for searching, filtering, organizing, and analyzing data can produce intermediate products that, in a very practical sense, make the raw data significantly more accessible and, in so doing, make freedom of information as much a practical reality as a formal commitment or value. However, these new technical tools create two problems. First, the very capacity to manipulate and mine public data may expose private information embedded within it; thus a formal balancing of interests is involved in the collection and publication of data for public purposes. Again, this is a problem that did not need to be urgently confronted in the past because of the practical limitations on teasing the private information out of the public database.

Furthermore, because many intermediate data products serve a public purpose, it is in the public interest for government to encourage the growth of markets for these products. That means creating incentives for the private sector to invest in their development. Generally, these incentives have taken the form of intellectual-property protection. Conflict then arises in determining what balance between the public nature of information and the private protection of intellectual property will maximize freedom of information as a practical reality.

In the following sections, such conflicts and tensions are examined in the context of specific kinds of public information and specific legal approaches.

6.3.2 Types of Information Subject to Freedom of Information

Primary Legal Information

"Primary legal information"—information having the force of law, such as parliamentary enactments, judicial decisions,[22] and comparable instruments from administrative agencies such as rules and orders—is the raw material of democracy. Most observers committed to freedom of information would agree that making primary legal information widely accessible to the public is not only consistent with individual rights but also important for effective governance. Indeed, if the public doesn't know the law, it can't follow it. In addition, if it doesn't have complete access to information about the operations of government, it can't exercise democratic oversight. Thus there is an overriding public interest in easy and inexpensive access to primary legal information.

An important and ongoing controversy related to the public's right to legal information is the issue of who may hold a copyright on information subject to disclosure under freedom-of-information laws. If private entities obtain information from public entities under such laws and then reorganize it, may they copyright the product thus created? If so, what does the copyright cover?

In the United States, these controversial questions have been raised in connection with the U.S. Congress's consideration of two database-protection bills[23] modeled in part on the European database-protection directive.[24] Specifically, both of these proposed bills would have granted certain property-like rights to database owners entirely apart from whatever copyright interest they did or did not hold; in general, these rights would have forbidden other parties from extracting large quantities of information from these databases in a way that caused financial harm to the database owner.

On the other hand, federal entities in the United States are precluded from copyrighting public information. In Germany, the situation is slightly more complicated. According to Article 5 of the Copyright Act,

---

[22]Germany is a civil-law country. Court decisions thus do not, in and of themselves, have legal force *erga omnes*, though the decisions of the upper courts have high persuasive authority. This does not, however, change the desirability of having easy and inexpensive access to their texts.

[23]H.R. 354 in the 106th Congress, the Collections of Information Antipiracy Act, and H.R. 1858 IH, the Consumer and Investor Access to Information Act of 1999.

[24]Directive 96/9/EC of the European Parliament and of the Council of 11 March 1996 on the legal protection of databases (O.J. 27/3/96 no L 77 p. 20).

"Laws, ordinances, official decrees and notices [and] also decisions and official grounds [for] decisions" cannot be copyrighted. The same applies to other official works published to satisfy the official goal of informing the public. But information collected and maintained by public agencies can be granted a private copyright when it is material actually written by private individuals.

In the United States, some courts have held that certain state and local laws can sometimes be copyrighted, and have forced third parties to refrain from reproducing or distributing primary legal information contained in such statutes and court decisions. For example, Peter Veeck posted on a private Web site the municipal building code for Denison, Texas. The text of this building code is actually owned by the Southern Building Code Congress International (SBCCI), a private, not-for-profit organization whose primary mission is to develop and maintain a set of model building codes. The SBCCI has developed the building code and gives it free to municipalities as an incentive for adopting it. However, sales of the code to engineers and architects is a revenue-generating enterprise for SBCCI, and thus it sued Veeck for copyright infringement. The case is working its way through the U.S. court system; in February 2001, a panel of the Fifth Circuit Court of Appeals upheld by a vote of 2-1 that SBCCI had the right to force Veeck to refrain from publishing these materials on the Web.[25]

It has been argued in the past that the private publication of government information is the only practical way to ensure its broad distribution, and that the incentive of copyright protection is necessary to encourage the involvement of the private sector. However, Internet and PC technologies have sharply reduced the costs and increased the ability of government agencies to publish their own material. As noted earlier, these same technologies have also created incentives for the private sector to create value-added products from the raw data produced by government agencies. The challenge is to develop appropriate criteria to protect private-sector innovations that enhance the usability of original government data without depriving the public of its access to that data.[26]

---

[25]The opinion of the panel can be found at <http://www.ca5.uscourts.gov/opinions/pub/99/99-40632-cv0.htm>. A press article on this controversy is in Daniel Fisher, 2001, "We Own That Law," *Forbes*, April 30, p. 60.

[26]This is a topic of ongoing debate in the United States. The Computer Science and Telecommunications Board is participating in a National Research Council project that addresses these issues for weather-related information.

Public Records Containing Personal Information

Public records that contain personal information create an obvious conflict between freedom of information and privacy rights. In principle, this is not a new concern, but advances in information technology have made it a practical concern. In the past, the cost and effort of extracting personal data from public records was so great that few attempted it. However, as such records are computerized and become available under freedom-of-information law, the threat to privacy becomes quite real.

Whether privacy or freedom of information takes precedence depends on the particular situation. If the invasion of an individual's privacy is limited and noninjurious, one might argue that the cost is worth the benefit of retaining the public's access to government information. On the other hand, if the interest in access to public records is purely commercial and unrelated to the democratic and integrative functions of freedom of information, then one might argue that protection of individual privacy should be given greater weight.

In addition to facilitating the mining of databases for personal information, technological advances affect the balance of rights in two other ways. First, information technology enables "profiling"—the linking of data from a number of different sources to create much more serious invasions of individual privacy than would be possible with any single record. The possibilities for such profiling are thus an element in judging the harm to individuals that results from granting access to public records, though the number of actual instances in which an individual has been harmed by profiling is apparently small. Second, and on the other hand, information technology also facilitates the anonymization of data, a practice that can help to protect privacy without compromising the public's access to the aggregated database.[27]

Some have argued that anonymizing data can reduce its worth because the process essentially blocks certain information that might, in fact, be useful. But that raises the question of whether the competing principles of privacy and public interest have, in the past, been thoroughly weighed in deciding what information on individuals it is appropriate for governments to collect. In the past, the government may have had no alternative but to gather more information than it had a right to gather, in order to glean the information that it needed and to which it was entitled. The practice may not have been challenged because, as a practical matter, there were limitations on the misuse of the private data. However, the

[27]Such an outcome depends on the particulars of the data in question, because sometimes even anonymized data can be assembled in such a way as to uniquely identify an individual.

mere fact that the government has collected or is in possession of the aggregated database does not mean that it is actually entitled to use all of the data or to use it for any purpose. Because technology increases the ability to link information, the potential for such misuse by government—and others—increases, and government agencies will have to revise their past approaches to collecting data and weigh the competing claims of privacy and public need more rigorously.

Notes, Drafts, and Intermediate Documents of Public Officials and Bodies

Documents that shed light on the administrative aspects of government's decision-making process (e.g., preliminary or internal drafts) present thorny problems, and how far a society should go in providing access to such documents is a matter requiring much further discussion.[28] On the one hand, transparency in the political and administrative decision-making process is of major importance in a democracy and one of the strongest arguments for a freedom-of-information principle. On the other hand, disclosure of every conversation and recorded thought between administrators or judges and their advisors would have a chilling effect on candid deliberation that would, in fact, reduce the quality of decisions. Government needs space and time in which to assess arguments and conduct internal debates with a certain degree of privacy of its own.

Technology (though not necessarily as part of global networks) again complicates matters. In the past, a good deal of highly informal conversation might have taken place on the telephone or in face-to-face meetings. It was *possible* to record these kinds of conversations, but not required.[29] When they were recorded, they might well have been subject to freedom-of-information requests (or subpoena, as Richard Nixon learned). The applicability of freedom-of-information regulations in these instances was often debated, even litigated. But the participants had an option that allowed them to control the balance between privacy privilege and the public's right to information; except where public meetings were involved (itself a question of definition), they could decide whether or not to record the conversation.

---

[28]It was discussed in the United Kingdom. See "Your Right to Know. The Government's Proposals for a Freedom of Information Act," presented to Parliament by the Chancellor of the Duchy of Lancaster by Command of Her Majesty, December 1997. Available online at <http://www.official-documents.co.uk/document/caboff/foi/foi.htm> (03.03.2000).

[29]Indeed, in many jurisdictions, it would be illegal to record such conversations—for example, if the recording were carried out by third parties or without appropriate notice.

Now, many of these same interactions are conducted through vehicles such as e-mail or bulletin board postings. Electronic records of these exchanges exist and are frequently the subject of freedom-of-information requests. In effect, technology has shifted the balance and the control without any change in the substantive social and political facts. In this, as in other instances, each society must determine if the shift is consistent with its balance of the values involved. The technology itself should not be the determining factor.

Records Associated with Publicly Funded Research

A relatively new area of contention, particularly in the United States, is the public accessibility of research data produced with government grants. Although the principle of openness in research is, in and of itself, an important value in the scientific community, freedom-of-information requests for scientific data in recent years seem to have been motivated by political agendas outside that community. As scientists have become more engaged in issues with strong political overtones—such as the health effects of tobacco, the environmental effects of industrial wastes, or the relative contributions of nature and nurture to I.Q., lawyers, lobbyists, and other advocates have sought access to scientists' raw data. The reasons for such requests vary, and how they are viewed depends on the eye of the beholder. What is seen by one party as a legitimate attempt to understand the basis of a scientist's conclusions can be seen by another as an effort to discredit or harass.

The matter has been further complicated by the heightened concern about scientific fraud. Public bodies, including congressional committees, have sought access to the notebooks of scientists in order to assess the veracity of their published works. They have used forensic approaches to determine the time sequence of notebook entries, the actual (expected) randomness in raw data, the inclusion or exclusion of data in final reports, and the laboratory instruments actually used in measurements. In so doing, they have tried to assess not only the integrity of scientists, but their competence as well.

In some respects, this is a rather new facet of the issue of privacy. That is, to what extent is the practice of one's profession—the way one thinks, how one creates, what one's personal style is like—a public activity for which the researcher must be accountable? Where should we draw the line between legitimate access and inappropriate revelation of one's personal information and idiosyncrasies? The balance to be struck must ensure accountability while respecting the intellectual process and avoiding the chilling effects of harassment or intimidation.

The U.S. Congress attempted to balance these considerations in a law recently enacted[30] that requires all recipients of federal research grants to disclose research data in accordance with the provisions of the Freedom of Information Act. However, the law defines the term "research data" as "the recorded factual material commonly accepted in the scientific community as necessary to validate research findings, but not" such things as trade secrets, commercial information, personnel and medical information, and any "similar information which is protected under law." In addition, it limits the application of the new provision to "research data relating to published research findings," which it defines as either "[r]esearch findings [that] are published in a peer-reviewed scientific or technical journal" or those that are "publicly and officially cite[d] . . . in support of an agency action that has the force and effect of law." It is too early to assess the effects of the law, because it is still being shaped as administrators develop rules for its enforcement and requests for information lead to court cases that will provide further interpretation. Certainly, the issue remains one of great concern to the scientific community.

6.3.3 Global Networks Affecting Freedom of Information

As with privacy, global networks exert direct and indirect pressure on national disclosure policies. Global networks are multiplying the options through which citizens can gain access to information and are making it more difficult for nations to maintain restrictive policies.

New Technical Options

In the past, even if the public was legally entitled to access governmental files, in practical terms it was not easy to exercise this right. In the earliest times, the citizen had to go to the appropriate office and transcribe excerpts by hand. Photocopiers significantly reduced the logistical burden on these efforts. But the digital representation of public documents means that they can be searched, stored, and combined at will. Moreover, if these files are available online, access becomes so comfortable that it can become a routine operation for citizens.

There has been considerable progress in this direction. Congressional legislation is available online; all of the opinions of the U.S. federal appellate courts are available in full-text form and in popular word-processing formats on the Web, and a growing number of state courts and agencies

---

[30]Office of Management and Budget's Appropriations Act for Fiscal Year 1999, Public Law No. 105-227. See FOIA Update, Vol. XIX. No. 4, available online at <http://www.usdoj.gov/oip/foia_updates/Vol_XIX_4/page2.htm> (03.03.2000).

also publish information on the Web. German authorities are moving into the same direction, albeit at a somewhat slower pace. All decisions of the *Bundesverfassungsgericht* are already available online free of charge. Other federal courts in Germany are planning to follow, and the European Commission has launched a similar initiative.

The Modest Effect of Globalization

Although the Internet has had a strong impact on national policies concerning free speech and privacy, its effect on FOI policies is much weaker because it is the disclosure of information held by *local* governments that is often at issue. Global networks do not change the local character of the source. Thus, even under changed technological conditions, each country can in principle pursue its own policy. However, for a number of reasons, this may be an unwise choice for nations where present policy appears to limit freedom of information, or at least to not promote it vigorously.

First, global networks expose people to new ideas from other places. Thus citizens in a more restrictive nation who see examples of governmental openness in other nations may demand more openness and access at home.[31] Given the pronounced differences in regulatory traditions, there is a great potential for such policy diffusion. Of course, it took hundreds of years for the legal structure providing for freedom of information to spread beyond the borders of Sweden (where the first law on the subject was enacted in 1766). But with the present high degree of connectedness between nations it is inconceivable that a concept such as freedom of information could long remain contained within the borders of one or a few nations. Other hastening factors include the concept's inherently democracy-promoting character, the United States' broad commitment to it, and its manifestation on the Web.

In the United States, freedom-of-information norms are expressed in a collection of federal and state statutes: the Freedom of Information Act of 1966;[32] the Paperwork Reduction Act of 1980 (revised subsequently in 1995);[33] the Federal Register Act of 1935;[34] and the Electronic Freedom of

---

[31]Of course, such change is possible only when the government of the more restrictive nation is responsive to the popular will. Indeed, some government—in general, those of the more authoritarian nations—may impose restrictions on access to certain Internet content precisely in order to *prevent* their citizens from seeing the openness of other nations.

[32]5 U.S.C. § 552.

[33]Paperwork Reduction Act of 1980 (94 Stat. 2825; 44 U.S.C. § 3503 note) [set out as a note under § 3503 of Title 44, Public Printing and Documents].

[34]44 U.S.C. § 1505.

Information Act of 1996.[35] Most American states also have freedom-of-information laws. These typically adopt the same norms as those of the federal laws. There are, however, some differences. Many states provide no deadlines for agency responses to private requests for information. Others are vague about the availability of judicial review. Still others require the identification of a legitimate private interest in the information requested. And some distinguish between requests that are made for personal reasons, which are favored, and those made by commercial entities for a profit-making purpose, which are not favored.[36]

Germany, on the other hand, has not yet established a Freedom of Information Act at the federal level. The only applicable provisions are those of the German Basic Law art. 5, subsec. 1[37] and the Federal Law on Administrative Procedure §§ 29, 30.[38] These legal instruments, however, actually express a principle of secrecy rather than openness, restricting provision of information on administrative procedures to persons who take part in the procedures or who might be affected by their outcomes. This tradition obviously does not give rise to a general public right to government information, and no other specific law addresses such access.

Still, there is currently some movement away from government secrecy and toward greater transparency, both in Germany and throughout Europe. The general approach is to build on the foundation of individual rights, beginning with the existing rights of participants in particular proceedings to obtain information pertinent to those proceedings. This is rather different from the American approach, which links freedom of information to democratic oversight of governmental operations and thus grants rights of access to all citizens. Nonetheless, the strategy has already been successful in several cases. For example, in 1994, the German Federal Freedom of Access to Environmental Information Act was adopted,[39] implementing a European Union directive granting access to environmental information held by public authorities.[40]

---

[35]Electronic FOIA Amendments Act of 1996, P.L. 104-231, 110 Stat. 3048 (Oct. 2, 1996), amending 5 U.S.C. § 552.

[36]Media requests, which obviously serve commercial, profit-making purposes, have always been given exceptional status in the United States under the protection of the First Amendment of the Constitution (see Chapter 8).

[37]Grundgesetz für die Bundesrepublik Deutschland of May 23, 1949 (BGBl. I S. 1) as amended up to and including Gesetz zur Änderung des Grundgesetzes of July 16, 1998 (BGBl. I S. 1822).

[38]Verwaltungsverfahrensgesetz vom 25 Mai 1976 (BGBl. I S. 1253), as amended up to and including Gesetz of August 6, 1998 (BGBl I 1998, 2022).

[39]BGBl. I, 1490.

[40]Council Directive 90/313/EEC of 7 June 1990 on the freedom of access to information on the environment, Official Journal L 158, 23/06/1990, p. 0056-0058. See <http://europa.eu.int/eur-lex/en/lif/dat/1990/en_390L0313.html>. Note that the directive allows a number

On the state level, the East German States of Brandenburg and Mecklenburg-Vorpommern provide a general right of access to information in their constitutions. General freedom-of-information acts were also enacted in Brandenburg[41] and Berlin[42] in 1998 and 1999, respectively. However, comprehensive nationwide or EU-wide legislation on freedom of information is not yet a reality, although it is becoming a goal. Indeed, the present coalition government in Germany has expressed its intention to enact a general freedom-of-information law on the federal level. In addition, Directorate General 13 of the European Commission has been working for more than 5 years on the development of a legal regime for freedom of information, seeking to implement the transparency guarantee of the Maastricht treaty. However, recently published drafts have been criticized for being too tentative (Box 6.9).

Second, the impact of global networks is not limited to disseminating a normative yardstick. A restrictive national policy with respect to freedom-of-information principles can be undermined to a certain extent by use of the Internet. Ironically, this became obvious recently as drafts of the European Community's freedom-of-information regulation were leaked and published on the Internet.

Third, and perhaps most important, economic considerations in a globalized world may provide an even stronger motivation for adopting freedom-of-information principles in Germany. As the European Commission's "Green Paper on Access to Public Information"[43] states, "Without user-friendly and readily available administrative, legislative, financial, or other public information, economic actors cannot make fully informed decisions." Therefore, the Commission notes, "the ready availability of public information is an absolute prerequisite for the competitiveness of European industry. In this respect, EU companies are at a serious competitive disadvantage compared to their American counter-

---

of exemptions that specify environmental information that can be withheld from the public. Specifically, it may be withheld if the release of the information affects the "confidentiality of the proceedings of public authorities, international relations and national defence; public security; matters which are, or have been, sub judice, or under inquiry (including disciplinary inquiries), or which are the subject of preliminary investigation proceedings; commercial and industrial confidentiality, including intellectual property; the confidentiality of personal data and/or files; material supplied by a third party without that party being under a legal obligation to do so; material the disclosure of which would make it more likely that the environment to which such material related would be damaged." In addition, requests for information may be refused "where it would involve the supply of unfinished documents or data or internal communications, or where the request is manifestly unreasonable or formulated in too general a manner."

[41]Akteneinsichts- und Informationszugangsgesetz (AIG) vom 10. März 1998 (GVBl. I S. 46).

[42]Berliner Informationsfreiheitsgesetz vom 15. Oktober 1999 (GVBl. I, S.561).

[43]COM (1998) 585 final.

BOX 6.9 No Secrets About Public Access Regulation?

Any citizen of the Union . . . shall have a right of access to European Parliament, Council and Commission documents subject to the principles and the conditions to be defined. (Article 255 of the Treaty establishing the European Communities [Amsterdam Treaty]).

The European Commission was charged with drawing up a draft regulation governing the public's "right of access" to documents from the Commission, Council, and European Parliament, according to Article 255 of the Amsterdam Treaty. The Commission's original intention was to publish a "communication" (discussion paper) and then draft a regulation. Drafts of this communication were leaked to Statewatch, a nongovernmental organization (NGO) that monitors state and civil liberties in the European Union, in April 1999. The document was widely circulated and subject to strong criticism by other NGOs, members of Parliament, and academics. In June 1999 the Commission decided to withdraw the publication of the draft communication from its agenda and proceeded instead straight to the draft regulation of the European Commission's "Proposal for a Regulation on Public Access to Documents of the European Parliament, the Council and the Commission." Statewatch again obtained "unpublished" drafts and published them on its Web site, criticizing the draft as "a new regulation which will completely undermine the intent and spirit of the Amsterdam Treaty to 'enshrine' the citizen's right of access to documents." Tony Bunyan, Statewatch editor, said, "We have obtained a copy and we intend to ensure that it is 'reproduced' as widely as possible so that civil society can register its anger that such a proposal could even be considered in a democratic Europe."

SOURCE: See <http://www.statewatch.org> (04.03.00).

parts, which benefit from a highly developed, efficient public-information system at all levels of the administration." In addition, public-sector information may itself be a vehicle for economic growth, as the public sector is the biggest single producer of information in areas such as legislation, statistics, culture, finance, geography, transport, and research. Box 6.10 provides more discussion.

Because nations can determine their own FOI policies that are, in their essence, nonoverlapping, there is no particular need for international harmonization of freedom-of-information laws. It is important, how-

BOX 6.10 Economic Significance of Access to Governmental Information

" . . . [I]t is important that efforts made by the public sector to render information accessible for commercial exploitation are recognized and rewarded. At the same time, if the private sector is to develop competitive products from public-sector information, the [source] materials must be available to them at a reasonable price.

"Pricing is therefore a crucial issue for the exploitation of public-sector information by the content industries. It largely determines whether they will [have] an interest in investing in value-added products and services based on public-sector information. American companies benefit from the fact that they can obtain U.S. public-sector information [at no cost].

"An American software firm is about to release a business mapping software product allowing users to find and illustrate points on the map, integrate maps in their documents, and identify the trends of their business on the map. The objective is to make it easy for business users in organizations of any size to use maps to make better-informed business decisions. Over 15 million addressed street-level segments are included for all U.S. and worldwide country-level boundaries. The estimated retail price of the product is $109.

"As an element of comparison, a German map-information company is offering geodata for [a single] German state . . . for a total of 9,728 DM + VAT 16%."

SOURCE: Excerpted from European Commission, 1998, "Green Paper on Access to Public Information," COM 585.

ever, to ensure that international treaties do not hamper national freedom-of-information policies. A case in point is internationally harmonized copyright law. So far, the pertinent international rules are silent with respect to copyrighting governmental information; neither the TRIPs agreements under the WTO treaty,[44] the Berne treaty,[45] nor the

[44]The TRIPS Agreement (Agreement on Trade-Related Aspects of Intellectual Property Rights) is Annex 1C of the Marrakesh Agreement Establishing the World Trade Organization signed in Morocco on 15 April 1994. It is available online at <http://www.wto.org/english/tratop_e/trips_e/t_agm0_e.htm>.

[45]Berne Convention for the Protection of Literary and Artistic Works of September 9, 1886, as amended on September 28, 1979, UNTS No. 11850, available online at <http://www.wipo.int/treaties/ip/index.html>.

World Intellectual Property Organization (WIPO) conventions[46] deal with the issue. If they were extended to such information, the potential for conflict between treaty obligation and FOI for government data would be obvious.

NOTE ADDED IN PROOF

In the wake of the horrific events in New York City and Washington, D.C., on September 11, 2001, the "Uniting and Strengthening America by Providing Appropriate Tools Required to Intercept and Obstruct Terrorism" (USA PATRIOT) Act was enacted into law (P.L. 107-56). Reflecting congressional concern that the legislative tools available to law enforcement were inadequate in an advanced-technology environment in which terrorists can freely travel and operate relatively free of the constraints imposed by national borders, the act expanded government authority to monitor Internet traffic, to compel disclosure of information contained in public and private records if approved by the judicial branch, and to share information collected in grand jury investigations with "any Federal law enforcement, intelligence, protective, immigration, national defense, or national security official in order to assist the official receiving that information in the performance of his official duties."[47] This legislation has implications for privacy interests of individuals vis à vis government, and a number of public interest groups have strongly criticized this legislation for weakening protection for these interests.[48]

In addition, in the freedom of information domain, the Bush administration has promulgated a policy that "discretionary decision by [a federal] agency to disclose information protected under the FOIA should be made only after full and deliberate consideration of the institutional, commercial, and personal privacy interests that could be implicated by disclosure of the information. . . . When [an agency] carefully consider[s] FOIA requests and decide[s] to withhold records, in whole or in part, [it] can be assured that the Department of Justice will defend [its] decisions unless they lack a sound legal basis or present an unwarranted risk of adverse impact on the ability of other agencies to protect other important records."[49]

---

[46]WIPO Copyright Treaty adopted by the Diplomatic Conference on certain copyright and neighboring rights questions, Geneva, on December 20, 1996 and WIPO Performances and Phonograms Treaty adopted by the Diplomatic Conference on December 20, 1996. Available online at <http://www.wipo.int/treaties/ip/index.html>.

[47]See <http://thomas.loc.gov/cgi-bin/bdquery/z?d107:h.r.03162:>.

[48]See, for example <http://www.cdt.org/press/011025press.shtml> and <http://www.epic.org>.

[49]See <http://www.usdoj.gov/oip/foiapost/2001foiapost19.htm>.

7

The Impact of Global E-Commerce on Local Values

7.1 INTRODUCTION

Given the great potential that the Internet offers for commercial applications, it is hardly a surprise that e-commerce has become a subject of intense interest. There is a growing literature on market opportunities, business strategies, transaction efficiency and security, electronic currency, intellectual property, tax policy, trade policy, and other regulatory issues related to doing business electronically. Indeed, the National Research Council has itself produced a number of reports relevant to several aspects of e-commerce.

This chapter does not aim to re-cover all this ground. What *is* of concern is the extent to which e-commerce affects the values of a society (and vice versa)—a more limited task, but still no small challenge. Indeed, there are at least three ways in which interactions between e-commerce and local or regional values might come about:

- To the extent that e-commerce encourages new business models, changes the relationship between seller and buyer, and challenges existing regulatory structures, it has the potential to alter certain traditional commercial values. Those values are often locally, regionally, and nationally specific, so that the effect of e-commerce on commerce itself can also be local, regional, or national.
- The continued growth of e-commerce raises the possibility that, either directly or through the institutions developed to regulate (or stimulate) the commercial uses of the global network, e-commerce may alter

the structure and/or operation of the Internet. These changes may affect the Internet's noncommercial uses as well. For example, the control of portals, the organization of browsers, the legal protections afforded to operating-system and application software, and even the control over URLs can have significant implications for all users. Indeed, the changes can alter the culture and values that characterized the "network of networks" during its formative stages.

- To the extent that commerce itself has a role in defining a local society, the changes brought about by e-commerce may affect some of the other local political and social values discussed in this report.

7.2 COMMERCE AND VALUES

Economic activity is often assumed, particularly in neoclassical models, to be largely or entirely driven by individual profit-maximizing behavior. In this utilitarian view, commerce is essentially a value-free activity. As long as institutions are properly designed to provide efficient markets with adequate property rights, freedom to enter into contracts, and strong protection against monopolies, competition and self-interest will do the rest.

The utilitarian assumption is useful for many purposes, but most observers (including economists) recognize that it is an incomplete description. The individual and group values and attitudes that are the subject of this report manifest themselves in the rich network of informal social institutions in which a market-oriented economic system is embedded. At the heart of these institutions is what might be called commercial values: personal motivation, the material dimensions of social status, and—perhaps most important—various aspects of trust. Buyers and sellers know the great value of trust and have developed ways of judging *whom* to trust. They understand that an untarnished reputation, credit rating, and reliability are essential to commercial success.

Although these fundamental values are, on the surface, much the same in most successful market economies, they manifest themselves in different ways in different nation-states. For example, Germany and the United States have very different concepts of contract. When a German firm sells a complex piece of equipment or system to another, the contract is typically no more than a few pages in length. In the United States, the contract for the same transaction might run to hundreds of pages. This difference arises, as a legal matter, out of the distinction between the civil law rules in Germany and the common law rules in the United States. The former tend to be broad and abstract, the latter quite specific as they are derived from case analysis and precedent. However, the very prevalence of those two different traditions reflects a profound value difference in the two countries. Germans appear more willing to trust the courts to "fill in the gaps" in a contractual relationship. Americans may look to the courts for redress, but expect the entire contractual relationship to be explicitly stated; what's written is what counts, and few would expect (or trust) the courts to go beyond a strict reading of the language of the contract.

Another difference in the manifestation of values between the two countries lies in how they define intellectual property. In the United States, patents and copyrights are property rights granted by the society. In Germany, they are innate or moral rights earned by an individual as a reward and recognition for his or her creation. Moreover, because it views intellectual property rights primarily as an effective stimulus to economic activity, the United States has been more flexible in defining what kinds of creative ideas are worthy of protection and has tended to extend intellectual-property protection to more and more activities, such as business processes. German law has been more cautious in allowing such extensions, perhaps coupling the deeper respect and greater protection for individual innovation with a narrower definition of what constitutes a creative act. In effect, the German system may place somewhat less emphasis on intellectual-property protection as a stimulus to economic activity and approach the issue primarily as a balance between individual rights and the rights of the public to have access to new ideas.

This governmental responsibility and concern for protecting the rights of the public is also evident in German attitudes and law concerning competitive practices. Germany places severe constraints on borderline marketing practices and exaggerated advertising claims, and competitors are quick to seek judicial relief when it appears that the line has been crossed. The consumer is assumed to be vulnerable and entitled to protection, and there are a host of default and mandatory rules in commercial law to provide that protection. In the United States, there is much less interference with market transactions, per se, and the order of the day is caveat emptor. On the other hand, the United States has product-liability laws that are much more severe than in Germany, and liability suits leading to very large jury awards are much more common in the United States.

These examples illustrate the values of commerce that relate to commerce itself. But commerce also provides some of the glue for a society. Its form and dynamics shape a society as much as commerce is shaped by it. Exchanging goods and services is a means by which people connect. The suburban malls and chain restaurants of most U.S. cities build different kinds of community relationships than the pedestrian-oriented, city shops and cafes of most European cities. And businesses are not only commercial but also social organizations. The GE employee who carries a laminated card enunciating the company's principles and commitments has not merely entered a business relationship but has become part of a defining social system. The German worker who has built a relationship with a specific corporation since his or her apprenticeship days has developed a social structure as well as a stable employment situation.

E-commerce enters the picture in two ways. First, network-related commercial values differ, at least in emphasis, from other commercial values. Second, by competing with local commercial systems and wresting market share from them, e-commerce can weaken their embedded values.

7.3 THE IMPACT OF E-COMMERCE ON LOCAL COMMERCIAL VALUES

7.3.1 The Globalization of Markets

Because global networks reduce the distance-related transaction costs of certain kinds of business, they may clearly increase the magnitude of international commerce and change the cast of participants. Electronic commerce may be of several kinds. Business-to-consumer traffic encompasses the range of transactions between firms and end users, from purchase of goods to information and financial services. Business-to-business transactions offer opportunities to develop efficient auction-based platforms for procurement and supply-chain management systems that are very attractive to large corporations. Business-to-government exchanges make it practical for many new and smaller players to enter the international market.

Commercial opportunities on the Internet both arise from and are limited by the fact that only digitized information moves through the network. This makes it a natural medium for activities that depend on the movement or manipulation of information—including words, numbers, symbols, and descriptors or digital representations of shape, color, and sound. Databases and the tools for using them, as well as many other kinds of software programs, obviously fit this description, and it is not surprising that a large fraction of Internet trade occurs in these "soft goods." But other kinds of digital content are fast catching up. Financial services are expanding and, as bandwidth increases, so is the flow of real-time audio and video files. Search engines have pioneered new ways of allowing interactive information retrieval. Furthermore, customized advice and support are increasingly being provided through the Internet.

Many kinds of tangible goods are also traded on the Internet, though still constituting a relatively small fraction of total activity. The advantages of the Net for hard goods come into play in different phases of the value chain: price-setting mechanisms, including auction formats, can be set up; procurement can be carried out electronically; and billing and maintenance services can be executed. These services are becoming more attractive as technical and regulatory issues related to security and anonymity are resolved.

The globalizing effect of networks on these types of commerce differs markedly. Trade in hard goods is less likely to be globalized than soft goods because the merchandise needs to be physically transported and is subject to the same delays and border controls as non-e-traded goods. Even for soft goods, globalization can be hindered by bandwidth capacity in different parts of the world. In this latter case, however, technical improvements in physical networks and wireless communications, and political developments that increase the openness of certain societies, will markedly reduce the barriers to global e-commerce.

One of those barriers is the difficulty of establishing the level of trust that has always been an important part of commerce generally and that has been built up in particular ways within local regions and nations. Some have argued[1] that the problem is exacerbated when information products are involved because of the lack of "transparency" of information. That is, it is difficult to judge a priori how well the product will serve the purpose for which it was purchased. In that sense, information goods can be categorized as "experience" or even "credence" goods. Experience goods are those whose quality can be judged only by use—i.e., after the purchase has become binding. With credence goods, the purchaser can never really assess the quality of the good.[2]

Technical approaches to credit validation, seals of approval, and cooperation among national governments can help to develop new approaches to trust building. Producers also spend a great deal on marketing, providing free information about the good, as well as samples or demonstration versions. Large firms in business-to-business transactions can use initial face-to-face meetings to establish the trust basis for an ongoing business relationship. Firms marketing branded goods or services over a long period of time will also have little trouble. But small businesses will not necessarily have these and other mechanisms available for generating trust across large distances and national borders. Intermediaries such as eBay, that solicit and publish the ratings of buyers and sellers, will undoubtedly have a greater role.

---

[1]See Bradford DeLong and Michael Froomkin, 2000, "Speculative Microeconomics for Tomorrow's Economy," in Brian Kahin and Hal R. Varian, eds., *Internet Publishing and Beyond*, Cambridge, MA: MIT Press.

[2]These concepts have been developed by G.A. Akerlof, 1970, "The Market for 'Lemons.' Quality Uncertainty and the Market Mechanism," *Quarterly Journal of Economics* 84:488-500. They have been applied to information in M. Kretschmer, G. Klimis, and J.C. Chong, 1999, "Increasing Returns and Social Contagion in Cultural Industries," *British Journal of Management* 10:61 ff.

7.3.2 Business on the Internet

There is an ongoing debate concerning the extent to which production and distribution decisions in the information economy differ from those in manufacturing industries.[3] But the emerging consensus is that e-commerce leads to fundamentally different "business models."

Network Effects

The spread of a hardware or software standard is accompanied by an exponential increase in the usefulness of that standard for its users, as more and more elements can be connected to an interactive system. According to "Metcalfe's Law," the value of a network increases in approximate proportion to the square of its numbers of users—or, to be more precise, the potential value, V, is proportional to n(n–1).[4] While some may disagree about the magnitude of the effect or the precise functional relationship between number of users and value, the benefit of communications technologies depends crucially on the number of those participating in their use. This effect has been observed in many consumer-product markets. Often, it leads to veritable "standards wars," as in the case of the two video recorder standards VHS and Betamax. It also applies in the production sector.

In every case, we find a shift away from competitive equilibria, in which there are many suppliers, and toward single-firm equilibria. These monopolists have a strong interest in locking customers into network relationships. Concepts like trust, reputation, loyalty, and commitment play a key role in the business strategies of online companies.[5] We also find new strategies for price setting, from giving away products to complex schemes of price discrimination.[6] Although it can be argued that competition remains intact—because of a fierce contest for the maintenance and eventual replacement of such network monopolies—the recent evidence

---

[3]Among the two leading contributions, Shapiro and Varian take a more conservative view, whereas Kelly foresees sweeping changes for fundamental concepts such as property and scarcity. See Kevin Kelly, 1998, *New Rules for the New Economy. 10 Radical Strategies for a Connected World,* Harmondsworth: Viking Penguin; and Carl Shapiro and Hal R. Varian, 1998, *Information Rules: A Strategic Guide to the Network Economy,* Cambridge, MA: Harvard Business School Press.

[4]For a survey of the literature, see Shapiro and Varian, 1998, p. 184.

[5]AOL, for instance, has launched a long-term campaign to increase customers' trust in its provider services.

[6]Shapiro and Varian offer the most detailed advice to the aspiring information entrepreneur, while at the same time demonstrating the economic logic behind the new strategies.

from the Microsoft case has shown that there is considerable potential for weakening the competitive process.

Production by Copy

In traditional markets, firm size is constrained by the ultimately increasing marginal cost of material resources. In markets for digital products, few material resources are needed for reproduction—which essentially consists of copying a file of binary digits. Once initial hardware costs are paid, digital copying costs are next to nothing. The largest supplier will have the lowest marginal cost and thus appear to be a "natural monopoly."

Obviously, the low cost of copying increases the incentive to command the largest share of a digital good market. It also poses problems for the protection of information products. Though the cost of assembling the original good may be very high, as in the case of new operating-system software or a movie, its digital reproduction involves a simple operation that can be carried out with little technical skill and equipment. In consequence, there is an incentive to "trespass."[7]

Properties of Information

Only information can be transformed into the digital signals that travel through global networks. Information makes its impact on users in a very specific manner: it does not change their physical state or modify their physical circumstances. Instead, it affects the users' thoughts, knowledge, or feelings. Users learn something new, or they gain pleasure, or they receive instructions to behave in ways that make them more successful.

The receipt of such signals by individuals does not destroy or alter the original message. In consequence, there is no rivalry in consuming an information good. This is the core reason why information is considered a public rather than a private good. In many cases, it is still easy to exclude those who do not pay for the consumption of the good, either through electronic walls, legal sanctions against unauthorized copying, or technical copyright-management systems (see below). Such interventions may meet the goals of an individual producer, but from a social-welfare perspective, there are inevitable losses in potential utility associated with them. That is the reason why patent and copyright statutes try to strike a tenuous balance between the temporary protection of exclusive property

[7]For a discussion of problems associated with a lack of excludability, see Bradford DeLong and Michael Froomkin, "Speculative Microeconomics for Tomorrow's Economy," 2000.

rights and the subsequent free use of new inventions, be they technical or artistic in nature.

The particular nature of information also accounts for its lack of transparency.[8] The qualities or potential defects of material goods are sometimes immediately visible. In the case of information goods, nothing can be gleaned from the appearance of a CD-ROM or a pdf file.

Producers react to this situation with a massive increase in the proportion of total expenses devoted to marketing. Prospective buyers receive free information about the good, or samples, or even demo versions in order to decrease their perceived risk. This amount of free publicity poses a problem in itself—the much-discussed "information overload"—when the entire public is exposed to these messages. On the other hand, the basic lack of transparency of information goods provides incentives to try out various schemes in order to reduce the likelihood of fraud or the delivery of inferior-quality products.

7.4 EFFECTS ON LOCAL COMMERCIAL VALUES

To the extent that global networks lead to significant increases in e-commerce, some local business ventures will clearly be subjected to competitive pressures, particularly where the transactions involve tangible goods. Of greater concern for purposes of this report, however, is the *value* competition—the degree to which Internet-based business creates tensions with local commercial values.

Because business conducted through the Internet has such different characteristics from local commerce, it requires a somewhat different set of commercial values. This is as true of e-commerce conducted within a single nation as it is of global e-commerce. In principle, individuals can adapt to operating with two sets of values, one for local commerce and another for e-commerce. But the more that traditional values become a burden or disadvantage in e-commerce, the less likely the separation can be rigidly maintained.

Globalization of e-commerce enters the picture in several ways. The degree of tension between Internet-commerce values and more traditional local ones is at least in part a function of the local value system—which, of course, differs from nation to nation. In effect, each nation faces a different challenge in resolving the discrepancies between local and Internet values. Moreover, if e-commerce transactions are global—that is, do bridge different nations—there must be some harmonization between the accommodations adopted by each of the nations.

---

[8]See DeLong and Froomkin, "Speculative Microeconomics for Tomorrow's Economy," 2000.

Commercial values, as noted earlier, are implicit in the design of the laws and the formal and informal institutions that give meaning and shape (and a regulatory framework) to such concepts as intellectual property, contracts, and competition. It is useful to examine how each of these is affected by e-commerce.

7.4.1 Intellectual Property

The recognition of intellectual property provides a means for societies to grant monopoly rights to an individual (or corporate entity) for some specified period of time. As pointed out earlier, these rights are granted to recognize and reward the inventor's creativity as well as to stimulate the creative process for the benefit of society at large. These two goals are balanced differently in each society, as a function of laws, formal and informal institutions, and other practical factors.

The legal institutions that have been developed to protect intellectual property include patents, copyrights, and trademarks.[9] Patents grant temporary rights to the inventor of a product or process that meets certain criteria of originality, usefulness, and non-obviousness. Copyrights grant temporary rights to the author or owner of a work of human expression. Traditionally, works of art, music, and literature were protected by copyright. Today, both copyright and, increasingly, patent protection has been extended to software programs and databases. Patents for software in particular have been controversial, and the practice is also not followed in all countries. Trademarks protect a visual symbol or label used as an identifying mark.

The growth of digital information and communications technologies has created a number of knotty intellectual-property problems, particularly with respect to copyright law.[10] A comprehensive discussion of the issues is presented in a separate CSTB report.[11] The comments that follow here are therefore quite brief and intended only as a summary and to touch on some recent developments.

Information and communications technologies raise issues in copyright law for several reasons. The technological capacity to manipulate, organize, and transmit information allows the generation of a large num-

---

[9]For completeness, one should include trade secrets in this group, as companies can take legal action against misappropriation of such secrets. But it is a category that is much less dependent on a specific legal structure than the others, and therefore is not treated here.

[10]In contrast, advances in molecular and cellular biology have had much greater impact on patent law.

[11]Computer Science and Telecommunications Board, National Research Council. 2000. *The Digital Dilemma. Intellectual Property in the Information Age.* Washington, D.C.: National Academy Press.

ber of new information products whose producers need (and, in many cases, deserve) intellectual-property protection. However, these products do not easily fit into one or another of the traditional intellectual-property categories. Copyright is attractive to most producers because protection can be obtained much more quickly and easily than is the case with patenting, and this has been of great value to them in a rapidly changing environment. But copyright protects only the expression of an idea, not the idea itself, leaving producers rather vulnerable to misappropriation.

For example, copyrighting the lines of code in a software program still leaves the program owner vulnerable; code can be altered to avoid copyright infringement, while the underlying design of the program is exploited. As another example, the organization of a database into a format that is much more usable than the raw (often public) data on which it is based adds value worthy of protection. But again, if the protection comes through copyright, small reformations of the data would allow others to avoid copyright infringement.

The problem is exacerbated in e-business because the same digital technologies that offer so many opportunities to create new information products and market them at very low marginal costs also make it extremely easy for others to copy those products. Indeed, they could make copies in such numbers that it might seriously reduce the size of the original producer's market. The producer's vulnerability is thus all the greater.

There are technical countermeasures, however. Copyright management systems—technologies that enable copyright owners to regulate and automatically charge for access to digital works—are now available.[12] They make it considerably easier to control the distribution of information and to trace who uses it (as well as when and how often), who copies it (legally or illegally), and who redistributes it.

Taken together, these factors are exerting pressure to change traditional attitudes toward copyright and traditional strategies for protecting it. Although copyright is a well-established element in intellectual-property protection, legal institutions have provided for "fair-use exceptions" and "first-sale limitations." In adopting these provisions, society and the law have recognized the practical limitations on monitoring every possible copyright violation and the relatively small damage to the value of intellectual property that limited and sporadic violations represent. In addition, by making the barrier to the public's unfettered use of information covered by copyright slightly porous, the system has achieved a somewhat better balance between private and public interests.

---

[12]See Julie E. Cohen, 1997, "Some Reflections on Copyright Management Systems and Laws Designed to Protect Them," *Berkeley Technology Law Journal* 12.

With the increased vulnerability that producers feel and the new tools available to them, copyright owners have generally become much less willing to tolerate the porosity that has, up until now, indirectly acknowledged and accommodated the communal property aspects of information. For example, source codes for programs are much more closely guarded than in the earlier days of information technology.[13] In addition, although database producers may only own the form of the data they market, they make efforts to restrict the easy availability of the (often) public data on which their information product is based. Major copyright holders, particularly the U.S. film industry, initially invoked provisions of international treaties in order to eliminate private copying, or fair use; these efforts were denounced as "copyright grab."[14] The issue is hardly settled, however, as the recent Napster controversy illustrates.[15] It has become clearer that illicit copying may not be as simple and inexpensive to monitor as originally thought; when such copying involves networks with several million users—representing a considerable potential market for property such as music files—copyright holders are aggressively seeking legal remedies. Thus, whether the solution ultimately lies in law or technical architecture remains to be seen.[16]

The suddenness of the changes has led to turbulence both in the diplomatic and judicial arenas. The Copyright Treaty adopted within the framework of the World Intellectual Property Organization (WIPO) by the Diplomatic Conference on December 20, 1996, requires contracting parties to provide "adequate legal protection and effective legal remedies against the circumvention of effective technological measures that are used by authors in connection with the exercise of their rights." This has given rise to a strong political reaction by groups committed to protecting

---

[13]A significant exception is the rise and continued growth of "open source" (OS) software development. OS development is a process in which many individual programmers collaborate to maintain, refine, and upgrade software. The primary example of OS development is LINUX, an operating system that is widely regarded as a highly robust operating platform. See, for example, Steve Weber, 2000, *The Political Economy of Open Source Software*, BRIE Working Paper 140.

[14]Pamela Samuelson. 1997. "Confab Clips Copyright Cartel," *Wired* 5.3, March.

[15]The Napster controversy concerned a service provided by Napster that the music recording industry believed operated in violation of copyright law. Napster did not copy copyrighted files; instead, it provided an index of titles, many of which were copyrighted, and enabled "matchmaking" between a person wanting a particular title and another person who already had that title. The latter would provide the former with the requested title, usually without compensation. In February 2001, the U.S. Court of Appeals for the Ninth Circuit upheld an injunction issued in the U.S. District Court for the Northern District of California that effectively shut down Napster. See *A&M Records, Inc. v. Napster, Inc.*, 239 F.3d 1004 (9th Cir. 2001), available at <http://www.riaa.com/pdf/napsterdecision.pdf>.

[16]Lawrence Lessig, 2000, "Architecting for Control," preprint, Stanford University.

free access to ideas and preventing interference with the "flourishing of cultural life."

The arguments have been joined in the discussions and debates surrounding the U.S. and EU legislation implementing the WIPO Treaty (the U.S. Congress has enacted the Digital Millennium Copyright Act (DMCA),[17] and the European Union promulgated Directive 2001/29/EC on the harmonization of certain aspects of copyright and related rights in the information society[18]). But these arguments have made clear that there are some significant differences between the European Union and the United States on some of the values underlying the current conflicts. The Europeans tend to emphasize the "moral rights" of the author. In contrast to pecuniary rights, moral rights are inalienable personal rights allowing an author to claim authorship and to prevent the mutilation or distortion of the work. Moral rights are rooted in natural law principles recognized by a number of European nations in civil law and in the Berne Treaty.[19]

Although the United States signed the Berne Treaty in 1989, it has been quite reluctant to grant such sweeping moral rights to authors and artists.[20] First (as the Napster case has shown), many in the U.S. public perceive that what is at issue is often the rights of owners rather than of authors or artists. Second, the United States has focused on the public value of information and the damage to research that excessive restrictions on "fair use" might cause.

The conflict is an excellent illustration of the challenge to local values that the new technologies represent. Moral rights are a component of continental European law that, if compromised, would certainly be perceived as the destruction of an important value. Indeed, an artist or writer's moral rights to a voice in all transactions involving a work of art have been introduced into the EU code. On the other hand, freedom of information has always been extremely important in the United States, and laws that

---

[17]P.L. 105-304, 112 Stat. 2860 (October 28, 1998).

[18]See <http://www.europa.eu.int/comm/internal_market/en/intprop/docs/index.htm>, or Official Journal L 167, 22/06/2001 P. 0010-0019.

[19]Article 6 bis(1), Berne Convention for the Protection of Literary and Artistic Works, No. 11850, 828 U.N.T.S. 221 (September 9, 1886) (revised 1908, 1928, 1948, 1967, 1971).

[20]As Howard B. Abrams puts it: "The fact of the matter is that the United States was anxious to join the Berne Union; and the Berne Union, and its governing body—the World Intellectual Property Organization—were quite anxious to have the United States as a member. Thus both parties have been more than willing to accept the fiction that the United States really has a right of respect, and the fact that the United States does not truly recognize moral rights will almost certainly be glossed over." See Howard B. Abrams, 1991, *The Law of Copyright*, New York, (Looseleaf) Vol. 2, § 18.02 [C][2].

might compromise it would also be perceived as the destruction of an important value.

Still, it now appears that e-commerce is leading to modifications in the underlying values of both the European Union and the United States. Where the final compromises will lead and what steps can be taken to ameliorate the perceived losses, however, are difficult to predict.

7.4.2 Contract and Consumer Protection

Successful market economies have always recognized the need to "level the playing field" between seller and buyer, particularly where the buyer is an individual consumer at a great power disadvantage with respect to typical producers and sellers. Governments have seen it as their role to provide this leveling by regulating advertising, contracts, and liability.

In an online economy, the fundamental issue is much the same—overcoming the power differential between seller and buyer—but a number of circumstances make it a somewhat more challenging task. Internet transactions will increasingly involve buyers and sellers in different nations with different commercial-law regimes. Of course, international trade is not, in itself, a new concept, and mechanisms for resolving jurisdictional disputes have long been in place. What renders the Internet situation different is that many of the buyers (and sometimes the sellers) are relatively unsophisticated, and they are not supported by the kind of legal structure that has allowed large commercial ventures to deal with such issues in the past. Thus it is likely that governments will be pressed to improve the transparency, efficiency, and reach of their mediation processes.

More than process is at issue, however. As pointed out earlier in this chapter, there are considerable differences between the European Union and the United States regarding consumer protection and the role of contracts. Europeans are more severe in restraining false advertising claims than are Americans. For their part, Americans are more literal in interpreting (and relying on) the specific wording of contracts to define and limit the obligations of seller and buyer. Yet Americans give consumers much more latitude to seek judicial relief and are more likely to hold producers financially liable for mishaps involving their products.

Thus the resolution of the different contract and consumer-protection approaches is more than a procedural problem. It begins with the need to establish the extent to which the parties have voluntarily consented to the terms of the contract. In the Internet world, with hypertext or icon-linked Web pages, contract terms may not be obviously and explicitly apparent to the buyer. Moreover, certain actions far less conscious than an explicit signature (box or button clicks online, opening a shrink-wrapped software package offline) may be taken as constituting acceptance of contractual terms. In certain cases, these terms may create continuing obligations related to the use of the product that contravene other laws in one of the constituencies involved.[21]

The problem continues with the need to resolve differences in views about the appropriate role of government in enforcing or supplementing contracts to protect consumers, which would appear to make the issue more complicated than merely one of negotiating the proper application of commercial law. Furthermore, which nation's values should apply in determining what is appropriate advertising? Should one take into account that a consumer in a country where advertising has previously been more constrained might be more vulnerable to exaggerated claims? Or, on the other hand, should a seller be expected to alter what amounts to a cultural standard by exhibiting more restraint when operating in the international setting? And should a seller be considered as "operating in an international setting" even *before* an actual transaction occurs? Finally, to what extent do competitors have standing to challenge, on the basis of laws (and their underlying values), the practices of sellers who are not in their country?

The technology of the Internet also enables a number of practices related to e-commerce that have no obvious equivalent in the non-Internet world. The practice of spamming, the use of cookies, the involuntary opening of other Web pages when one connects to a particular URL address, are all far more intrusive than sales and advertising practices offline. Therefore, each practice raises new challenges to governments in balancing the rights of sellers and consumers. Although attempts can be made to extend present law to cover these new practices, they appear to be sufficiently different from existing situations that a deeper consideration of the underlying conflicting values should first take place.

7.4.3 Competition

The Internet changes the competitive environment of commerce. Because the information space is unlimited and the entry cost is low, small entrepreneurs can enter the marketplace easily. And because direct communication between customer and entrepreneur is enhanced, transaction costs are lower. For both these reasons, the Internet appears to facilitate greater variation and diversity. Most importantly, as new niches of promising business activity are identified, large numbers of (initially) small business entities may occupy them.

---

[21]See Margaret J. Radin, 2000, "Humans, Computers and Binding Agreements," *Indiana Law Review* 75:1125.

On the other hand, the Internet especially facilitates enterprises whose success depends on network effects—"winner-takes-all" situations for companies with significant market share—which further facilitate their growth and market dominance.

This effect leaves competition and antitrust policy in a quandary: can market domination continue to be viewed as a threat to competition if gaining a (temporary) monopoly is the central strategic guideline for competitors in information-goods markets? The only actions likely to continue to be viewed as violations will be "unacceptable practices" by the temporary-monopoly holder to perpetuate that position. Even then, it may be difficult to agree on what is "unacceptable," given the long tradition of practices like tie-in sales and product bundling.

The obvious illustrative case for such violations, *U.S. v. Microsoft*,[22] is, of course, still not quite settled. However, it has already provided both the legal and the economic fields with a wealth of new insights.

Among other issues, an important aspect of the case was Microsoft's behavior during the market introduction of its Web browser, Internet Explorer. The techniques it used to push the then-incumbent standard browser, Netscape's Navigator, out of the market led to the claim that Microsoft extended its operating-system monopoly by unfair means. The trial proceedings have developed at length the arguments around "temporal natural monopolies," and the case illustrates two major controversies: whether, and how much, the use of market power should be limited; and the extent to which antitrust law should be restraining.

The network nature of global communication gives rise to another major current issue. Because the networks of competing firms are connected into larger nets, interconnection can be successively leveraged in ways that effectively exclude specific competitors. Of course, such measures can be billed (or even deliberately designed) as technical incompatibilities.[23] Exclusion can also be practiced at the basic hardware level. For example, in the absence of regulation preventing the restriction of access to last-mile telephone lines and cable networks, companies can preserve monopoly positions despite fierce price and service competition.[24]

---

[22]United States Court of Appeals for the District of Columbia Circuit, June 28, 2001, *United States of America v. Microsoft Corporation*; appeal on District Court of Columbia Circuit, 97 F. Supp. 2nd 59 (D.D.C. 2000)—Final Judgment; see also 84 F. Supp. 2nd 9 (D.D.C. 1999)—Findings of Fact and 87 F. Supp. 2nd 30 (D.D.C. 2000)—Conclusions of Law.

[23]There is also an OECD report on various countries' responses to related questions: "Competition Issues in Electronic Commerce," DAFFE7CLP (2000)32, January 2001.

[24]See Francois Bar et al., 1999, "Defending the Internet Revolution in the Broadband Era: When Doing Nothing Is Doing Harm," Berkeley: BRIE Working Paper N. 0137, August.

In the United States, antitrust has in recent years focused on economic policy, and has been aimed at enhancing efficiency. Germany has always shared that goal, but influential politicians believed that antitrust policy should also serve to protect the political process from excessive economic influence and power.[25] In the United States, on the other hand, there has been a great reticence to mix economic and political issues, as well as a greater willingness to let the market work. However, there are signs that the two systems may be converging, at least where the Internet is concerned. Still, given the track record on recent U.S.-European controversies—concerning civil-aviation subsidies, airlines' landing-rights policies, and in the major differences between U.S. and European authorities on a proposed GE-Honeywell merger—it would be a mistake to assume that the two systems are converging rapidly.

7.5 THE IMPACT OF E-COMMERCE ON GLOBAL NETWORKS

The second chapter of this report reviewed the history of the Internet and emphasized how its growth and structure were influenced by the interests and attitudes of its developers and by the "Netizen" culture, which influenced the form of this network of networks and, in turn, was supported and reinforced by that network architecture. This history illustrates the nature of technology development—an interaction between technology's "push" and the "pull" exerted by its users and adapters of a technology, an example of both "soft determinism" and "path dependence."

But the evolution of a technology does not stop at some arbitrary point. As the user community changes, the "pull" factors change, and the architecture and operating systems continue to evolve. One important current question is the extent to which the explosion of e-commerce will so shift the makeup of the user community, and so influence the structure and operation of global networks, that network values will be substantially affected.

The commercial opportunities offered by the Internet are largely related to the privatization of digitized information and, to a lesser extent, the means for obtaining and using it. On the other hand, one of the great strengths of the Internet is its ability to support and encourage public uses of information for a range of political, social, cultural, and personal purposes—obtaining it, using it, sharing it, and being able to accomplish those functions quickly, unthreateningly, and inexpensively. These are not en-

[25]For a comparative view, see several articles by David Gerber, Chicago-Kent School of Law.

tirely conflicting goals (and they together explain, in part, why there are markets for information products). However, it certainly seems prudent to be alert to ways in which e-commerce could drive alterations—in architecture, hardware, software, and regulation—that could inhibit other Internet activities and their related values. Some of these are outlined in the following paragraphs.

One of the more obvious areas of potential conflict concerns privacy, the subject of Chapter 6. Many of the commercial opportunities offered by new technologies are based on obtaining and using more complete information about consumers—their needs, tastes, and patterns. Having such information allows sellers to locate individuals who may want their services and to customize those services; developing databases that aggregate such information helps companies to plan marketing strategies. The motivation to acquire such data stimulates development of the requisite technologies—cookies, analysis of purchase records, data mining and matching—but their availability increases the potential threat to privacy.

It is important to keep in mind that this is not merely a conflict between the interests of information-product producers (or traders) and of individuals whose concern is protecting their own privacy. In fact, the individual may well realize that having the benefit of products and services customized to his or her needs depends on some other person or corporation gaining access to his or her personal information. For example, individuals may *want* the convenience of online booksellers calling certain new books to their attention, and they might appreciate the life-saving potential of a hospital's emergency room having easy access to records of their blood type and allergies.

Given the recognized usefulness of these new commercial services and their enabling technologies, the response has been not so much to preclude the gathering of information as to regulate its misuse (or its use without an individual's permission). But there are those who argue that in the long run we may actually see a devaluation of privacy per se; that is, there may be an increased willingness to relinquish certain control over one's private data in return for the perceived value of services based on the easy availability of that data.

Another area of potential conflict concerns freedom of information. It is, of course, the enormous growth in the availability of information through the Internet that has created many of the market opportunities for new kinds of Net-based intermediaries. The search engines, the derived databases, the rapid official-document publication services, and the news-scanning services all help users to sort through the information overload in order to find what they actually want. These products truly enhance the availability of information, and they reinforce one of the most significant values offered by a networked world.

But these products can also compromise freedom of information in two ways. First, there is a constant pressure on the system to protect and increase the value of a product that uses an underlying data set or open information source by extending intellectual-property protection to the underlying information, thereby making it less available to the public generally. The protests of many in the scientific community about the WIPO Copyright Treaty and the Digital Millennium Copyright Act stemmed from this kind of concern about restrictions on the availability of scientific data for use in research.

Second, there is concern that the commercial availability of derived data products will reduce the incentive for public agencies to make the same data available in convenient alternative forms. For example, if private entities mine the census data in various ways and sell the resulting products, the raw data may still be available to the public; but the incentive for government agencies to develop intermediate products (which might be inferior to the private products but still a lot more useful than the raw data) will be much reduced. And if the full, searchable text of judicial decisions or legislative actions is available from a commercial firm for a fee, these texts may still be available to the public in hard copy, but there will be less incentive for the government to provide this information online or as quickly.

Another area of potential conflict arises from the development of technologies to monitor the distribution and use of commercial information products. The purpose of these technologies is to trace who accesses such products, how often they do so, and what they do with them for purposes of billing (and subsequent marketing). These technologies can also limit access to paying subscribers, and filter information to serve clients or to conform to the requirements of law. But technologies developed for one use are, of course, available for other uses. Filters used to block offensive material from reaching a user's computer can be used by governments to filter political information. Systems for monitoring how and when people access commercial data can be deployed by governments to keep track of whom citizens communicate with and what information they receive.

Clearly, there are a number of countries in which these kinds of uses of the technology are common today. Many argue that, even though technically feasible, it is unlikely that such practices will be politically sustainable over an extended period of time. Nevertheless, it is clear that the continuing development of these and similar technologies has the potential to create a network architecture whose inherent properties no longer promote the freedom and anonymity of the early days of the Internet.

A final example relates to the practicalities of accessing and transmitting information. One of the most important characteristics of the Internet is the sheer volume of information that it permits users to access or communicate. The continual improvement in chip performance and bandwidth leads to ever-expanding capacity that, unlike the electromagnetic spectrum, is almost without limit. In principle, this should all but eliminate competition for a share of the communication space, a major issue in broadcasting and telecommunication.

But in practice, the average user depends on intermediaries such as search engines to sort through the information overload of the Internet. At the very least, both users and providers need search engines to help them find each other. A smaller but still significant number of users rely on host providers. These intermediaries are commercial entities, and one rational business strategy for them is to offer information providers greater prominence in the information universe—a first-page location in the list of "hits" for certain key words, for example, or more direct and convenient linkages from user to favored provider—for a price. In effect, market forces can tilt the playing field for information. Whether or not this occurs on a grand scale will depend on whether the market rewards intermediaries more for the quality and breadth of their service to information users than for their service to information producers.

7.6 THE IMPACT OF E-COMMERCE ON LOCAL, SOCIAL, AND POLITICAL VALUES

The impact of e-commerce on values is generally not separable from its impact on *local* values. Privacy, freedom of information, and the right of free speech, as discussed in earlier chapters of this report, are local values, though their precise interpretation may differ from one locality to another. Therefore many of the issues raised in this chapter can be interpreted as potential impacts on local values.

Over and above those issues, however, is what may be labeled the decoupling of commerce and community, which the expansion of e-commerce may well provoke. Commerce, particularly local commerce, is a social activity that promotes community connections, reinforces community values, establishes community identity, and supports community development. Some kinds of market activity, of course, must always be local—for example, the provision of food, housing, and much of health care. However, competition between local commerce and global e-commerce is not only possible but already evidenced in a number of business arenas. Online booksellers such as amazon.com compete with local bookstores, for example, and mail-order retailing, once primarily a phenomenon of rural areas, is now equally commonplace in large cities. As noted earlier, such activities are likely to remain a small part of the total value of e-commerce, but their local effects may be significant nonetheless.

Because the United States has already seen the replacement of many kinds of local businesses by large chains, the social change prompted by retail activity on the Internet may be less obvious than in Europe. On the other hand, the receptivity to online retailing in the United States may be greater than in Europe precisely because it is the continuation of a pattern that has already been accepted.

Depending on how the tax consequences of e-commerce ultimately play out, there may be additional, and significant, impact on local political and social life. It is not our intention in this report to offer a comprehensive analysis of Internet taxation. However, it should be noted that in the United States, with its many local tax authorities and its heavy dependence on sales tax to run local government, a significant shift from local to Internet commerce would have serious ramifications. On the face of it, this would put local businesses (which are taxed) at a competitive disadvantage, and it would certainly reduce the funds available for local social services. One interesting possibility is that the United States may respond to these pressures by moving toward a European-style value-added tax.

It would be a mistake to think that e-commerce inevitably leads to a weakening of local social and political structures. Many of the Internet's service functions, which comprise a far larger fraction of e-commerce activity than does brick-and-mortar retailing, may serve to stabilize communities by reducing the tight coupling of job and residence location.

In the United States, for example, small rural communities whose existences were threatened by the failure of family farms have been able to remain intact by creating employment in information-network services—e.g., airline-reservation centers and credit-card processing centers. In addition, telecommuting has been growing in the United States, allowing families more choices with respect to child-rearing arrangements. Indeed, the virtual mobility of labor permitted by global networks can have significant effects on policies, institutions, and social patterns—regional social infrastructure (e.g., housing, health care, and transportation), immigration law, dress standards, eating habits, and others.

In all these examples, locality is important because it determines whether the value set will be receptive or resistant to the opportunities of e-commerce. The attractiveness of telecommuting is likely to be relatively high in the United States, where commuting distances are getting longer and longer and the dearth of efficient, inexpensive public transportation is a growing problem. As noted above, the issue of Internet taxation may be much less important in Europe than in the United States. On the other hand, the threat to the local nature of commerce may be more serious in the European setting. What remains an interesting question is whether these various patterns of acceptance or tension will lead to changes in local values or to a pattern of e-commerce development that differs noticeably from the penetration pattern of global networks themselves.

8

Governance in Cyberspace: Multi-Level and Multi-Actor Constitutionalism

8.1 INTRODUCTION

This report has identified a number of specific social, political, and economic values, and has explored the ways in which global networks may challenge them or shift the traditional balances between them. The report is by no means exhaustive, but it does illustrate the kinds of problems that may arise as global networks expand even further.

The question is how to deal with these problems. When is it appropriate to intervene? Which regulatory tools are likely to be most effective and which ones less so? Should global networks be governed and, if so, in what way? That is, what are the appropriate goals and functions of global-network governance? How should it be structured? And which actors should be involved in its design and its operation?

8.2 GOVERNANCE

In general, stable governance require commonly accepted operating principles, structures, and responsibilities, and sometimes authorities or agencies. At the very least in an Internet context, some authority (or authorities) must oversee certain technical operations such as address assignment and domain-name administration.[1] But for political, commercial, and social issues, what is the relevance of traditional means of

[1]See OECD, 1997, *Internet Domain Names: Allocation Policies*, OECD Document GD(97)207, Paris. See also Chapter 7.

regulation? What role might commercial law play in governing certain aspects of the Internet? What new approaches to governance should be considered? Note that the issue is not whether governance is relevant to the Internet, but rather how such governance should be conducted, with what scope, and at what cost.

8.2.1 Is Regulation Necessary? Technical Solutions, Intermediaries, and Self-help

Prior chapters have pointed out that technical solutions can be found to help deal with some of the problems created by global networks. For example, filtering systems can help end users to separate desired from undesired information. New methods for identification (e.g., electronic signatures), electronic payments (e.g., digital cash), and privacy protection (e.g., encryption) can strengthen the safety and reliability of network-based commercial transactions. Regulations may be necessary to facilitate the use of these tools or to monitor their effectiveness, but the regulations can be designed to build on and enhance the technical tools rather than to replace or impede them.

In addition, the market creates incentives for intermediaries in the electronic marketplace to offer services that protect the interests of its customers—both content providers and users. Users, for example, can choose an Internet provider that offers a selection of Web sites suiting the user's tastes while blocking sites the user would prefer not to see.[2]

Users can, of course, help themselves rather than depend on intermediaries. For example, an avalanche of organized e-mail protests to a spammer's address can effectively shut down the spammer's e-mail service.[3] Global networks themselves, as an efficient source of information distribution and of group organization, help like-minded individuals to find and help one another. Consumers can exchange opinions on products and services, warn others of unfair practices by merchants on the Net, and organize groups to take action to protect their interests.

---

[2]For example, AOL blocked its gateway for e-mails from a company called "Cyberpromotions" because the majority of its users disliked getting the direct advertising of that company via e-mail.

[3]Spam is unsolicited and unwanted e-mail. Spammers are broadcasters of such messages, which are usually advertisements. For more information on organized technically based approaches to prevent spam, see <http://mail-abuse.org/rbl/>.

8.2.2 Informal Rules

In the world of global networks, informal sets of rules of behavior, such as "Netiquette," are common. They can exist as an explicit code of conduct in a certain community or as an implicit agreement about behavior.

None of these rules, whether explicit or not, is binding in a legal sense, and they are weak tools for compelling behavior in a person unwilling to submit to them voluntarily. There are, of course, social means of enforcement that can be effective in relatively closed groups, where the threat of excluding the individual might be a significant one. Such groups might be virtual communities of hackers, people who share special interests, and even some Internet businesses. But these are very special cases in a networked world with millions of users, which is expanding at a rapid rate. For most cases in which rules are necessary, legal tools of one sort or another will often—perhaps even usually—prove more effective.

8.2.3 The Limited Power of Traditional National Regulation

The Internet and some other global networks allow anyone to transfer information-based material, easily and at minimal cost, from one country to another. They even allow a person to move in a virtual sense from one country to another without a passport, visa, or work permit. These new exit options reduce the regulatory power of the individual nation-state because its traditional tool for regulation—public law—generally applies only within its own borders. Although extraterritorial enforcement of national laws is possible in principle, this generally presupposes that the nation-state can exercise jurisdiction over some element of the transnational activity—e.g., by seizing local property or by restricting access to its market.

But although the power of the nation state to regulate is reduced, it is not eliminated, even in the Internet world. The fact that the network is global does not mean that all communications and transactions on it are between people in different countries. The end points for many exchanges are within the same country. Chat room users often wish to communicate with partners in the same national community, especially for language reasons and because of the increased likelihood of meeting in real life. E-commerce, especially retail purchases, largely takes place within one country. These kinds of activities can still be regulated by a single nation-state, even though the bits may travel anywhere in the world on the way from sender to receiver.

And even when one or more of the parties involved in an Internet exchange is outside the territory of a particular state, the state's power is not necessarily as limited as it may seem at first glance.[4] The behavior of the party who is within the country can certainly be regulated; for example, such a person might be prosecuted for downloading illegal content from the Net. More importantly, Internet traffic usually goes through the hands of local intermediaries such as Internet service providers or credit-card agencies. These intermediaries are prime targets for national regulation. They can be required by law to block, or at least provide no support for, an activity in cyberspace that is illegal in the particular country. Still, this is an imperfect and a costly solution. It is imperfect in that the creation of new uncontrolled intermediaries is often technically and economically easy. And it is costly in that disempowering the intermediaries risks slowing the national penetration rate of the Internet, with all of the attendant economic and social consequences.

8.2.4 International Legal Harmonization

Some analysts regard the international harmonization of laws as the only way to meet the challenges of global networks.[5] International cooperation in implementing and enforcing rules can be accomplished through agreements that assign responsibility for regulation, or through harmonization of the regulations themselves. The problem is that states tend to balk at cooperating when their own laws and attitudes toward a particular issue differ from those of the state whose laws they are asked to enforce. Therefore, only when there is consensus about an issue is international cooperation likely to be achieved quickly and effectively.

That reality is illustrated by the fields in which the G-8 states consider coordinated action. For example, the Conference of the G-8 Ministers of Justice and Interior held in Milan on February 26-27, 2001, issued a communiqué in which pedophilia and sexual exploitation, money laundering, and corruption were identified as areas of common concern.[6] In these subjects, the underlying attitudes are similar in all industrialized countries, and the need for regulation is obvious.

But even when there is agreement in principle, regulation will not be a high priority for some nation states if there is no perceived potential harm to their economic development. Consequently, few nation-states

[4]A more detailed discussion of these issues can be found in Jack Goldsmith, 2000, "The Internet, Conflicts of Regulation, and International Harmonization," *Understanding the Impact of Global Networks on Local Social, Political and Cultural Values*, Engel and Keller, eds.

[5]Willem Calkoen uses drastic imagery in his plea for harmonization: "The issue is rapidly becoming one of whether we choose to have laws or live in a lawless society" (in "Harmonization of Laws and the Internet," *International Business Lawyer*, April 1998, pp. 146 et seq.).

[6]See <http://www.g8.gc.ca/2001/Milan_Justice_Interior-e.asp>.

will invest any significant resources in cooperative enforcement, and some may want to use cooperation as a lever to extract concessions from the international community on completely separate matters that *are* of political or economic importance to them. The problem is that even a single noncooperating state can be a serious challenge to a consistent international regulatory framework where the Internet is concerned. That country can create a "regulation leak" that enables highly mobile content providers to evade international regulation; or, if the country includes a significant enough group of network participants, it can, de facto, force its own regulatory structure on the international community.

8.2.5 The Use of Internationally Coordinated Commercial Laws

To what extent might commercial law, rather than public law, be used to regulate global networks? The central actors in commercial law are private parties freely shaping their own legal relationships through contracts and, when necessary, suing each other in the courts. The state takes an auxiliary role by offering the legal protection of the courts, which interpret and judge the validity of contracts, protect people's interests in the contracting process, and help them in the enforcement of legal titles. But even these limited roles provide the state with mechanisms that can be used to protect local values in a networked world.

Contracts have, in fact, become popular tools for the governance of Internet transactions. Access to a Web site is often made conditional on clicking an "I agree" button, which is taken to indicate that the site visitor has agreed to, though has not necessarily read, a long list of terms and conditions to which the statement refers. If the participating computers are appropriately programmed, the actual agreement can even be concluded by the two machines without any explicit action by humans. Moreover, the first contract can be made conditional on holding to these same conditions any other parties to which the digital good is later sold.

The private laws of the United States and Germany both start from the principle that individuals should be free to conclude a contract with anyone they wish, and to decide on its terms. Basically, the role of contract law is limited to giving these contracts legal validity. The normative argument is that if the two parties have agreed to the contract, the law has no reason to intervene. At most, it offers to fill in details, using "default rules" that supplement the wording of the contract, if the parties have not explicitly or implicitly ruled them out.[7]

---

[7]German law is much more active in this respect, resulting in complex transactions being contracted on no more than a few pages, whereas similar U.S. contracts can have hundreds of pages.

This restraint on the part of the legal system does not extend to situations in which the fact of consent is in doubt, or where systematic power differences are likely to unbalance the outcome. This is why contract laws in both countries also have mandatory rules, which contracting parties cannot waive. To the extent that those rules differ between countries, they add complexity to the enforcement of contracts in which the parties are in different jurisdictions, but many of those have been dealt with in the past.

Online transactions raise a number of additional questions that have and will continue to challenge specific mandatory rules, as well as their coordination across national boundaries. Is a simple click enough for consent on unusual or highly burdensome contract provisions? Must the substance of the provisions to which the click refers be controlled by the courts? Should some provisions, such as an anti-reverse-engineering clause, be prohibited when they are actually legal under patent law?

Default rules also offer a way in which contract law can insert local values into the governance of international commercial activity. Although default rules, unlike mandatory rules, can be changed, both parties to the contract must explicitly agree to do so. This has two governance effects: changing a default rule is costly, and it is revealing. A party who asks for a change signals the other that the change has some particular value. The other party will then wonder why such a change might be rational for the first party, leading to a more explicit focus on the underlying values (and value differences) that gave rise to the default rules in the first place.[8]

Last, but not least, there is tort law, which offers opportunities to regulate by establishing liability for damage caused by certain kinds of conduct. This allows the state to establish a financial incentive for a private entity to refrain from such conduct. The weakness in the approach, of course, is that the behavior is not proscribed but merely made costly, so that the person contemplating some socially undesirable enterprise can decide whether or not to proceed by first doing a cost-benefit calculation. Therefore tort law cannot, in any absolute sense, protect vulnerable people.

Procedural law offers other opportunities to influence the legal relationship between private parties. In effect, the state can use this instrument to establish a right of action by a third party, or by a class or group; in fact, the state could authorize itself to act on behalf of a third party, as it often does in protecting the rights of minors. Procedural law can also be used effectively in a trial to establish rules on accessing information relevant to the trial, to ascertain facts, or to specify the burden of proof to be used in reaching judgments.

---

[8]This idea plays a prominent role in what economists call mechanism design. See Douglas G. Baird, Robert H. Gertner, and Randal C. Picker, 1994, *Game Theory and the Law*, Cambridge, 147-153 passim.

The central advantage of regulation by commercial law lies in the reality that national commercial legal systems are much better coordinated internationally than are systems of public law. In commercial international law, there are conflicts-of-law rules that determine the applicable national law. The rules of the international law of civil procedure regulate the authority to adjudicate on national jurisdiction, and they regulate the recognition and enforcement of foreign judgments as well. In contrast to public laws and regulations, which have essentially no effect beyond a state's borders, commercial law's role in accepting foreign legal action (e.g., in enforcing foreign judgments) is no peculiarity; rather, it is an everyday process in civil courts.[9]

That is not to say that rules governing conflict of laws are neutral or totally balanced in their effect. In fact, negotiation of those rules is another point at which the state can indirectly extend its regulatory intervention. Jurisdictional rules can be established that give an advantage to either plaintiffs or defendants, that favor content providers over users (or vice versa), or that extend a state's regulatory power by giving its residents or citizens no choice about jurisdictional venues. On the other hand, rules can be constructed to give the greatest influence to states with the least regulatory restrictions by allowing parties to a dispute to "forum shop."

Some of the commercial-law conflict rules currently used in the offline world may not be suitable in their current form for a global virtual arena like the Internet, and some rethinking will be necessary. The process of adaptation will require a certain flexibility in the application of existing conflict rules in order to fit the kinds of cases that are likely to arise in the context of the Internet.[10] For example, rules based on the location of the plaintiff or the defendant are much less meaningful in the Internet world,[11]

---

[9]Cf. Wolf Osthaus, 2000, "Local Values, Global Networks and the Return of Private Law. On the Function of Civil Law and Private International Law in Cyberspace," in Christoph Engel and Kenneth H. Keller, eds., *Governance of Global Networks in the Light of Differing Local Values,* Baden-Baden, p. 209-236.

[10]This may be easier in the traditionally more flexible Anglo-American system than in the fixed-connection system of Continental-European design. But the tendency to a more open approach in the continental Conflict of Laws system can already be ascertained. A good example is provided by the rules of the Rome Convention on the legal order governing contractual relations. According to Art. 4 of the Convention, as a rule, the law of the nation to which the contract has "the strongest connection" is to be applied. A list of assumptions in par. 2 intends to fill out this term for the regular case. But if there is any closer connection to the law of another state, the judge is free to apply this law (Art. 4 par. 5).

[11]See Matthew Burnstein, 1998, "A Global Network in a Compartmentalized Legal Environment," in Katharina Boele-Woelki and Catherine Kessedjian eds., *Internet, Which Court Decides? Which Law Applies?* Kluwer Academic Publishers, Dordrecht, the Netherlands, pp. 23, 27 et seq.

and a rigid adherence to notions of location would provide easy opportunities for people to evade the law by adjusting their virtual location.

There may well be a temptation to find convenient but inappropriate analogies to Internet cases in existing commercial law, not least because particular interpretations may serve perceived national interests.[12] With each nation-state making such interpretations in its own interest, the result could be an unraveling of the carefully developed commercial-law coordination regime and an accumulation of inconsistent regulations, comparable to what exists in the area of public law. Indeed, it could result in a loss of international willingness to recognize and enforce foreign judgments in civil-law matters. It would be far better at the moment to consider Internet cases individually and de novo, accumulating experience that might ultimately be used to identify valid abstract norms.

As promising as it is, the potential of commercial international law should not be overestimated. Regulation by commercial-law systems can lead to practical problems in which the individual actors are not able to defend their rights. The most important restriction relates to money: the commercial law system requires the parties to pay the costs of litigation, a serious financial burden to those involved. Even if litigants ultimately obtain a favorable judgment and are reimbursed for the cost of litigation—no certainty in any event—the up-front costs can be enormous. [13] Gathering evidence, prosecuting the case, and dealing with delays all take time and money. Furthermore, these costs multiply with every appeal and even more when judgments must be legitimized and executed in another state.[14] In many cases, the cost and uncertainty discourage a person from ever pursuing a legal remedy, though in the American system, class-action suits have been one answer to this problem.

On the other hand, it is also true that defendants, particularly those without "deep pockets," are disadvantaged by a costly legal system and

---

[12]Here in particular, the U.S.-wide "governmental interest approach" could undergo an undesired renaissance.

[13]Here, the national costs associated with litigation are important. The German solution, that all costs follow the event, is advantageous providing one wins. But a victory in court is never sure. The American system, by which everyone bears their own costs, harbors the danger that the party has to split an award with his or her lawyers. This is not always compensated for by the high levels of compensation for pain and suffering, structured settlements, or punitive damages. Therefore lawyers find themselves hunting cases and are content with being remunerated only with a share of the amount awarded (contingency fee).

[14]According to an investigation carried out by the E.U. Commission, the costs for lawyers and courts for the enforcement of a judgment worth 4,000 marks, even within the common market, amounts to 5,000 marks. See Enquete Commission, "Future of the Media in the Economy and Society: Germany's Way in the Information Society: Fifth Report on Consumer Protection in the Information Society" (Bundestags-Drucksache 13/11003), p. 26 (with further references).

therefore more likely to settle claims regardless of their merit. No equivalent to class action suits exists in this case, and an unfortunate consequence of excessive dependence on commercial law may be that certain content providers or intermediaries will adopt a protective strategy to avoid liability, with a resultant chilling effect on freedom of expression. An additional interesting problem in the application of commercial law to the Internet is the difficulty of identifying a defendant with some certainty and establishing his or her location. One cannot sue a domain name or an IP address per se. (There is an exception, however, where trademark protection is concerned. The U.S. Anticybersquatting Consumer Protection Act gives the trademark owner the option to sue "in rem." In practical terms, this means that he or she can sue the domain name without even knowing who has registered it.[15])

Of course, even if a defendant has been identified, enforcing a judgment may be quite difficult because of the high mobility of persons and capital.[16] In the physical world, and where parties are subject to the jurisdiction of the same government, those who win judgments against clearly identifiable parties often have available such enforcement mechanisms as attaching a person's property or garnishing wages. It may well be that the Internet world will require new mechanisms (for example, withdrawing a domain name, or striking the IP addresses from domain servers and routers) for enforcing judgments that relate to important assets in this new technological setting.[17]

8.2.6 Self-regulation Without State Intervention

Many have argued that the state should refrain completely from attempting to regulate the Internet and instead allow network participants to regulate themselves. Indeed, many claim that this kind of self-regulation is already occurring, and that there is a workable set of rules in place for cyberspace, quite independent of national borders. Variously called "cyberlaw," "lex informatica,"[18] or "common law of the Internet," its pro-

[15]In this regard, the EU directive on distance selling also is a (weaker) step in the right direction. It stipulates that a consumer, even before concluding a contract, needs to be informed about the (real) identity of his contracting partner (Art. 4 I lit. a).

[16]Peter Swire. 1998. "Of Elephants, Mice, and Privacy: International Choice of Law and the Internet," *The International Lawyer* 32:991, 1024.

[17]Henry H. Perritt, Jr. 1998. "Will the Judgement-Proof Own Cyberspace?," *The International Lawyer* 32:1123, 1132 et seq., 1139 et seq.

[18]Joel Reidenberg. 1996. "Governing Networks and Rule-Making in Cyberspace," *Emory Law Journal* 45: 911-929; Aron Mefford, 1997, "Lex Informatica: Foundations of Law on the Internet" available online at <http://www.law.indiana.edu/glsj/vol5/no1/mefford.html>.

ponents point to "lex mercatoria" (the law of the marketplace in international business) as an example.[19] Although these are technically not laws, they are rules that have evolved through a process of self-regulation that was essential in the development of the Internet precisely because its activities transcended national boundaries. The effectiveness of such self-regulation, what might be called "soft law," depends on such social pressures to conform as the threat of exclusion from membership in a group where membership confers benefits.

As valuable as soft law can be in many areas, it does raise certain problems. First, and obviously, private enforcement measures are not always effective. If the issue is sufficiently important or the inappropriate behavior sufficiently disruptive, people whose rights are threatened may try to call on formal state-based institutions to enforce the soft law. But states' willingness to act may depend on whether the self-regulatory structure exists within the context of some legal framework. If not, the soft law may be seen as an ad hoc agreement among Net participants that is not a matter for legal authorities.[20]

Some might argue that the nation-state should enforce the self-regulation rules as it would a contract. That may work in certain circumstances, but not if the "contract" contains provisions that are inconsistent with mandatory rules—i.e., nonwaivable rules of national law.[21]

Furthermore, there is a question as to whether all participants have contractually accepted the pertinent rules of cyberlaw merely because they are using the Internet. In principle, one possible approach to giving contractual status to a given set of rules—associated, perhaps, with a particular Web site or service—would be to require all users, at the time of logging in,[22] to declare their willingness to accept the rules. But it is highly questionable whether such a vague commitment concerning future, hypothetical actions could have legal validity.

An even larger question in a self-regulatory scheme is how to avoid a tyranny of the majority that violates the interests of the minority. How would a party with much weaker bargaining power be protected against rules imposed by a party with much greater power?[23] How would due

---

[19]Cf. Burnstein, 1998 (supra note 11); David Johnson and David Post, 1996, "Law and Borders: The Rise of Law in Cyberspace," *Stanford Law Review* 48:1367 et seq. (especially pp. 1387 et seq.).

[20]In German law, for instance, Art. 4 II EGBGB, which only refers to the choice of the"law of a state," provides a clear answer: mandatory rules of national law that would be applicable according to the general Conflict of Laws rules cannot be avoided by reference to nongovernmental rules.

[21]Goldsmith (supra note 4) 1200.

[22]Burnstein (supra note 11), pp. 31 et seq., suggests such a negotiation. Following the expression shrink-wrap, he calls for "click-wrap-contracts."

[23]Goldsmith (supra note 4) 1200.

process be ensured? The notion of self-regulation arose at a time when Internet users were a relatively homogeneous group with strongly shared ideals. Informal rules had as much, or even more, effect on behavior as legally binding rules. Such an "Internet community" would be a mere illusion today, given not only the commercialization of the Net but also its burgeoning use for many social, political, and cultural purposes. The protection of local values quite often amounts to nothing more (or less) than the recognition and protection of the differing ideas of many small groups that are unable to have any significant influence on the rules in a self-regulatory regime.

For Europeans and others, the majoritarian nature of a self-regulatory scheme raises the concern that American legal concepts and American cultural values will dominate the Internet, and further, that American interests will be served by its orientation. This has been characterized as "Americanization by the back door."[24] As people from other cultures seek their own opportunities to participate in the Internet, the concern about "Americanization" may well be broadened to a concern about "Westernization" or even the specter of "neocolonialism."

Interestingly, some proponents of self-regulation may find themselves having second thoughts if commercialization of the Internet leads to the creation of powerful economic interests that can exercise a very strong influence on the direction of the informal or de facto rules. Where economic transactions take place between equally strong partners, self-regulation can be a usefully flexible and effective tool. But when stronger and weaker participants come together on the Net, self-regulation cannot guarantee a desirable result. Similarly, if self-regulation leads to greater influence for market-driven processes, local values can lose out. In these cases, some participation by the state seems necessary.

8.2.7 Hybrid Regulation

As noted in other chapters of this report, a number of experts have suggested that the best approach to governing the Internet is to combine a number of different regulatory and policy tools, selecting those that work best for particular purposes and in particular circumstances. Obviously, this leads to a rather complex system of governance, but the fact is that the globally networked world is itself complex, which is why no single regulatory approach seems adequate. This use of a panoply of tools and actors, formal and informal, governmental and nongovernmental, national and international, is labeled hybrid regulation.

---

[24]Very clear on that point is Peter Mankowski, 1999, "Wider ein transnationals Cyberlaw," *Archiv für Presserecht*, p. 138 (140).

What Does Hybrid Regulation Mean?

In a sense, hybrid regulation is a misleading term. It is not so much *regulation* as a broader concept of governance, taken to mean the system of institutions and processes used to influence the conduct of individuals and groups. Governance, from this perspective, is about the allocation of power—not only in a public setting but within private associations as well—and exercised by a multitude of actors at different levels of authority and operation.

This system of governance involves a number of challenges: coordinating the legal and political actions of national governments; adding and integrating new forms of transnational institutions such as the European Union; making use of diplomatic conferences or permanent international organizations such as the ITU or WTO, when appropriate; and recognizing and facilitating voluntary self-regulatory mechanisms involving industry, labor, public interest, and other community interest groups.

Applied to cyberspace, with its multitude of activities and many constituencies, governance may basically serve an "umbrella" function, asserting certain normative principles, explicitly recognizing the set of agreements and arrangements that deal with the subjects of public international law, and providing some level of legitimacy to the principles and self-regulatory schemes that govern, respectively, business, civil society and other nongovernmental entities. Put differently, one can envision a hybrid regulatory regime in which government provides a framework for private self-ordering that meets certain minimum requirements established by the framework.[25] Over time, this might well lead to an even more limited role for the nation-state, as new actors appear who assume regulatory powers that have traditionally been state responsibilities.

Public institutions also share authority at the level of global governance. New nongovernmental actors with transborder reach, such as multinational or transnational enterprises,[26] internationally organized public-interest groups, and other nongovernmental organizations (NGOs), increasingly exercise influence and assume responsibilities complementary to, or in cooperation with, established public actors in the international legal community.[27] Global networks, of course, play an important

[25]See Henry H. Perritt, Jr., 2000, "The Internet Is Changing the Public International Legal System," *Kentucky Law Journal*, 88:885-955.

[26]Klaus W. Grewlich. 1988. *Transnational Enterprises in a New International System*, Alphen aan den Rijn.

[27]James Rosenau and Ernst-Otto Czempiel, eds. 1992. *Governance Without Government*. Cambridge.

role in helping these new entities evolve positions on various issues and in empowering them to act.

Developing a public international-law structure that enables the integration of binding public international law, "soft law," self-regulatory arrangements, and nonbinding self-policing measures might, in the long run, change the nature of international law itself. Gradually, a scheme of governance that was originally designed to achieve some sort of workable coexistence among sovereign actors might develop its own normative demands, along with procedures for new institutions to address them.

Interest in Hybrid Regulation

Hybrid regulation is not a new concept. Indeed, governance in both the United States and Germany relies on several levels of federalism, including national, state, local, and district law and regulation. Further, trade associations often make their own rules on competition and antitrust, and various interest groups such as NGOs lobby, draft regulations, and get them approved by legislative or administrative bodies. Against this background, hybrid regulation just adds another—international—level.

Governments on both sides of the Atlantic appear to be willing to consider hybrid forms of governance in a number of domains, though they generally speak in terms of opening markets and minimizing government interference. For instance, at the G-7 Conference in Brussels in February 1995, the following policy principles were endorsed by the conferees: promoting dynamic competition; encouraging private investment; defining an adaptable regulatory framework; providing open access to networks; ensuring universal provision of, and access to, services; promoting equality of opportunity to the citizen; promoting diversity of content, including cultural and linguistic diversity; and recognizing the necessity of worldwide cooperation, with particular attention to less-developed countries.

These principles have been refined in statements and reports emerging from a number of international governmental meetings, such as the 1997 Ministerial Conference on Global Information Networks in Bonn and the 1998 Organization for Economic Cooperation and Development (OECD) Ministerial Conference, "A Borderless World: Realizing the Potential of Global Electronic Commerce," in Ottawa. The Ministerial Declaration issued after the Bonn Conference, as well as a parallel "Industrial Declaration" put forward by the private sector, asserted that if there was to be further expansion in electronic commerce, a number of key strategies would have to be adopted. For example, regulation would have to be as light-handed and flexible as possible; legal rules applicable to global information networks would have to be consistent across borders; and telecommunications markets would have to be opened up to effective competition. It would also be necessary to allow market forces to drive the development of open technical standards; to avoid discriminatory taxes on the use of information networks; and to provide a high level of intellectual-property-rights protection for the creation, storage, and distribution of cyber-content.

Businesses also seem to be open to self-regulation under a governmental umbrella. For example, at the 1998 OECD Ottawa Conference, business spokespersons proposed a set of fundamental principles "to shape the policies that govern electronic commerce, if the promises of electronic commerce are to be fulfilled."[28] It included the following:

- The development of electronic commerce should be led primarily by the private sector in response to market forces.
- Government intervention, when required, should promote a stable, international legal environment, allow a rational allocation of scarce resources, and protect the general interest. Such intervention should be no more than is essential and should be clear, transparent, objective, nondiscriminatory, proportional, flexible, and technology-neutral.
- Mechanisms for private-sector input and involvement in policy-making should be promoted and widely used in all countries.
- Regulation of the underlying telecommunications infrastructure, where necessary, should reduce impediments to competition, enabling new services and new entrants to compete globally in an open and fair market.
- A high level of trust should be pursued by mutual agreement, education, further technological innovations to enhance security and reliability, the adoption of adequate dispute-resolution mechanisms, and private-sector self-regulation. Business should make available to users the means to exercise choice with respect to privacy, confidentiality, content control, and, under appropriate circumstances, anonymity.

The apparent enthusiasm for new governance approaches should not, however, obscure two realities. First, the more important that telecommunications, information services, electronic commerce, and global information networks become to national societies and economies, the less likely

---

[28]OECD Ministerial Conference. 1998. "A Borderless World: Realizing the Potential of Global Electronic Commerce," A Global Action Plan for Electronic Commerce Prepared by Business, with Recommendations from Governments, 7-9 October 1998, Ottawa, Canada, OECD Document SG/EC(98)11/REV2, 5 October 1998.

it is that governments will relinquish all controls. Second, on the flip side, withdrawal of controls—i.e., liberalization and deregulation—will only work if international cooperation becomes more stable and reliable and the right balance is struck between subsidiarity, harmonization, and the transfer of some authority to new entities—international or private.

Constitutionalizing Public International Law to Facilitate Hybrid Regulation

Effectively managing the changes inherent in the global evolution towards an information society is a challenge involving many constituencies and rules at once. It would appear more effective and appropriate to explicitly engage all of these constituencies, rather than to rely on the traditional monolithic concept of national sovereignty. This approach would be tantamount to "constitutionalizing" public international law that in the past has served little more than a coordinative function for sovereign governments. Public authority would become the joint and separate responsibility of a multiplicity of coordinated authorities, with nation states being but one of the elements of this system.[29]

In addition to multilevel authority, the system would have a multiplicity of actors.[30] In its umbrella function, this constitutionalized international legal system[31] might establish normative principles, agreements, and procedures pertaining not only to subjects appropriate for public international law but also to self-regulatory schemes that would apply to business, labor, civil society, and other nongovernmental entities. In the most optimistic scenario, this umbrella function, at first little more than a compilation of arrangements, might ultimately lead to integration of the public and private, the traditional and newly emerging, and regulation by law and the process of self-regulation.

---

[29]See, in this context, Ingolf Pernice, 1999, "Multilevel Constitutionalism and the Treaty of Amsterdam: European Constitution-Making Revisited?," *Common Market Law Review* 36 :703 (709).

[30]Klaus W. Grewlich, 1999, *Governance in Cyberspace—Access and Public Interest in Global Communications*, Den Haag/London/Boston (Chapter Ten).

[31]Ernst U. Petersmann, 1999, "How to Constitutionalize International Law and Foreign Policy for the Benefit of Civil Society?," *Michigan Journal of International Law* 20; Hannes L. Schloemann and Stefan Ohlhoff, 1999, "'Constitutionalization' and Dispute Settlement in the WTO—National Security as an Issue of Competence," *American Journal of International Law* 93:424.

9

Information Networks and Culture

9.1 INTRODUCTION

The interaction between global networks and local cultures is clearly an important dimension of the study of global networks and local values generally. Both "culture" and "values" are terms with a number of meanings. Culture and values are obviously not entirely independent of one another. Values are embedded in cultures and, to a certain extent, derive from those cultures. At the same time, values are part of the glue that gives the culture cohesion and identity. Chapter 3 discusses the term "values" in some depth; this chapter takes on the same task with respect to culture.

Other chapters in this report have dealt with local differences on such matters as privacy, pornography, and hate speech—subjects that can properly be viewed as manifestations of local cultural differences. Not only do different cultures attach different weights or varying levels of importance to each of these issues, but they even give alternative meanings to the terms we use to identify them. These differences then affect the social, political, and legal tools that each society is willing to employ in dealing with the issues' challenges.

In this area perhaps more than any other, the limitation imposed by focusing this study on two nations that are more alike than different becomes obvious. As the introduction to this report points out, although there are a number of differences between American and German cultures, in the context of the world's overall cultural diversity they are quite similar. Both are modern and wealthy nation states with strong, technologically based market economies and highly educated populations. Each has been strongly influenced by Western European history and tradition (a significant, though now-decreasing, fraction of the U.S. population traces its family origin to Germany) and they have comparable distributions of religious affiliations among their people. They also share an alphabet, and their languages are closely related.

In contrast, most people elsewhere in the world live in cultural settings far different from those of the United States or Germany. Their differences make clear that the introduction of global networks in many of those settings challenges, and is challenged by, a variety of local cultural values that are not relevant to the American or German cases.

The committee was thus faced with a dilemma: to ignore a topic of obvious relevance to the study generally because it could not be explored adequately within the limited framework of U.S. and German culture, or, at least for this chapter, to remove that geographical constraint in order to address the broader issues. The committee chose the latter course, arguing that in this, the penultimate chapter of the report, it is reasonable to highlight some questions that might well be explored more comprehensively in a later study by a committee with a far broader range of regional expertise than the present one. Thus, what follows should be viewed as an introduction to the range of issues that need to be considered in assessing the potential cultural impacts of global networks.

"Culture" is a term with many meanings. It covers art, literature, and music; it refers to various dimensions of identity, including the linguistic, national, local, ethnic, and religious; it is sometimes described in terms of social solidarities or epistemic connections, which run the gamut from single-issue interests to professional occupation; and it depends on level of education, social and professional status, and age. Culture is also a moving target, affected by economic, social, political, and technological changes, even as it affects each of them. Global networks are clearly one of those changes, but it would be a major challenge to separate out this one factor from the many others associated with globalization that are also bringing about cultural evolution.

Anthropologists, sociologists, historians, and economists have written much about the dynamics of technological change, with most rejecting a rigid technological determinism. They instead emphasize that transformations over time result from interactions between new technologies and the existing social and economic circumstances.[1] To interpret these interactions, cultural theorists have given us a certain structure that cat-

---

[1]Robert McC. Adams, 1996, *Paths of Fire: An Anthropoligist's Inquiry Into Western Technology*, Princeton, NJ: Princeton University Press; Leo Marx, 1964, *The Machine in the Garden: Technology and the Pastoral Ideal in America*, Oxford: Oxford University Press; Nathan Rosenberg, 1994, *Exploring the Black Box: Technology, Economics, and History*, Cambridge: Cambridge University Press.

egorizes cultural patterns according to "social solidarities."[2] This provides some insight into not only the nature of the interactions between technologies and cultures, but also the limitations on how far the former can go in altering the latter. Although such writings provide a framework for analyzing the interaction of global networks and local cultures, they also make clear that the analysis must be approached comprehensively if it is to advance our understanding.

Looming large among these questions to be considered is the specter of cultural hegemony—the concern of many that the architecture and software of global networks so strongly reflect the language, values, and interests of the United States that other cultures will be either disadvantaged or displaced as these networks exert an ever-increasing influence not only on the language of commerce and discourse, but on community hierarchy and organization, business style, education, and entertainment programming as well.

There are many other questions as well. Some have suggested that class cultural differences within societies may be more significant than differences between societies in assessing the effects of global networks. On the other hand, age differences may be more telling than either class or nationality. Or, perhaps, as others have suggested,[3] the Internet in and of itself may be giving rise to a new culture, relatively homogeneous in its values, and quite distinct from the local cultures in which its members are otherwise embedded.

From still another perspective, we need to be able to distinguish transient effects from long-term consequences. To what extent do cultural factors merely have an effect in the short term—say, in slowing the adoption of or accommodation to global networks—and to what extent do they influence or entail permanent cultural changes? And of course, how much are particular cultures economically or politically disadvantaged relative to others in the short or long term?

The sections that follow provide some amplification of these issues, based on discussions that took place during the committee's deliberations.

---

[2]Michael Thompson. 1999. "Global Networks and Local Cultures: What Are the Mismatches and What Can Be Done About Them?," in *Understanding the Impact of Global Networks on Local Social, Political and Cultural Values,* Christoph Engel and Kenneth H. Keller, eds., Law and Economics of International Telecommunications, Vol. 42. Baden-Baden: Nomos.

[3]See Esther Dyson, 1997, *Release 2.0.* New York: Broadway Books, p. 52.

9.2 CULTURAL HEGEMONY

The very essence of global networks is the power they give individuals to participate actively, either as providers or recipients of information. Low cost of entry, wide penetration of networks, and the transparency of Web-browsing software all contribute to this characteristic. In principle, any individual or group can easily distribute information to a seemingly unlimited audience, and at minimal cost. Also in principle, anyone can select—or block—information from the vast universe of sources available throughout the world.

But the practical reality is somewhat different. Networks provide an infrastructure whose actual characteristics are determined as much by which people and groups use and design them as by their innate potential. When one group or nation constitutes a significant, even dominant, fraction of the users and providers, then the network's hardware and software—"the code," to use Lawrence Lessig's term[4]—and the preponderance of its available information, are likely to reflect the culture of that group or nation.

The language used on Web sites is clearly one measure of this kind of dominance, and indeed, a very large fraction of all Web sites use English. In a world of networked communication, language takes on an importance even greater than that in broadcast or entertainment media because it affects not only how well one can understand what is said or written but how effectively one can communicate. Language in that sense is a form of power, and thus the requirement that one communicate in an unfamiliar language is, effectively, a restriction on freedom of speech.

Those who raise the issue of cultural hegemony point out that the effect could go even deeper. With native speakers of English being the single largest linguistic group of network users,[5] market considerations dictate that a large fraction of the software written for use in conjunction with networks will also be developed in English. At present, for example, it is estimated that American companies develop about 80 percent of packaged software. Thus, English is the language not only of communication but also of programming. Further, there is more impetus to focus on digital coding for the Roman alphabet, and such programs are likely to be more effective than coding for other alphabets. As a result, those techniques that increase the efficiency of Web and document searches, transmission rates, and the like will be better developed for the Roman alpha-

---

[4]Lawrence Lessig. 1999. *Code and Other Laws of Cyberspace*. New York: Basic Books.

[5]Native English speakers now represent approximately 45 percent of the online population. See United States Internet Council, 2001 State of the Internet Report, Press Release November 12, 2001. Available from <http://www.usinternetcouncil.org/>.

bet and the English language than for other modes of written communication.

With the disproportionate representation of one language and culture driving both the creation of and the market for operating systems, databases, other reference materials, digital music, advertising, e-business, and the range of services, the fear is that the content available on global networks will primarily reflect that one culture. To the extent that the Internet, through its efficiency and ubiquity, begins to dominate the social and intellectual life of a community or nation, this would be tantamount to cultural hegemony. If technological path dependence reinforces this pattern, the hegemony could be long lasting.

How realistic are the fears? With respect to the Western industrial nations, it appears that they are overdrawn. Although a snapshot of the present situation does, indeed, reveal the overwhelming dominance of the English language and American content globally, there is little evidence that other languages and cultures are being displaced now or are likely to be so in the future. In a de facto sense, language zones have already been created in many parts of the developed world. Most German, French, and Japanese computer and Internet users can conduct all of their day-to-day activities in their native languages, as content providers have already translated information for local usage. Furthermore, space for new, culturally localized content is virtually unlimited; it can and will be added as the penetration of networks and computers continues in the countries of the industrialized world. The growth in the flow of bits may introduce information traffic problems, but existing content will not necessarily have priority over new content.[6]

Similarly, there is no overwhelming technical barrier to the localization of software, even when it has not been written specifically for a given region.[7] The major software firms separate the source code of programming languages, operating systems, and applications from linguistically

---

[6]This is not to say that priorities cannot and will not be established that affect access to certain kinds of material or its effective speed of transmission. Internet service providers already have the technical capacity to do that, using filtering or blocking technologies to create various degrees of transparency (a measure of the extent to which the network itself exerts influence on the ability of individuals to access content). The point here is that, unlike broadcasting, the earlier content and service providers gain no great advantage that would allow them to limit access to their services or exclude those who follow.

[7]Localization refers to the rewriting of software programs from the original language in which they were developed to the language of the locality in which they will be used. However, more than language is involved because cultural differences may well require that colors, numbers, box sizes, names, dates, and icons be changed for the program to work in the new cultural setting.

and culturally specific elements in order to allow them to be adapted to local circumstances.

There is no reason to think that such adaptation will be difficult. The cultural barriers to applying information technology in a variety of everyday activities in developed nations appear to be modest. Although neither computer hardware and software nor networks have, in fact, spread through most other industrial societies to the extent that they have in the United States,[8] they appear to have been widely accepted. Indeed, in some respects, other nations have led the United States in using information technology in everyday life.

For example, in 1981 France deployed Minitel, a national videotext system using telephone lines, to send text and graphics from mainframe computers to home terminals. By the late 1990s, Minitel had 15 million users, or about 25 percent of the French population. They use it for applications ranging from personal ads and pornography to online banking, travel services, and directory assistance—all with online billing (charges are added to a user's phone bill). Furthermore, because Minitel is a "pay-by-the-minute" service, some analysts argue that the transition from Minitel to the Internet will be "gentler" for Minitel users than the transition for most Internet users from "free" content to "for-pay" content.[9]

Thus it appears likely that the use of information networks will reflect local values rather than replace them wholesale with foreign ones. To be sure, they will provide a quite-new medium for the expression of those values, much as electronic "chat rooms" have replaced community-center meetings and electronic auctions have replaced weekend antique-hunting expeditions for some people in the United States. The new forms will not necessarily look like the old ones but will clearly be influenced by them, and the result will be new patterns of interaction and new cultural forms that are less indicative of cultural hegemony than of cultural evolution.

The e-commerce approaches currently being adopted only reinforce these conclusions. A key element in the strategy of most firms has been to attract prospective customers and to earn their loyalty by providing them with free products and services of interest, and then to use the attention—and potential loyalty—thus garnered to market other products and services.[10] Clearly, this requires sensitivity and responsiveness

---

[8]The Scandinavian countries are an exception to this general statement, reflecting their small size and economic and social homogeneity. The city state of Singapore is another special case.

[9]See John Tagliabue, "Online Cohabitation: Internet and Minitel; Videotex System in France Proves Unusually Resilient," *New York Times*, June 2, 2001, Saturday.

[10]The easy and wide availability of information on the Internet has created an environment in which people are generally unwilling to pay for content except in very specific areas

on the part of e-firms to the cultures of the people whose attention the e-firms are trying to attract.

The situation is far more complex in the developing world, which itself is hardly homogeneous. In the newly industrialized countries of East Asia, economic globalization is considered a key to development; rather than being seen as a threat to local culture, global networks are considered a tool that will be advantageous for those societies. Moreover, Asian leaders have often argued that their hierarchical societal structures facilitate the kind of educational system and disciplined behavior that make rapid adaptation of new technology relatively easy, without leading to social disruption or undesired changes in cultural values.

The city-state of Singapore advertises itself as the most computerized and networked nation in the world. The homogenizing influence of the Internet is of little concern because Singapore is already an extremely homogeneous society that has served as a major regional financial center and home to multinational corporations for years. Its authoritarian government has apparently been successful in convincing its population that accepting the imposition of tight discipline is the price of prosperity. In such a society, heavy-handed measures can be used to control undesired public manifestations of foreign cultural influences.

China has undertaken the ambitious Golden Bridge project to provide broadband networks throughout the densely populated regions of the east and south of the country. Fiber-optic backbones, microwave intermediate transmission, and local wired distribution systems are being complemented by the development of multimedia software and the training of end users to build a network-based economy. The official, centrally defined standardizations of the written Chinese language—its ideographs—and the ways of entering them from a keyboard are making it possible to rapidly adapt Western software as well. (Major U.S. software vendors are also seeking to customize their software for users whose first written language is Chinese.) Indeed, the reinforcement of language standardization, which is a by-product of information networks, is consistent with China's cultural agenda.

Both Singapore and China have, of course, sought to exploit the use of networks in support of their economies while, at the same time, preventing the distribution of other kinds of information and programming to their people. Their concern is a political rather than a cultural one: preventing information networks from being used to encourage and enable organized opposition to government authority.

---

such as pornography or current business information. Therefore "bundling" is a common practice, offering a good deal of free content in the hopes of attracting consumers to purchasable goods and services.

In the long run, it is likely to be impossible to achieve that goal. The technical structure of the Internet makes it relatively simple to track the flow of information from one node to another, but interdicting that flow is relatively difficult. Although it is possible to block certain Web sites or groups of Web sites—even all of the material originating from a certain country—the ever-changing array of mirror sites, domain names, host service providers, and transmission routes makes for a constantly moving target and an increasingly challenging task, as Chinese authorities have discovered.[11]

Therefore, rather than being able to use the relatively benign (because essentially invisible) tool of preventing "undesirable" information distribution, governments must use the more heavy-handed approach of sanction and punishment after the fact to discourage further distributions. But as the density of network nodes and the bandwidth of transmission lines increases, the likelihood of "leakage" becomes greater and the sanctions necessary to discourage it must be made increasingly severe. The practical problem, which seems all but impossible to surmount, has become that of preventing the severity of the sanctions from becoming the very destabilizing force that the governments had sought to avoid through the control of information flow. Chapters 5 and 6, which deal with freedom of speech and privacy, respectively, explore these issues in greater detail.

The more difficult question to answer is whether the political changes that information technology is likely to bring about in these countries over the long run will also give rise to significant cultural changes. It is a question related to the much larger issue of the connection between political structure and cultural values. Many East Asian leaders have argued that the proclaimed political agenda of Western nations, and of the United States in particular—encouraging the spread of democracy—is in fact a manifestation of cultural hegemony. At issue is whether the self-proclaimed hierarchical nature of many East Asian nations is a consequence or a determinant of their political structure (as well as their educational systems, research goals and productivity, legal structures, and the like). Would political democratization change culturally determined structures in the same way regardless of whether the stimulus for the change were global networks (as might be the case in Singapore or China) or economic failure and environmental degradation (as in the former Warsaw Pact) or the failure of a military venture (as in Argentina)? These are questions that future studies should examine.

---

[11]See, for example, Jennifer Lee, "Punching Holes in Internet Walls," *New York Times*, April 26, 2001.

To the extent that cultural values do define political structures or are linked to a society's position on a variety of other issues from human rights to child labor to environmental protection or the protection of religious and ethnic minorities, they are not necessarily neutral. In that sense, the protection and preservation of historic cultures is not an absolute imperative. Thus, labeling attempts to change certain cultural values, whether through global networks or by other means, as cultural hegemony may be accurate but not necessarily dispositive.

India offers an example entirely different from the authoritarian regimes of East Asia in several respects. As a democratic nation committed to preserving the many traditional cultures of its several states, India regards language diversity as an important cultural value. In contrast to the situation in China, the monolinguistic nature of the Internet works against that value. The problem is exacerbated by the fact that the Internet's language is largely English, which has played a special role in India as the link language of the nation and the language of power and wealth. Thus, rather than being a barrier to the penetration of Internet culture, the language is a vehicle for bringing it into the society and skewing a delicate balance.

Because English is so accessible to the educated classes in India, including the large cadre of technically trained software developers, there is little motivation to localize software. Indeed, the dominance of the United States in computer hardware and software, as well as in network content, creates a ready market for the talents of Indian software engineers precisely because of their familiarity with the English language. Thus it appears that software as well as network content oriented toward the English language and American culture is likely to continue to be the norm for some time, setting the stage for possible long-term cultural hegemony in India—at least for Internet-related activities.

Are there factors that may ameliorate this trend? Two suggest themselves. First, although English has functioned as the link language across the many cultures of India, only about 5 percent of its people are fluent in it. Tradition and legal structures have promoted the use of vernacular languages in local commerce and even in government business. Therefore it is possible that the Internet will not penetrate the Indian society to a significant extent. The cost would be a loss of the economic and social gains that the Internet promises; the gain would be the preservation of cultural diversity.

Second, through its long and rather special colonial history, Indian elites have learned to maintain a dual cultural identity, living in two worlds simultaneously. They functioned effectively in the English-dominated governance structure and civil service of the country, while preserving their historical cultures within their own communities. If this duality can be maintained for long enough, the market (possibly U.S. companies but more likely Indian ones) may awaken to the opportunity presented by a country the size of India, where the population of many of its cultural subgroups exceeds by far that of most other entire nations. We may then see the kind of localization of software that would allow a positive social construction of global networks to fit local cultural needs and desires.

Nevertheless, a major unanswered question that needs to be continually re-asked is whether the cultural duality will actually continue. It is possible, after all, that the very power of networks in shifting the modes of business, education, entertainment, and communication will change the pattern.

In many ways, India is an interesting testing ground for the limits of social and cultural construction. Precisely because its technical and business elites can function in either the hegemonic culture of the English-speaking world or in the local and highly diverse cultures of the Indian subcontinent, networks can penetrate India without requiring or even bringing about change. On the other hand, if the efficiencies and opportunities of networks encourage elites to shift more of their daily political, social, and economic activities into the network-dominated culture even without any localization, the shift may disrupt the delicate cultural balance on which Indian democracy is based. In effect, the elites may become the intermediaries that give electronic networks the leverage to alter the culture of the society.

There is still another scenario, different from the East Asian and South Asian examples. It is essentially a reactive and narrow nationalism—even a zealous isolationism—brought about by the perceived fear of the threat to traditional cultures that economic globalization represents. In the view of those who lead this reaction, globalization is a juggernaut that carries with it Western social and cultural values that are anathema to the "invaded" society. What adds to the fear is that globalization has been so successful, both as an economic strategy and as a dominant cultural force.

Electronic networks play a role in this economic globalization, although the trend toward globalization was well under way before the Internet had achieved any significant penetration.[12] Nevertheless, they not only play an important current role in globalization, they have come to symbolize it. They also reinforce the influence of English-speaking elites. Localization is not a solution in the view of reactionary national

---

[12]For example, international financial networks have been important to the global economy for at least several decades. See Walter B. Wriston, 1992, *The Twilight of Sovereignty*, New York: Charles Scribner's Sons.

leaders because the essence of these networks—their egalitarian nature, tolerance of diversity, market-driven character, and rhythms of social intercourse—are values that cannot be changed merely by localizing software. The network culture itself—in which shared interests and attitudes rather than familial connections establish group linkages and where geography, history, and connection to the land mean almost nothing—is unacceptable.

Some have argued that the vigor of the reaction in these Asian societies is driven by leaders' concerns that their culture will be perceived as inferior because it cannot produce the same economic results as the invading network-dominated culture.[13] Challenged in this way, they seek not to adapt the new technologies to their circumstances but to look inward; their hope is that a purer adherence to their own cultural values not only will be a successful strategy but also will demonstrate its superiority to Western culture.

This scenario, then, is not so much one in which cultural hegemony is at issue; instead, it is one of cultural conflict based on a clash of values. Much has been written about this phenomenon—for example, Barber's *Jihad vs. McWorld*, Huntington's *Clash of Civilizations*, and Friedman's *Lexus and the Olive Tree*.[14] These authors postulate that the clash of values arises because of differences between Western cultures, with their push toward globalization, and more traditional Middle Eastern cultures. However, there is also the possibility that the incompatibility is between the local culture and the innate characteristics of the network. The question is, Does the Internet represent a technology that is just not sufficiently flexible to be "socially constructed" to serve the values of these societies or are local political and religious forces preventing them from getting to the point where such a proposition could be tested?

But certain real-world experiments now in progress could provide some preliminary answers to this question. The migration of people from the developing to the developed world is creating relatively cohesive diasporas of various ethnic and religious groups that have not had a significant presence in the Western world until now. The ways in which networks are adapted to the use of these communities—for example, to preserve and transmit language and culture within and between these communities—may indicate whether "localized" networks might ulti-

---

[13]Bernard, Lewis. 1999. "The West and the Middle East," *Foreign Affairs* 76(1):114-130.

[14]Benjamin R. Barber, 1996, *Jihad vs. McWorld*, New York: Ballantine Books; Samuel P. Huntington, 1998, *The Clash of Civilizations and the Remaking of the World Order*, New York: Touchstone Books; Thomas L. Friedman, *The Lexus and the Olive Tree*, New York: Farrar, Straus and Giroux.

mately be a positive force in the nations that are, at present, actively excluding them.

9.3 GLOBAL NETWORKS AND CLASS ISSUES

A rather different approach to examining the influence of electronic networks on cultural values is to consider their effects on different social groupings within a given society. The issue of education and level of literacy was raised above in connection with India. But it is hardly a situation unique to India. In a world in which more than half of all people have never made a telephone call, it is clear that networks penetrate most societies in a highly skewed way. The most benign consequence is that global networks will be irrelevant to the groups not directly touched by them, in much the same way that the formal economy and legal structure of a number of countries can be irrelevant to the everyday economic and cultural life of certain rural or ethnic groups within those countries.

More worrisome, networks may give rise over time to increasing disparities between those with access to them and those without such access—the so-called "digital divide." The most obvious potential effects have been described: more economic activity mediated by networks means less activity in traditional markets and fewer linkages with traditional society. Networks confer power to organize politically and to gain access to information, education, and even health care, thereby increasing the autonomy of the privileged relative to the less privileged and decreasing the interest of the privileged in the institutions that serve the less privileged.

The educational system in Latin America provides an interesting example of how the support of societal institutions can be skewed by the interests of the privileged. It is often noted that higher education in Latin America is better funded relative to primary and secondary education than in most parts of the world. Indeed, in view of the inadequacy of that region's primary and secondary education funding, many would argue its higher education is *over*funded. The reason for the investment disparity is relatively clear. The middle and upper classes in most Latin American countries usually receive their primary and secondary education in private schools but turn to public universities afterward. Therefore they have little motivation for supporting the former and an obvious interest in supporting the latter.

The educational system bears an obvious relationship to the preservation of a society's culture. So, too, do many other institutions whose influence may be less direct. Will network databases available to elites cut down on the perceived need for public libraries? Will Web-distributed music and film, available only to a subset of society, undercut support for local entertainment venues? Will the intensity of telephone-line usage for data transmission actually reverse the slow gains that have occurred in making telephone service available to a wider cross section of society? Whether the effects are transitory or long lasting is a question that needs study. The answer depends on the extent to which initial network developments in a given society "lock in" hardware and software, reducing future flexibility in introducing more appropriately localized structures.

Within Western industrialized societies, some have cast the problem in different terms. Jacques Arlandis,[15] for example, has argued that in the networked society the power and behavior of various professional groups are being changed, thus shifting the relationships between them and altering the values, modes of discourse, and structure of the society. His emphasis is on the interactive nature of the change. The network's potential resonates differently with each group in the society, revealing aspects of the group's values. In turn, each group seeks to influence the network's development in different ways.

Examples of these effects on professional groups abound. In the practice of medicine, for example, the local physician is no longer the unquestioned expert for all patients. The availability on the Internet of enormous amounts of data (of widely varying quality) on the treatment of disease has shifted the balance of power between patient and physician, diminishing the absolute authority that physicians long enjoyed in determining what was best for a patient. Telemedicine—the ability of specialists to deliver treatment without being in the physical presence of the patient—promises to offer patients a much higher degree of collaboration and consultation between general practitioners and specialists in deciding on treatments. Both of these changes represent significant shifts in the nature of a professional culture.

Still another example: network-stimulated changes in copyright protections and related fair-use exemptions have the potential to change long-established patterns of sharing and using scientific data—that is, the culture of the science community. Whether this will shift the traditional balance between open, "pre-competitive" scientific research and commercialization of scientific applications remains to be seen.

The proximity of computers and networks to the everyday life of the society gives rise to a resurgence of power for experts, creating a new elite and enormous rewards for technological innovation. And the ability of many technologically literate professionals to master the new systems

---

[15]Jacques Arlandis, 2000, "The Clerk, the Merchant and the Politician," in *Governance of Global Networks in the Light of Differing Local Values*, Christoph Engel and Kenneth H. Keller, eds., Baden-Baden: Nomos.

gives them access to sources of useful knowledge not available to others, and confers the advantages that come with such knowledge. Journalists and other intermediaries lose legitimacy as more people are connected directly to sources of information. At the same time, a new class of intermediaries may arise from among those experts who have the skills to create value-added products within the world of electronic databases and services.

To the extent that the cyberworld facilitates the formation of epistemic groups without regard to geographic boundaries, it provides a lifeline to individuals who live *within* geographic boundaries; thus cultural diversity in real space is actually promoted by the anarchy of cyberspace. On the other hand, the virtual society of the network can become a substitute for the geographically bounded society, drawing individuals away from the real political and social world and leaving it even more homogeneous, if somewhat reduced in richness.

For merchants, it is not the anarchy of cyberspace that is attractive but its efficacy as a marketplace. For this group, the value of the networked world is its sameness; commerce looks the same across the world. Thus growth of global commerce shifts the relationship between merchants and politicians, requiring them to form a partnership that changes the balance in a society in which politicians had previously been the arbiters of competing interests, only one of which was that of the merchants. Politicians, or at least governments, must now represent the interests of "their" merchants in such issues as copyright, privacy protection, standards development, and taxation, to cite just a few.

Arlandis suggests that many of these issues can be understood, or at least analyzed, in terms of the technical, economic, and social forces that move a society. All three are influenced by the cyberworld and all three, in turn, influence the development of that world. But crucial to the argument, and important to framing future research questions, is the fact that these are not independent forces; they themselves interact, and local society as well as the networked society depends on their collective effect.

9.4 PUBLIC AND PRIVATE SPACES

Not all of the cultural phenomena affected by global networks relate to groups or classes. The shifting relationship between public and private spaces, essentially an issue concerning individuals in the society, is one of the most interesting and complex brought about by the cyberworld. That boundary, in both principle and practice, has been largely determined by cultural norms. Which people know about us and what they know, what they physically see of us, how we feel about it, and the extent to which we control it differ widely from one culture to another.

Some aspects of this issue—in particular, those related to privacy, which refers rather specifically to the right to control the distribution and use of information about oneself—are discussed in Chapter 6 of this report. It is noted there that even in cultures as closely similar as the United States and Germany, there are deep differences in perspective. In the wider world, the differences are much more profound. How and where one entertains, the candor and directness with which one expresses ideas, and how publicly and under what circumstances one displays one's body parts are all related to the boundary between public and private spheres but follow no obvious, logical, or consistent pattern.

In Japan, one is more likely to share a community bath with strangers than to express an opinion directly to them. In the United States, the use of one's social security number merely for purposes of identification has become a major public issue, but it is widely expected that just about everyone in a small community will know who has visited you in the past month and what you ate.

The public/private space boundary may not be rational, but in the physical world it is more or less clear how to maintain it. If one does not want a private conversation heard publicly, one does not carry it out loudly on a bus. If one wants to maintain a private living space, one does not entertain there. If one wants to discourage telephone calls, one does not allow the listing of one's telephone number in the directory.

On the other hand, there are community norms that reject excessive protection of privacy. A covered face might be reflective of modesty in a Muslim society, but it would generate great suspicion on a street in Europe or the United States. An unsigned letter to the editor would not be published in most Western countries (although anonymity in voting is a basic tenet of democracy). For public officials in the United States, there is almost no element of their lives that the public or the media is willing to accept as private.

Information networks present a challenge to these cultural norms in a number of ways. First, the technologies themselves have the potential to shift the boundary between public and private space in *either* direction, depending on circumstance and the sophistication of the user. Encryption technologies can increase the effective domain of private space; on the other hand, connecting to the Web can, in itself, expose the contents of one's computer to inspection or alteration and thus provide a public incursion into previously private space. Most discussions of this issue have emphasized the latter point rather than the former, in large part because of the threat posed by the naiveté of Web users and the surreptitious nature of information-gathering technologies.

Technological sophistication and aggressiveness enter the picture because the actual shift is affected by the vigor of attempts to penetrate the boundary and the defenses mounted to prevent it. In certain circumstances, a code name may be sufficient to prevent a person's identity from being known in a chat room; in other cases, a so-called secure encrypted message may be intercepted and decoded by a person or organization with sufficiently advanced decryption technology.

But the larger cultural question concerns the effect of decoupling one's physical presence and geographical location from the world of bits, in which ideas, opinions, and virtual intimacy can flourish disembodied. An often-referenced *New Yorker* cartoon shows two dogs conversing in front of a computer monitor with one saying, "Yes, but on the Internet, they don't know you're a dog."[16] This is a world in which "local space" is not equivalent to "private space," where the safe expression of candor in speech or the embarrassment-free expression of intimacy to strangers is possible.

A question for future study is whether the existence and experience of such a world will shift behavior patterns within one's local setting or merely provide an alternative space in which values and behavior can differ from those of everyday life. If the former scenario prevails, global networks will provide a means for relaxing culturally imposed conformity and for encouraging individuality. Whether this is viewed as a good or bad thing will, of course, depend on the local cultures in which the new behavior patterns arise. If the latter scenario more accurately captures the reality, the question is whether those already inclined to seek such a dissociation of body from thought will selectively populate the world of bits or whether the cyberworld will, in itself, create the motivation to change patterns of behavior for those who choose to become "Netizens."

The concept of Netizens, of course, carries with it the idea that there really is a distinct cyberculture composed of individuals, drawn from many different local cultures, who share a number of characteristics and values. In this view, the significant divide is between this group and essentially all geographically centered (and hence locally centered) cultures. Within the cyberworld, there is no requirement to meet anyone's physical needs, ideas are more easily dissociated from any specific individuals, and tangible consequences of ideas are limited. This leads to a culture that places a great deal of value on removing any restriction to the flow of

---

[16]Cartoon by Peter Steiner, *The New Yorker*, July 5, 1993, p. 61.

[17]See, for example, John Perry Barlow, "A Declaration on the Independence of Cyberspace," available online at <http://www.eff.org/pub/Publications/John_Perry_Barlow/barlow_0296 .declaration>.

ideas, much less value on their critical assessment, and an absolute antipathy to any hierarchical structure that might be superimposed on a world entirely defined by ideas.[17]

This kind of cyberculture is, in many ways, a utopian anarchy; it clearly offers a strong contrast to locally centered cultures of almost any kind. But is it necessarily a threat to those local cultures? And is it an ineluctable prototype of global networks? In the committee's view, these two questions are related, and the answer to both is no. The rapid growth of the Internet as a source of information and services, and as a medium for commerce, continues to increase the diversity of individuals who use it, as well as their purposes in using it and the extent to which they use it. The Netizens who pioneered these networks and created for a period of time a fairly well-defined epistemic group, now constitute a rather small minority of Net users much as they constitute a rather small minority of each of the many societies from which they come. These pioneers embraced an *absence* of structure, which has meant that the evolution of network culture has not been controllable by any group; the resulting culture is, and will continue to be, far from homogeneous.

9.5 GENERATIONAL PHENOMENA

To what extent are other cultural conflicts primarily issues of transition that will resolve themselves over time? Edward McCracken, former president and CEO of Silicon Graphics, Inc., describes an intriguing generational phenomenon that is apparent even within his high-technology, information-based company.[18]

Members of the most senior generation—those who trained and began their careers before digitized information technology had emerged—never become completely comfortable with the gestalt of modern information technology: its opportunities and the altered ways of thinking and working that it entails. For the middle generation—those who grew up with the new technology—computers and networks are overwhelming objects of interest. Many of these individuals are the computer "nerds" and "hackers," the creative people who treat the optimization of hardware and software, and the development of new ways of doing old things, as fascinating and satisfying ends in themselves. They are also the Netizens discussed in the previous section.

---

[18]Edward McCracken, "Innovation and Information Technology in the 21st Century," Keynote speech, Science and Technology Day, University of Minnesota, April 3, 1997.

For the younger generation, information technology in all of its manifestations appears to be viewed primarily as a set of tools, taken almost as much for granted as hammers and screwdrivers. To be sure, the analogy can be overdrawn. Information technology continues to develop at an extraordinary rate, while hammers and screwdrivers work much as they have for hundreds of years. Therefore the improvement of these new tools remains a creative enterprise, a fact that makes them objects of continuing attention. But the trend seems clear: they are moving toward becoming transparent systems, simply the means for carrying out the activities of a society and achieving its goals.

Can this observation be generalized to the connection between global networks and culture? Cultural resistance may be a phenomenon of the "senior" generation, cultural distortion a characteristic of the "middle" generation, and social and cultural construction the final stage in the transition. That optimistic scenario would be constrained by two phenomena: "technological lock-in," the phenomenon of path dependence in which initial technological choices limit future flexibility, and "technological unsuitability," the essential conflict between the structure and dynamics of a new technology and the cultural/social system on which it is being imposed.

The concept of transition is important in another respect. Some cast the issue of information technology and culture as a choice between the preservation or loss of existing cultural values. This seems to the committee a false dichotomy in that it conveys the notion that cultural norms are static. In fact, it is difficult to conceive of a dynamic society in which natural and social history, demographics, and intersocietal intercourse do not alter cultural norms. Technological change is clearly one, but only one, of the factors that bring about evolutionary change. These include language, art, myths, and music, as well as political and economic structure, occupations, housing, food, education—indeed, the totality of human activity.

But the pathway of change is very much affected by existing cultural traditions, and the outcome of change is largely defined by those traditions. A McDonald's restaurant in Beijing does not make Beijing into Peoria, even though it makes Beijing something different from what it was. The challenge in the development of new technologies, as Thompson has noted, is to emphasize "inflexibility reduction."[19] The premise is that it is impossible to predict all of the social and cultural effects of a new technol-

[19]Michael Thompson, "Cultural Theory and Technology Assessment," manuscript prepared for European Parliament, Office of Scientific and Technological Options Assessment, Luxembourg, October 1995.

ogy on the institutions of society; those institutions themselves include a mixture of individuals and groups that fall into different "social solidarities," each of which will affect and react differently to the technology. There is therefore a need for experimentation and iteration in the construction of technological applications. This requires both attention to the interactive effects as they occur and the capacity to make adjustments in response.

Examining the impact of global networks on local cultural values must therefore be viewed as an ongoing challenge. Ability to predict the changes is less important than alertness in observing them and creativity in responding with altered designs—not with the goal or expectation that global networks should not or will not alter detailed local cultural patterns of behavior, but to ensure that the changes do not disconnect the cultural present and future from the past, or alter the balance of solidarities in a way that is unacceptable to the society they affect.

10

Principles and Conclusions

For reasons outlined in Chapter 1, the committee came to the conclusion early on that an exhaustive study of the impact of global networks on local values was not possible within the constraints of time, focus, and group composition under which it was operating. Nevertheless, in the course of the symposia it hosted and the discussions it held, the committee was able to make some tentative judgments about some of the pertinent issues that may serve as a starting point for later studies.

10.1 GOVERNMENTS AND THE EVOLUTION OF LOCAL VALUES

As noted in Chapter 3, the values of a society are both formal and substantive. Because the world is increasingly diverse and interconnected, the committee believes that modern societies are better served by values that emphasize process and mutual respect than by those that seek to establish orthodoxies. Such an emphasis would give priority to formal values over substantive ones, though substantive values continue to have importance in defining a society or culture.

Considerable historical evidence suggests that the values of a society change over time. Thus, rather than seeking an unchanging status quo in which social and cultural values are frozen for all time, governments of modern societies might well choose a role in guiding such evolution, while ensuring the existence of a healthy process that is conducive to such change.

Governments could choose to intervene directly in the process. However, direct government intervention is hard to legitimate in a liberal state where value formation is a social rather than a governmental process. In addition, a coherent plan is hard to design, especially if it seeks to change the overall balance among values. Governments may be able to implant a single new value in the minds of the citizens or erase a single older value, as totalitarian governments have shown. But affecting the processes as values evolve is a much more ambitious task, the pursuit of which would necessarily aim at controlling thought rather than action; such an attempt would be inappropriate for democratic societies striving to maintain the rule of law.

A second approach is to regulate the mechanisms that affect the process. Consider, for example, the Internet as a possible influence on the evolution of local values. Governments do have a continuing and long-term role in ensuring that, on balance and in aggregate, communication informs rather than manipulates, and that it serves the purposes of democratic society with respect to universal access and the balance of social and political power.

Nevertheless, the Internet is not the only influence on the evolution of values; there is a multitude of other influences. Thus the Internet policy of government should be part of a larger strategy aimed at promoting the healthy evolution of a society's value set, in response to the many changes occurring as that society becomes better educated, more diverse, and more fully connected to the wider world around it.

10.2 DEMOCRACY

Policy interventions to channel or direct the impact of global networks on democracy and political institutions are fraught with difficulty, and it would be naive to expect that political leaders would make neutral decisions where their own future power base is concerned. Even if that were not the case, it would still make sense to be cautious, even modest, about making explicit recommendations. The fact is that the structure and influence of global networks are constantly evolving, and the normative goals that would presumably be served by such policy efforts continue, as they have been for centuries, to be in dispute. Nevertheless, or perhaps with these caveats in mind, the committee concludes the following:

- To the extent that policymakers believe that action is necessary, their focus should be on outcomes rather than on tools or modalities. Thus they should seek to define what outcomes are desirable and undesirable rather than seek to regulate one particular instrumentality such as the Internet. The Internet is only one factor, albeit an important one, in globalization and modernization.

• Networks such as the Internet (that is, systems capable of multinode generation and receipt of information) and broadcast media (that is, few generators to many recipients) each have, in principle, advantages and disadvantages in promoting democratic goals. Network-based information resources are probably more effective in providing access to information and to political forums, and to the maintenance of a plurality of ideas, although network users have the ability to determine what information reaches them, thus limiting what ideas can reach people. Broadcast media do a better job of integrating a society because they expose the broad population to a relatively common pool of information. Acting together, they can facilitate plurality with integration; they also provide certain checks and balances in the polity.

• Global networks create new opportunities for direct democracy, and policymakers in each country should consider how these opportunities might best be used. They should decide how—and whether—direct and representative processes should be rebalanced to maximize legitimacy in both "input" (the voices of citizens) and "output"(policy actions resulting from those processes).

• Policymakers should assess whether the postulated disintegrating effect of global networks is actually felt in their polities. Has there, for example, been a recent trend toward single-issue constituencies?

• If global networks are seen as competing with established mechanisms for the provision of public goods, it becomes clear that research is needed into what one might call antitrust rules. The goal is to devise *workable* competition among the variety of political arenas.

• Despite a host of pressures toward greater internationalization and multilateral activity (especially in the European Union), actual change may be slow and painful. Countries give up previously sovereign rights and powers only grudgingly, if at all.

10.3 REGULATORY STRUCTURE

An alternative to command-and-control regulation is the use of self-regulation and intermediation within a statutory framework. With hybrid regulation, a credible threat of state intervention stimulates self-regulatory activities, and overt state involvement is unnecessary once the self-regulatory activities are under way. (A supranational entity, an international organization, or well-organized societal forces may also have the same effect.) Because global networks are characterized by a complex system of private, public, and quasi-public forces, a stable system is easier to achieve when stakeholders can take an active part in shaping their roles. Command-and-control regulation often attacks a well-balanced status quo; because hybrid regulation builds on the status quo, it is more likely to be successful.

Improved prospects for a new hybrid system of governance for global networks are consistent with the shifting boundary between public and private international law. Policy statements by national governments, and the actual establishment of a number of hybrid regulatory approaches, are promising signs that new forms of international governance will help implement the recommendations of this report.

10.4 FREE SPEECH

As noted in Chapter 5, the United States and Germany both recognize a constitutional right to freedom of expression. However, the interpretations of that right in the two countries are significantly different. As importantly, the *weights* given to that right, in comparison with other values, are different in the two societies as well. As a result, the legal structures and protections that have developed to implement the right are also different, exemplifying why harmonization of nations' laws related to freedom of expression on the Internet is likely to remain quite difficult.

The nature of today's Internet is a significant impediment for national authorities who wish to unilaterally implement laws and regulations that reflect national substantive values. At the same time, national pride and substantive cultural values are unlikely to be abandoned, so that a homogenization of values among nations—particularly with respect to the most restrictive or the least—is also unlikely to occur.

There are some areas, such as child pornography, where there is more-or-less universal agreement on the substantive values to be protected. International treaties that harmonize rules appear to be well within reach for these few, but important, areas. Generally, the more homogeneous the group of nations, the more likely it is that treaty solutions covering content will be practical. Even if the group of nations is small, it can still be useful in providing a model for harmonization and a bloc for bringing pressure on nonsignatory nations to respect the treaty's provisions.

To reduce the tensions and chaos that national differences create for a global activity, governments could cooperate in a number of ways. Nations could work together to discourage content providers from using the regulatory environment of one country to circumvent the regulations of another. They could establish an international information agency (or support private or quasi-public organizations) to help providers understand each nation's regulatory standards and structures. Finally, they could update and extend to the networked world the mechanisms that currently exist for dealing with circumstances in which domestic laws conflict.

Given the limited effectiveness of unilateral command-and-control rules regulating content, commercial law, self-regulation, and encouragement of intermediation (perhaps driven by the threat of imposing regulation) are options for national action in the appropriate circumstances.

- Commercial law is a useful tool when material on the network injures a clearly identifiable party (e.g., a Web site has published libelous material about a person or has violated a person's legally protected privacy). However, ccommercial law does not work well if large groups are indirectly or only potentially affected—for example, when child pornography endangers children, hate speech intimidates minority groups, or Nazi ideology threatens democratic government.
- Voluntary self-regulation on the part of the parties directly exposed to material on the Internet—through site-identification and labeling schemes, age-verification software, or the provision of filtering software, for example—is attractive in some ways, because it offers the potential for greater diversity of material to be accessible through the Internet, enhanced freedom of expression, and customization of controls to fit the needs and desires of the individuals involved.
- Intermediaries, such as host providers, can play a useful role in offering the public a regulating or authenticating service. That is, host providers can market their Internet access software by promising to include certain kinds and quality of content and exclude others. Hosts would compete with each other on the basis of the cluster of options they offer as well as over their software-based filtering systems (although the rigidity of these latter technical tools is a clear disadvantage).

Finally, government should provide means for improving the media competence of the users. An oversight function for government will remain important in striking a balance between the preservation of the individual right of freedom of expression and other legitimate goals of a democratic society.

10.5 PRIVACY

Privacy regulation must cover both online and offline transactions, either through the Internet or private networks, and must include comprehensive and consistent protection regardless of whether data are collected, held, manipulated, or disseminated by public sector or private sector entities. The United States faces particular challenges in this respect because its many sector-specific regulatory approaches are so different from (and indeed often inconsistent with) each other.

The existence of transborder data flows creates a strong need for harmonization, or at least convergence, of national legislative regimes, particularly among developed countries. Because the United States and Germany, as well as Europe more generally, share a number of values concerning privacy rights, harmonization is not out of the realm of possibility. However, subtle but important differences in cultural views about the appropriate role of the government make it unlikely that explicit, uniform, legislatively based regulations will ever be agreed on.

Hybrid approaches that combine self-regulation with a legislative framework that establishes general principles—as well as mechanisms for monitoring and enforcement—appear much more likely to provide flexibility, customization, and quick-response capability in the dynamic world of global networks.

10.6 FREEDOM OF INFORMATION

There are few international tensions related to inconsistencies in national freedom-of-information laws, as this is an area in which individual nations can control compliance with their own statutes. However, freedom of information is so vital to the proper functioning of a democracy that it is reasonable to endorse an upward harmonization of national standards toward the comprehensive law-based regime in place in the United States. That regime takes as a premise the right of citizens to access virtually all public documents (with narrowly drawn exceptions), though in practice the extent to which U.S. government agencies adhere to this regime varies widely. Among the few exceptions, in addition to national-security matters or judicial proceedings, are the privacy rights of individuals. Advances in technology make it generally easier to anonymize data in government records, thereby allowing their release without compromising privacy.

Primary legal information—including laws, judicial opinions, and administrative rulings—should not be excluded from freedom-of-information regimes merely to protect a property interest of a private entity that uses the data to create value-added databases. If copyright protection is granted to such entities, it should not cover the raw data on which the information product is based.

Government institutions should encourage the trend of using Web sites and the Internet to increase the availability of public information.

10.7 TECHNOLOGY DEVELOPMENT

The network of networks appears to be what *The Economist*, in July 1995, called "the accidental superhighway." In its early stages the Internet was promoted and funded, but not designed, by the U.S. government. At no time did some kind of master plan exist to guide the Internet's evolution. The history of the Internet's technology suggests that it would be a mistake for governments to seek to control the future development through comprehensive action plans. There are alternatives to centralized approaches, such as coordination and self-regulation, though these pose challenges both within particular countries and globally. Such approaches require accommodating new forms of hybrid public-private international regimes, which may be experimental in the near term (as discussed in Section 10.3).

The core of the Internet's technology—the TCP/IP protocol stack—developed in a niche that sheltered it from market selection for many years. This incubation was very useful, and it suggests that creating and protecting other niches may be beneficial in keeping options for technological development open. The challenge will be to provide suitable, timely exposure to market realities while avoiding the propping up of what might not be viable.

10.8 CULTURE AND TECHNOLOGY

Generally speaking, cultural hegemony arising from global networks does not appear to be a major concern for developed nations. Technologies are available that allow localization of the language and culture of networks, the cost of entry of information providers of all kinds is low, and saturation of available bandwidth by early users does not appear to be a serious problem.

There is more reason for concern about cultural hegemony with respect to nations in the developing world. Here, too, the technological capacity exists to localize networks, but the incentives to do so are often marginal. Moreover, in certain of these societies, networks may exacerbate social stratification, reinforcing the power of elites and upsetting cultural balances that have developed over time. Of particular concern is the possibility of "technological lock-in" during these next several years as the structure and use patterns of the Internet develop.

An untested postulate, put forward by a number of East Asian and Middle Eastern countries, is that there is a strong connection between their cultural values and their political structures—and that global networks can be a threat to both. An examination of how electronic networks have been adopted in the growing diasporas of ethnic groups from these countries might provide further insights on this question.

Global networks appear more likely to change the culture of and relationships between various groups *within* societies, as defined by profession and level of education rather than by national identity. These changes result from the groups' different ways of using the Internet, the different interdependencies among groups that thereby occur, and the consequent changes in the modes of operation of certain professionals that affect activities unrelated to electronic networks as well as those directly related to the networks.

Networks are profoundly challenging the traditional and culturally defined conceptions of public and private spaces. It is not yet clear whether this will lead to two worlds—real space and cyberspace—with different rules and mores concerning privacy, or whether there will be spillover effects that create tensions or changes in local cultural practices. A separate cyberworld of "Netizens" is not likely to achieve any permanence, even as electronic network penetration and use grow over the years to come.

Finally, many of the observations about the cultural effects of global networks are likely to be transitory. Global electronic networks will cause a sea change resulting more from continual, dynamic evolution than from any one-time adjustment that remains fixed. Thus, long-term changes in the nature of local culture are certainly probable, but not predictable on the basis of phenomena currently being observed.

Appendix

Biographies

A.1 COMMITTEE MEMBERS

KENNETH H. KELLER, *Chair,* directs the Center for Science, Technology, and Public Affairs at the University of Minnesota. He also holds an appointment in the Department of Chemical Engineering and Materials Science. His research examines the intersection of science and technology with international politics and economics. His recent writings have dealt with technology and national sovereignty, the environment, the globalization of research and development, and policy issues in high technology medicine. He has spent most of his career at the University of Minnesota where he joined the faculty in 1964, became vice president for academic affairs in 1980, and University president in 1985. He was senior fellow for science and technology at the Council on Foreign Relations from 1990 to 1996. He has chaired and served on a number of public and private boards and advisory groups and is a member of the Commission on Physical Sciences, Mathematics, and Applications of the National Research Council, and the boards of RAND's Institute for Education and Training and the Science Museum of Minnesota. He chairs the Medical Technology Leadership Forum and is vice chair of the board of LASPAU: Academic and Professional Programs for the Americas. He earned a master's degree and doctorate in chemical engineering from Johns Hopkins University, and was named a distinguished Johns Hopkins alumnus in 1996.

KENNETH W. DAM is Max Pam Professor of American and Foreign Law at the University of Chicago Law School. Mr. Dam was elected to the

Order of the Coif while at the Law School; he was also a managing editor of the Law Review. In 1964, he was visiting professor at the University of Freiburg. Mr. Dam has published five books: *Federal Tax Treatment of Foreign Income* (with Lawrence Krause); *The GATT: Law and International Economic Organization; Oil Resources: Who Gets What How?; Economic Policy Beyond the Headlines* (with George Shultz); and *The Rules of the Game: Reform and Evolution in the International Monetary System*. He was law clerk to Supreme Court Justice Whittaker and then an associate with the New York firm of Cravath, Swaine and Moore. He joined the Law School faculty in 1960, but in 1971 he left to become assistant director of the Office of Management and Budget, where he was concerned with national security and international affairs. In 1973, he was executive director of the Council on Economic Policy, which was responsible for coordination of U.S. domestic and international economic policy. He returned to the University of Chicago Law School in 1974. He served as provost of the university from 1980 to 1982. He served as deputy secretary of state from 1982 to 1985 and then as vice president for law and external relations with IBM from 1985 to 1992. In 1992, he took leave from IBM to serve, on an interim basis, as president and CEO of the United Way of America in order to clean up a scandal in that organization and to put into place a new system of controls and governance. In early 2001 he was nominated by President Bush to be Deputy Secretary of the Treasury, and he is currently on a leave of absence from the Law School.

PAUL A. DAVID is professor of Economics at Stanford University, and, since 1994, also holds a Senior Research Fellowship at All Souls College, Oxford. He currently is Extraordinary Professor of the Economics of Science and Technology in the Faculty of Economics and Business Administration at the University of Maastricht. Paul David is known internationally for his contributions in several fields, including economic history, economic and historical demography, and the economics of science and technology. The development of "the new economics of science" has been a focal point of his most recent research and writings, and he continues to direct the High Technology Impact Program of the Center for Economic Policy Research at Stanford. He has served as a consultant to the U.S. National Academy of Sciences, the United Nations Commission on Trade and Development, the United Nations University Institute on New Technologies, the World Bank, the Organization for Economic Cooperation and Development, and other public organizations.

KENNETH KENISTON is Andrew W. Mellon Professor of Human Development and Director of Projects in the Program in Science, Technology, and Society at the Massachusetts Institute of Technology. He is the author of seven books and more than 100 articles and chapters. His most recent works are, with D. Guston, *The Fragile Contract* (1994), and with J. Ker Conway and L. Marx, *Earth, Air, Fire, Water: Humanistic Studies of the Environment*. He is the Director of the MIT India Project at MIT, a part of the MIT International Science and Technology Initiative (MISTI). In recent years, Professor Keniston's research focused on information technology and development in India. His research in India focuses on such topics as Indic language software (or the absence therof), and on Indian projects and research to close the "digital divide" within India and between India and the so-called Northern nations. In the fall of 1999, he was Sir Ashutosh Mukerjee Visiting Professor at the National Institute of Advanced Studies at the Indian Institute of Science in Bangalore; he has lectured at a number of Indian institutions including IIT-Chennai, IIT-Mumbai, the Confederation of Indian Industries, and private firms. He was a member, Carnegie Commission on Higher Education (1964-1971); director, Behavioral Sciences Study Center, Yale Medical School (1967-1971); chairman and director, Carnegie Council on Children (1971-1977), author of its report, All Our Children; and member, Board of Overseers of Harvard University (1973-1979); Guggenheim Fellow for study of engineering education (1982); evaluator, Guggenheim Foundation for Latin American applicants (1988-); member, Committee of Selection for the MacArthur Prize Fellowships (1973-1979); member, Committee of Selection for the Guggenheim Fellowships (1991-1994). He has been a Visiting Scholar at the Ecole des Mines (Paris); Visiting Professor at the University of ParisV (Sorbonne); Visiting Professor at the Centro de Estudios Avanzados de Ciencias Sociales (Madrid). He has been a consultant on a number of projects in Venezuela, Kuwait, Mendoza (Argentina), Malaysia, Politecnico of Torino, Italy, Petroleum Institute in Dhahran, Saudi Arabia. He is currently a member of the National Research Council/Max-Planck-Institute (American-German) working group on Global Networks and Local Values. He is a member of the Council on Foreign Relations and the American Academy of Arts and Sciences. Keniston was educated in part at the Colegio Nacional de Buenos Aires (Central). He graduated magna cum laude from Harvard College, with a thesis on the political philosophy of José Ortega y Gasset. He received his D. Phil. in Social Studies from Oxford University, where he was a Rhodes Scholar at Balliol College. He has taught at Harvard University, where he was a Junior Fellow; in the Departments of Psychology and Psychiatry at Yale University; and at the Massachusetts Institute of Technology, where he has been Director (1986-1992) and Director of Graduate Studies (1992-1996) of the Program in Science, Technology, and Society.

HENRY H. PERRITT, JR., is dean of Chicago-Kent College of Law and vice president of the Downtown Campus of Illinois Institute of Technology. He is the author of more than 70 law review articles and 15 books on technology and law and employment law, including the 730-page *Law and the Information Superhighway*. He served on President Clinton's Transition Team, working on telecommunications issues, and drafted principles for electronic dissemination of public information, which formed the core of the Electronic Freedom of Information Act Amendments adopted by Congress in 1996. During the Ford Administration, he served on the White House staff and as deputy under secretary of labor. He serves on the Computer Science and Telecommunications Policy Board of the National Research Council. He was a member of the interprofes-sional team that evaluated the FBI's Carnivore system. He is a member of the Bars of Virginia, Pennsylvania, the District of Columbia, Maryland, Illinois and the United States Supreme Court. He is a member of the Council of Foreign Relations and of the Economic Club and is secretary of the Section on Labor and Employment Law of the American Bar Association. He earned his B.S. in engineering from MIT in 1966, a master's degree in management from MIT's Sloan School in 1970, and a J.D. from Georgetown University Law Center in 1975.

ROBERT SPINRAD retired from XEROX Corporation, as Vice President of Technology Strategy in 1998. He joined Xerox in 1968, and over the years has held a variety of computer science positions, including that of Director of Xerox PARC (Palo Alto Research Center). Before his career with Xerox, Spinrad was a Senior Scientist at Brookhaven National Laboratory and Project Engineer at Bulova Research and Development Laboratory. Spinrad received a Ph.D. in Electrical Engineering from the Massachusetts Institute of Technology. He received his M.S. in Electrical Engineering, and B.S. in Engineering from Columbia University. Spinrad was a Bridgham Fellow at Columbia and a Whitney Fellow at MIT. Spinrad has served in various advisory and oversight roles at Harvard University, Stanford University, the Massachusetts Institute of Technology, the University of California, EDUCOM, the National Science Foundation, the National Academy of Sciences, the National Academy of Engineering, the National Research Council, the American Association for the Advancement of Science, the Council on Library and Information Resources, the Council on Foreign Relations, Bell Telephone Laboratory, the Defense Department's Advanced Research Projects Agency, Livermore National Laboratory, the RAND Corporation, the International Institute for Applied Systems Analysis, Digital Pathways, Inc., the McGraw-Hill Encyclopedia of Science and Technology, and The Information Society. Spinrad is on the Board of Advisors for the Berkeley

Center for Law and Technology and on the National Reconnaissance Office Advisory Council. He is also a member of the National Academy of Engineering and the National Research Council's United States/Japan Task Force on Corporate Innovation.

A.2 THE GERMAN DELEGATION

CHRISTOPH ENGEL, *Chair of the German Delegation*, was born in 1956, and he took the first state exam for lawyers in 1981 at Tuebingen University. After 2 years as assistant at the Tuebingen Law Faculty, he was for 9 years a research fellow of the Hamburg Max-Planck-Institute on foreign private law and conflicts of law. He took his second state exam for lawyers in 1987 and received a degree of doctor juris in 1988. In 1992, the University of Hamburg gave him tenure (habilitation) for public law, economic law, European law, and public international law. From 1992 through 1997, he held a chair for media and communications law at Osnabrueck University. Since 1997 he is co-director of a newly founded institution within the Max-Planck-Society, the Project Group on the Law of Common Goods at Bonn. His main fields are public law, economic law, media law, environmental law, and the impact of social sciences, in particular economics, on law. He is a member of the Scientific Council with the German Minister of Economics.

KLAUS W. GREWLICH is a professor in the European General and Interdisciplinary Department at the College of Europe/Bruges. From 1990 to 1995 he served as Executive Vice President (Director General) Business Development and Board Representative at Deutsche Telekom, Bonn and from 1996 to 1997 as Director General and Member of the Board of an Industrial Confederation in Brussels. Dr. Grewlich has held positions in the European Space Agency and in the OECD Madrid, in the Cabinet of the EC Commission in Brussels, and was Member of the Foreign Policy Planning Group and Director for International Technology and Telecommunications Policy in the Federal Foreign Office, Bonn. He received his Dr. Jur. from the University of Freiburg, his Dr.sc.econ. from the University of Lausanne/HEC, and his LL.M. from the University of California, Berkeley. Dr Grewlich is the author of various publications, particularly in the field of international economic relations, public international and European law, international technology policy, government-business relations, and communications, including the books *Direct Investment in the OECD-Countries* (1978), *Transnational Enterprises in a New International System* (1980), *Europe in the Global Technology Race* (1992), *Conflict and Order in Global Communications* (1997), and *Governance in Cyberspace* (1999).

BERND HOLZNAGEL is a professor of law and director of the Institute for Information, Telecommunication and Media Law at the University of Münster, Germany. After completing his law and sociological studies at the Free University in Berlin in 1984, he participated in a post-graduate law program at McGill University in Montreal where he received a Master of Laws (LL.M.) degree in 1985. After receiving his Ph.D. from the University of Hamburg on *Dispute Resolution through Negotiation* in 1990 and passing the second state exam in law in 1991, he began to write his thesis, "Broadcasting Law in Europe," which was completed in 1996 and received a special award from the European Group at Public Law. In 1997 he was announced as professor for constitutional and administrative law at the University of Münster. In the same year he founded the Institute for Information, Telecommunication and Media Law. His involvement in research projects covers areas such as access problems in the multimedia age, legal frameworks of data protection and data security, and new media in university teaching. In 1998 he was a visiting professor at the University of Virginia (Charlottesville) teaching "European Community Law" in the fall term. Since 1999, he has been a faculty member of Oxford University's summer school for incoming law students. His consulting work on the international level includes media law courses in Moscow and Ljubljana (with the Council of Europe), as well as working as an expert on the legal problems concerning Bosnian election law, residence law, data protection and I.D. cards (with the Phare Project financed by the European Commission). Furthermore, he was a member of the European Expert Group for the preparation of the Working Group "The Right Regulatory Framework for a Creative Media Economy" at the April 1998 Birmingham Conference organised by the European Community. Currently he is a co-editor of the Law Journal "Multimedia and Law" and co-initiator of the "International Journal of Communications Law and Policy," which is a joint project of the Universities of Münster, Oxford, Warwick, and Yale. In addition, he has published numerous articles in several German law journals relating to various problems concerning German administrative law.

MICHAEL HUTTER is professor of economic theory and director of the Institute for Economy and Culture at Witten/Herdecke University, the first private university in Germany. He received his Dr. rer.pol. with a summa-cum-laude thesis on the logical structure of property rights and his Dr. rer. pol. habil. with a study on the production of pharmaceutical patent law in Germany, Italy, and the United States. His current research interests focus on the role of communication in economic theory, and on applications of social systems theory on the economics of the Arts, media industries and networks, and monetary systems. Dr. Hutter was educated at Portland State University (B.A. Math., 1970), University of Washington (M.A. Econ., 1971), and the University of Munich (Dr. rer. pol., 1976, and Dr. rer. pol. habil., 1986). He taught at Claremont McKenna College and at the University of Munich before joining the faculty of Business Administration and Economics at Witten/Herdecke University in 1987. He was dean of the faculty from 1992-95, and he was president of the Association for Cultural Economics. He serves on the editorial board of the Journal of Cultural Economics, the European Journal of Law and Economics, and Soziale Systeme. He has published in the areas of cultural economics, history and theory of money, history of economic thought and economic methodology.

RAYMUND WERLE is principal research associate with the Max-Planck-Institut für Gesellschaftsforschung, Köln (Max-Planck-Institute for the Study of Societies, Cologne). He is head of the MPI Research Group on Network Development and Standardization in Telecommunications. His research is focused on the institutional conditions and the structural consequences of technological and scientific innovations, in particular in the information and telecommunications technology industry. It includes the development of telecommunications and data networks, the Internet in particular, and their structural and societal consequences. He has published in the area of science and technology studies, development and governance of large technical systems, but also in the sociology of law and the legal profession and research methodology. He received a Diploma (M.A.) in Economics and Sociology and a Ph.D. in Political Science. He was educated at the Universities of Bonn, Cologne, Mannheim and at the State University of New York at Stony Brook (postgraduate DAAD fellow). He held research and teaching positions at the Universities of Bielefeld, Mannheim and Heidelberg and at the Research Center on Nuclear Energy in Karlsruhe. In 1997 he was Visiting Scholar at the Center for Technology, Policy and Industrial Development (Research Program on Communications Policy) at the Massachusetts Institute of Technology (MIT). He is chair of the Coordination Committee of the Research Network "Sociology of Science and Technology" (SSTNET) of the European Sociological Association.

A.3 STAFF

JOACHIM DÖLKEN is a research assistant with the Max-Planck-Project Group on the Law of Common Goods at Bonn and currently enrolled in the preparatory program ("Rechtsreferendariat") for the second state exam for lawyers. He received his first law degree (J.D. equivalent) with a focus on commercial and competition law in 1995 from Osnabrück

University. Since 1992, he was a junior research assistant with the chair for the Law of the New Media at Osnabrueck University. From 1995-1996, he was a visiting scholar at the University of Chicago Law School (ERP-scholarship of the Ministry of Economics and the National Scholarship Foundation). His work is on antitrust law related to convergence in multimedia markets.

HERBERT LIN is senior scientist and senior staff officer at the Computer Science and Telecommunications Board, National Research Council of the National Academies, where he has been study director of major projects on public policy and information technology. These studies include a 1996 study on national cryptography policy (*Cryptography's Role in Securing the Information Society*), a 1991 study on the future of computer science (*Computing the Future*), a 1999 study of Defense Department systems for command, control, communications, computing, and intelligence (*Realizing the Potential of C4I: Fundamental Challenges*), and a 2000 study on workforce issues in high-technology (*Building a Workforce for the Information Economy*). Prior to his NRC service, he was a professional staff member and staff scientist for the House Armed Services Committee (1986-1990), where his portfolio included defense policy and arms control issues. He also has significant expertise in math and science education. He received his Ph.D. in physics from MIT in 1979. Apart from his CSTB work, he is published in cognitive science, science education, biophysics, and arms control and defense policy.

LORENZ MÜLLER is Higher Executive Officer in the administration of the German Bundestag on temporary leave of absence. He was Research Assistant of the Parliamentary Study Commission "Future of the Media in the Economy and Society—Germany´s Road into the Information Society," which finished his work in June 1998. After 4 years as a journalist, he studied law and arabic and islamic studies in Hamburg and Damascus. He took his first and second state exam for lawyers in 1991 and 1995 in Hamburg and received a degree of doctor juris in 1996 with a thesis on the relationship between modern islamic theory and the idea of human rights. Currently he is a Research Assistant with the Max-Planck-Project Group on the Law of Common Goods at Bonn.

WOLF OSTHAUS, born in 1971, received his first law degree (J.D. equivalent) with a focus on international private law and comparison of law in 1997 from Osnabrueck University after studying at the Universities of Osnabrueck, Paris (XII), and Florence. He is a research assistant with the

Max-Planck-Project Group on the Law of Common Goods at Bonn and also a member of the Graduate College "Internationalization of private law" at the University of Freiburg/Germany (DFG scholarship). His Ph.D. thesis, which is supervised by Prof. von Bar, Osnabrueck, will be on the rights to information in the international tort law.